The Life and Teachings
of
TSONGKHAPA

The Life and Teachings
of
TSONGKHAPA

Edited by

ROBERT A. F. THURMAN

Translations by

Sherpa Tulku, Khamlung Tulku, Alexander Berzin,
Jonathan Landaw, Glenn H. Mullin, and Robert A. F. Thurman

WISDOM PUBLICATIONS
IN COLLABORATION WITH THE LIBRARY OF TIBETAN WORKS & ARCHIVES

Wisdom Publications
199 Elm Street
Somerville, MA 02144 USA
wisdompubs.org

Library of Congress Cataloging-in-Publication Data
Names: Thurman, Robert A. F., editor, writer of introduction. | Sherpa Tulku. | Khamlung Tulku. | Berzin, Alexander. | Landaw, Jonathan. | Mullin, Glenn H. | Tsong-kha-pa Blo-bzang-grags-pa, 1357–1419. Works. Selections. English.
Title: The life and teachings of Tsongkhapa / edited by Robert A.F. Thurman; translations by Sherpa Tulku, Khamlung Tulku, Alexander Berzin, Jonathan Landaw, Glenn H. Mullin, Robert A.F. Thurman.
Other titles: Life and teachings of Tsong-khapa
Description: [Revised edition]. | Somerville, MA: Wisdom Publications, 2018. | Includes bibliographical references. |
Identifiers: LCCN 2017048509 (print) | LCCN 2017058805 (ebook) | ISBN 9781614294399 (e-book) | ISBN 9781614294276 (paperback)
Subjects: LCSH: Dge-lugs-pa (Sect)—Doctrines—Early works to 1800. | Tsong-kha-pa Blo-bzang-grags-pa, 1357–1419. | Dge-lugs-pa lamas—Tibet Region—Biography. | BISAC: PHILOSOPHY / Buddhist. | PHILOSOPHY / Eastern. | RELIGION / Buddhism / Tibetan.
Classification: LCC BQ7950.T753 (ebook) | LCC BQ7950.T753 E5 2018 (print) | DDC 181/.043—dc23
LC record available at https://lccn.loc.gov/2017048509

ISBN 978-1-61429-427-6   ebook ISBN 978-1-61429-439-9
22 21 20 19 18   5 4 3 2 1

Cover design by Tim Holtz. Interior design by Partners Composition. Set in Diacritical Garamond Pro 10.5/12.5.

Reverence to the Guru, Mañjughoṣha!

Contents

Preface

⚛

Since the opening of the Library of Tibetan Works & Archives in the 1970s, a number of Tibetan texts have been translated by our Research and Translation Bureau and brought out in print as part of our publishing program. Several of these were by or centered on the life of Lama Tsongkhapa (1357–1419), an important teacher who had been born in eastern Tibet and later spent many years traveling from one monastery or hermitage to another in search of the various lineages of the Buddhist teachings. His studies and practice explored the full range of Prātimokṣhayāna, Mahāyāna, and Vajrayāna teachings as found in all the schools of Buddhism then extant in the Land of Snow Mountains.

Studying with almost four dozen masters from all traditions of Tibetan Buddhism, the order he established was in fact the first major attempt at combining all Buddhist lineages in Tibet. One could say that the Gandenpa, New Kadampa, and eventually Gelukpa order taught the first appearance of the curriculum of what might be called "indigenous Tibetan Buddhism." The earlier traditions in existence at the time were mainly rooted in the teachings of specific Indian masters, such as Padmasambhava for the Nyingma, Virūpa for the Sakya, Tilopā and Naropā for the Kagyü, and so forth, whereas Tsongkhapa's tradition represented a synthesis of the several dozen most important schools of early-fourteenth-century Tibetan Buddhism. The eighteen volumes of writings that had issued forth from his pen were to act as a major inspiration in Tibetan cultural history, ushering in a renaissance of religious prose and poetry. The resulting effects on art, architecture, and folk culture were a natural product of his creating festivals such as the Great Prayer Festival of Lhasa and of the numerous master artists and craftsmen he used in his building and restoration work, as mentioned below in *A Short Biography*.

In the spring of 1979 Prof. Robert Thurman of Amherst College, Massachusetts, visited Dharamsālā on a sabbatical. Prof. Thurman is indeed one of the Western world's foremost scholars on the life and works of Lama Tsongkhapa, and the LTWA was most pleased when Prof. Thurman kindly agreed to collect together the various monographs by or related to Tsongkhapa that the LTWA had previously published in English translation, and to complement these with any of his own works that were unpublished.

The text of "A Short Biography" is based on an oral teaching by Geshé Ngawang Dhargé as translated by Khamlung Tulku and Sherpa Tulku, compiled by John Marshall and edited by India Stevens. It has been revised and reedited for this publication by Michael Richards and Kevin Garratt. It was first published by the LTWA in 1975 as *A Short Biography and Letter of Jey Tzong-k'a-pa*.

Song of the Mystic Experiences of the first section of this anthology, as well as the first three items in part 5, were translated by Glenn H. Mullin and Losang N. Tsonawa in accordance with the commentaries of Geshé Ngawang Dhargé, Gen Sonam Rinchen, and Geshé Losang Tenpa. They were first published by the LTWA in 1978 as *Four Songs to Jey Rinpoche*.

"Lines of Experience," "A Letter of Practical Advice on Sutra and Tantra," and "The Prayer of the Virtuous Beginning, Middle, and End" were translated by the team of Sherpa Tulku, Khamlung Tulku, Alexander Berzin, and Jonathan Landaw in accordance with the commentary of Geshé Ngawang Dhargé. The first of these was originally published as a monograph by the LTWA in 1973 and then reprinted in 1974 in a revised edition. The second originally appeared under the title *The Graded Course to Enlightenment* (New Delhi: Statesman Press, 1971) and in a revised edition under the title "A Brief Exposition of the Main Points of the Graded Sutra and Tantra Course to Enlightenment," in *A Short Biography and Letter of Jey Tzong-k'a-pa* (Dharamsālā: LTWA, 1975), with reprintings in 1975 and 1976. For this, their third edition, all three of these works have been retranslated by Alexander Berzin, with the assistance of Ven. Amchok Rinpoche, librarian at the LTWA, in "A Letter of Practical Advice on Sutra and Tantra."

The remaining pieces in the collection have all been translated by Prof. Thurman, some in the earlier years of his work with Tibetan literature and some—notably the "Garland of Supremely Healing Nectars"—specifically for this collection. The Library is most appreciative of the spirit of thoroughness with which Prof. Thurman approached the subject.

Although Lama Tsongkhapa is one of the most important figures in Tibetan religious and philosophical history, very little material by or about him has appeared in English to date. It is hoped that this small effort will contribute in some way to the Western world's growing knowledge of Tibet, her culture, philosophy, and religion, and the figures of Tibet's past who inspired and influenced the trends of Tibetan thought.

Gyatso Tsering
Director, LTWA, October 1981

Introduction

T his anthology of some of the important works of the great Dharma master Tsongkhapa Losang Drakpa (1357–1419) is presented for the general reader and the practitioner of the Buddha teachings to give her or him an introduction to the transformative life and profound teachings of that great lama. Most of the translations contained here were done some time ago and published as booklets and xerox manuscripts. Mr. Gyatso Tsering requested me to gather these translations together, adding some explanatory notes and translating newly some special pieces that round out the collection. It was decided from the beginning not to attempt to impose any standard terminology or even transliteration system on the works done by different translators, leaving each with his own style and taste. The key purpose of the anthology is to grant access to the useful teachings, the greatness of which always goes back to the greatness of the teacher. Tsongkhapa himself begins his *Great Stages of the Path to Enlightenment* (*Byang chub lam rim chen mo*) by elucidating the greatness of Jobo Jé, Atīsha Dīpaṃkara Śhrījñāna (982–1054 CE), whose *Lamp for the Enlightenment Path* served as the model for the *Great Stages*.

Since this book was originally put together in the 1970s, I have spent the decades further studying and trying to understand the amazing example and profound teachings of Lama Tsongkhapa, and I do not regret a single moment of those long efforts. I have also come to appreciate his role in Tibetan history, and indeed in world history, as I have come to see him as an axial figure in the mid-second-millennium CE world transformation Westerners think of as "the European Renaissance," which I think of as a global phenomenon. We in the West are still only dimly aware of the Renaissance transformations in the other great streams of Eurasian civilizations, those of

India, East Asia, Persia, Central Asia, and West Asia, as well as in the even less recognized (as dramatically interrupted by various colonialisms) changes in Sub-Saharan Africa and the Americas. What I think nowadays is that the essence of Tsongkhapa's great achievement is his fully nondual realization of the nature of reality, wherein his critical and intuitional wisdom realized Śhākyamuni's discovery of the equivalence of emptiness and relativity. Such thoroughgoing nonduality saves the deepest meditators from getting stuck in some version of the experience of empty space as "the absolute," "nirvana," "real voidness," and so on, and thereby upon return losing the relatively absolute lightning energy of universal compassion for all self-bound sentient beings. Tsongkhapa's invariable central theme, then, is the inconceivable union of transcendent wisdom and committed compassion that naturally makes the enlightened person the spontaneous servant of all suffering beings, not their master. He understood that a buddha enjoys living out her or his timeless (or all-time) nirvana without wavering from being blissfully engaged in the deliverance of all the time-bound misknowing and unnecessarily miserable beings. Granted there is something a bit intimidating in such a vision—Nāgārjuna called it "frightening to the timid" (*bhiru-bhīṣhanam*), such a "voidness the womb of compassion" (*śhūnyatā-karuṇā-garbhaṃ-stong nyid snying rje snying po can*), this profound (*gaṃbhīraṃ*) enlightenment in performance (*bodhi-sādhanaṃ*). Thus Lama Tsongkhapa's teaching has been disturbing to some at that deep level, though mainly very beneficial to scholars and practitioners of all the Tibetan orders for its profound humanism, its inspiring confidence in the ability of human beings of any era to realize their highest potentials of knowledge and compassion and embody them in lives dedicated to love and benefit, and therefore its proof by example of the durability of the Buddha's reality, his providing of refuge from the storms of delusion, hatred, and greed, and his liberating educational arts and sciences.

It is a great pleasure for me now to have this opportunity to update the book, thanks to the kindness of the officers and staff of Wisdom Publications, and the head and staff of the Library of Tibetan Works & Archives (LTWA), who are collaborating to bring out a new edition of the LTWA original. This time we have edited the entries a bit more than we did decades ago, as Buddhist studies has progressed since then, and it may help the reader to follow some of the main concepts from translation to translation, minus the confusion that arises when the same Tibetan word is translated with very different English terms. We have not done that completely, however, leaving the flavor of the different translator-authors' works largely in place.

The book is divided into five parts. The first begins with a short biography recounted by the late Venerable Geshé Ngawang Dhargyey from a number of traditional sources, notably the *Haven of Faith* by Khedrup Jé (1385–1438 CE). This biography is supplemented by Tsongkhapa's own *Song of Realizations*, a spiritual and educational autobiography, and *Song of the Mystic Experiences* by Jamyang Chöjé Tashi Palden (1379–1449), a record of Tsongkhapa's visionary experiences.

The second part presents Tsongkhapa's teachings on the *Stages of the Path to Enlightenment* (*lamrim*), including the quintessential summary given in revelation by the Bodhisattva Mañjushrī, the briefest version written by the master himself, and a lucid version of the overall path written in a personal letter to a close disciple. It concludes with a prayer for the accomplishment of the path.

The third part gives Tsongkhapa's enlightenment poem, his *Praise* (to Shākyamuni Buddha) *for* (his teaching of) *Dependent Origination,* written on the morning of Tsongkhapa's attainment of complete realization in 1398, as well as his middle-length version of the cultivation of wisdom through transcendent insight (*lhag mthong*).

The fourth part shows his lyrical and mystical side, including praises of the two emblematic bodhisattvas, Mañjushrī and Maitreya, a descriptive prayer for rebirth in the pure land of Amitābha, and a dialogue between the great Nyingma master Lhodrak Khenchen Namkha Gyaltsen (1326–1401) and the supernal bodhisattva Vajrapāṇī in the presence of Tsongkhapa himself. His Holiness the Dalai Lama's senior tutor, the late Very Venerable Kyapjé Ling Rinpoche, would invariably fold his hands in reverence upon the mention of the Lhodrak Namkha Gyaltsen, and express his thanks to that master for dissuading Tsongkhapa and his close disciples from going on pilgrimage to Bodhgaya in India in the late 1390s, telling them how the Dharma was no longer much appreciated in India and it was more important they stay in Tibet to stabilize the Dharma in the Land of Snows.

The final part includes three praises of Tsongkhapa written by his disciple Khedrup Jé, the Seventh Dalai Lama Kalsang Gyatso (1708–1757), and the Eighth Karmapa Lama Mikyö Dorjé (1507–1554), respectively. The entire collection concludes with the famous invocation of Tsongkhapa, *Lord of Tushita's Hundred Gods.*

Special thanks must be given to His Holiness the Fourteenth Dalai Lama, the clarity and inspiration of whose presence has been essentially instrumental in getting most of this work done; to the late Kyapjé Yongzin Ling Rinpoche, who clarified a number of points in my own translations; and to the late Denma Lochö Rinpoche, who saved me from a number of mistakes. And of course my deep thanks are always due to my first teacher who introduced me to the wonderful teaching of Tsongkhapa, the Venerable Geshé Wangyal.

Thanks are also due to the translators and teachers who contributed to the various works collected here: to Geshé Dhargé, who shared his clear vision of Tsongkhapa's life and its impact on Tibet up to the present day; to Sherpa Tulku, Khamlung Tulku, Alex Berzin, and Jonathan Landaw for their dedicated contributions; to Glenn Mullin, who got me moving on it; and to Gyatso Tsering, the dedicated and able director of the Library of Tibetan Works & Archives, who saw it through to completion. On this new edition, great thanks are due to Daniel Aitken, Mary Petrusewicz, Jason Dunbar, and the rest of the talented and skillful staff at Wisdom Publications.

In spite of all this excellent help and inspiration, I am sure there are errors still undetected, at least in the works I translated, for which I alone assume responsibility, inviting others to contribute criticism and improvements toward an eventual final edition of Tsongkhapa's works, along with its scholarly sources in the Tibetan Tengyur, the most important scholarly task I have set myself for this lifetime.

Robert A. F. Thurman
Jé Tsongkhapa Professor of Indo-Tibetan Buddhist Studies,
Columbia University
President, Tibet House US
President, American Institute of Buddhist Studies
Director, Columbia Center for Buddhist Studies
June 9, 2017, Sagadawa Day

BRIEF NOTE on transliteration conventions:

When spelling Sanskrit words or names, we adopt a convention of adding an "h" to "ś," "ṣ," and "c"—that is, giving "śh," "ṣh," and "ch"—while keeping diacriticals familiar to scholars to distinguish long vowels. I cannot understand otherwise how the general reader of English who does not know Sanskrit can properly pronounce these words. Tibetan names of people and places are written phonetically, and not standardized, as there are not yet universally accepted systems for doing so.

PART 1

LIFE, LIBERATION, AND
ACCOMPLISHMENTS

The first chapter in this part, "A Short Biography," was taught by Geshé Ngawang Dhargé in Dharamsālā at the Library of Tibetan Works & Archives, translated in the main by Khamlung Tulku. Its major source is Khedrup Jé's *Haven of Faith*, the standard short biography that is usually printed at the beginning of Tsongkhapa's *Collected Works*. I have a complete draft translation of this work, which will be forthcoming sometime soon. It is included here essentially to give the reader an idea of the many-sided marvel of the life of this great scholar, saint, and teacher-adept.

The second chapter is included to show, in Tsongkhapa's own words, the extreme breadth and depth of his education and experience, as well as his own sense of gratitude to Mañjuśhrī, his final guru. I translated this myself.

The third chapter balances the picture of his vast learning with a sketch of the richness of his mystic experiences, the catalog of his visions sounding like an iconographic encyclopedia.

1   A Short Biography

❦

The great Nyingma teacher Lhodrak Khenchen Namkha Gyaltsen once asked the Bodhisattva Vajrapāṇī to describe the qualities of Lama Jé Tsongkhapa; but since these were innumerable, Vajrapāṇī was unable to do so. To hear the complete biography of the Lord Tsongkhapa would take at least a year. This brief exposition has been compiled merely as an introduction for English-speaking readers.

Tsongkhapa, popularly known as Jé Rinpoche, was born in 1357, the year of the bird, in the Tsong Kha region of Amdo Province, in eastern Tibet. His father, who was bold but unassuming, energetic yet taciturn and reserved, was constantly engaged in thoughts of the Teaching and recited the *Expression of the Names of Mañjushrī* each day. His mother, a guileless and very kind woman, was always chanting the six-syllable mantra of Avalokiteshvara—*oṃ mani padme hūṃ*. They had six sons, Tsongkhapa being the fourth.

During the time of Buddha Shākyamuni, Tsongkhapa, in a previous incarnation, was a young boy who offered the Buddha a clear, crystal rosary and received a conch shell in return. The Buddha then called his disciple Ānanda to him and prophesied that the boy would be born in Tibet, would found a great monastery between the areas of Dri and Den, and would present a crown to the statue of the Buddha in Lhasa and be instrumental in the flourishing of the Dharma in Tibet. The Buddha gave the young boy the future name of Sumati Kīrti, or, in Tibetan, Losang Drakpa.

All this occurred exactly as the Buddha had prophesied. The conch shell that the Buddha had given the boy was unearthed during the building of Ganden monastery and, until 1959, could still be seen in Drepung, the largest monastery in Tibet. The crown still rests on the head of the Buddha statue in Lhasa.

Over a thousand years after the passing of Śhākyamuni Buddha, further prophesies relating to Jé Rinpoche were given by the lotus-born guru Padmasambhava. He predicted that a fully ordained Buddhist monk named Losang Drakpa would appear in the east near the land of China. He said that this monk would be regarded as being an emanation of a bodhisattva of the greatest renown and would attain the complete enjoyment body of a buddha.

During the year of the monkey, which preceded his birth, his parents had unusual dreams. His father dreamed of a monk who came to him from the Five-Peaked Mountain (*Wu-tai-shan*) in China, a place particularly associated with Mañjuśhrī. This monk required shelter for nine months, which, in the dream, his father gave by accommodating him in their shrine room for that length of time.

His mother dreamed that she and one thousand other women were in a flower garden, to which a boy dressed in white and carrying a vessel came from the east while a girl dressed in red and holding peacock feathers in her right hand and a large mirror in her left came from the west. The boy went to each of the women in turn and asked the girl if the woman would be suitable. The girl repeatedly rejected them until the boy pointed to Tsongkhapa's mother, whom she indicated as the perfect choice. The boy and girl then purified Tsongkhapa's mother by bathing her, and when she awoke the next day she felt very light.

In the first month of the year of the bird, Jé Rinpoche's parents again had striking dreams. His mother saw monks coming with many different ritual objects, saying that they were going to invoke the statue of Avalokiteśhvara. When the statue appeared, it was as big as a mountain, yet as it approached her it diminished in size, finally entering her body through her crown aperture.

Tsongkhapa's father dreamed of Vajrapāṇī, who, from his own pure realm, threw down a vajra, which landed on his wife.

Just before giving birth, his mother dreamed of many monks arriving with offerings. When she inquired about their purpose they replied that they had come to pay their respects and gain an audience. Simultaneously, the boy in white from her previous dream appeared and pointed to her womb. With key in hand he entered it and opened a box, from which came the golden statue of Avalokiteśhvara. This statue was stained, and a girl in red appeared and cleaned it with a peacock feather. This dream symbolized that Tsongkhapa would be an emanation of Avalokiteśhvara as well as of Mañjuśhrī. The same morning, Tsongkhapa was born without causing any suffering to his mother. At the time of his birth an auspicious star appeared in the sky. These portents were ample evidence of the birth of someone remarkable. In this respect Jé Rinpoche's birth resembled that of the Buddha.

Prior to these events, Tsongkhapa's future great teacher, Chöjé Döndrup Rinchen, had been in Lhasa and had learned that upon his return to Amdo, he would find a disciple who was an emanation of Mañjushrī. After Tsongkhapa's birth, he sent his chief disciple to the parents with a protection knot, some relic pills, and a letter of greeting.

At the age of three, Tsongkhapa took layman's vows from the Fourth Karmapa Lama Rölpai Dorjé and received the name Kunga Nyingpo.

When Tsongkhapa's parents invited Chöjé Döndrup Rinchen to their home, the lama brought horses, sheep, and a huge number of gifts, which he gave to Tsongkhapa's father. When the lama requested the father to part with his son, the father was delighted at the prospect of his child being with such a great teacher and allowed him to leave with the lama.

Before taking the novice vows, Tsongkhapa received many tantric initiations and teachings, including the Heruka empowerment, and was given the secret name of Dönyo Dorjé. When he was seven, he fulfilled his yearning to take the novice vows, receiving them from his teacher. It is here that he was given the name of Losang Drakpa, which, forty years later, was to become the most talked about and controversial nom de plume in central Tibet.

Tsongkhapa attached greater importance to guarding his vows than he did his eyes or his own life. He had entered the mandalas of Heruka, Hevajra, Yamāntaka, and other deities before receiving ordination, and was even performing self-initiation meditations on Heruka when he was only seven. Before self-initiation is allowed, a major retreat of the specific deity must be completed.

His eminent teacher took care of him until he went to central Tibet at the age of sixteen. Before the statue of Shākyamuni Buddha in the Lhasa Cathedral, he offered prayers to enable his completion of all the stages of sutra and tantra in order to mature and lead other trainees to enlightenment.

Chöjé Döndrup Rinchen proffered advice in poetical form to the effect that Tsongkhapa should first study and master the *Ornament of Realizations* (*Abhisamayālaṃkāra*) and then approach the other four great treatises. The lama further suggested Tsongkhapa's lifelong choice of meditational deities to whom he should make offerings and with whom he should feel perpetually inseparable. The following deities were to be cultivated accordingly: Yamāntaka for the continuation of his practice, Vajrapāṇī for freedom from interruptions, Mañjushrī for increase in wisdom and discriminating awareness, Amitāyus for long life, and the three Dharma protectors—Vaishravaṇa, the six-armed Mahākāla, and Dharmarāja—for protection and for the availability of prerequisites while practicing.

On his departure, his master came with him as far as Tsongkha Kang, from where Tsongkhapa went on alone, walking backward with his hands folded at his heart and reciting the *Hymn of the Names of Mañjushrī*. When he reached the line "Those who do not return to cyclic existence never come back," he had tears in his eyes, for he realized that he would never return to Amdo.

Traveling with Denma Rinchen Pal, in autumn of the year of the bull (1373), Tsongkhapa arrived at Drikung, a five-day journey from Lhasa, where he met the head lama of the Drikung Kagyü monastery, Chennga Chökyi Gyalpo by name. This great lama was his first teacher after leaving his original master and tutored him during his stay at the monastery on various topics such as the altruistic mind (*bodhicitta*) and the five sections of the *Great Seal* (*Mahāmudrā*). He also met the great doctor Könchok Kyap, who taught him the major medical treatises, and by the time he was seventeen he had become an excellent doctor. Thus his fame was already spreading even in the early years of his study.

From Drikung, Tsongkhapa went to the Chödra Chenpo Dewachen monastery in Nyetang, where he studied with Tashi Sengé and Densapa Gekong. Furthermore, Yönten Gyatso taught him how to read the great treatises and continually helped him with the *Ornament of Realizations*. Within eighteen days he had memorized and assimilated both the root text and all its commentaries, and he soon mastered all the works of Maitreya Buddha. He then gained a complete understanding of the *Perfection of Wisdom* (*Prajñāpāramitā*) *Sūtras* at great speed and with little effort. His teachers and fellow students with whom he debated were astonished at his knowledge and, after two years of studying the *Perfection of Wisdom Sūtras*, he was recognized, at the age of nineteen, as a great scholar.

That year Jé Rinpoche debated at the two biggest monasteries of the day in Tibet: Chödra Chenpo Dewachen and Samye. He now became very famous in U-tsang, the central province of Tibet, and undertook an extensive tour of it. First he visited the great monastery of Zhalu, where the renowned translator Khenchen Rinchen Namgyal, a direct disciple of the founder of the monastery, gave him the Heruka initiation. He went on to Sākya, the center of the Sākya tradition, in order to debate further on the major treatises and thereby increase his understanding of them. But upon arrival, he learned that most of the monks had gone to debate at the distant Karpu pass so instead he went to Zhalu and met the great lama Demchok Maitri, who initiated him into the Thirteen Deity Yamāntaka practice. Later he returned to Sākya, but the debaters had still not returned, so this time he went to Sazang and met the great Sazang paṇḍit Mati, who gave him extensive teachings. Returning a third time to Sākya, he was able to take the required examinations on the *Perfection of Wisdom Sūtras*.

He then continued on his travel around the other monasteries of U-tsang, engaging in more and more debates. There are many stories concerning the miraculous visions of those present at these places as well as Tsongkhapa's ever-developing great realizations and insights. Jé Tsongkhapa continued with many other required debates at various monasteries on the systems of philosophical theories and the five major treatises. As he had a great admiration for Nyapön Kunga Pal, whom he met at Tsechen in U-tsang and from whom he received many discourses, he went to him and requested instructions on the *Perfection of Wisdom Sūtras*, but this master was unwell and referred him to his disciple, the Venerable Rendawa (1349–1412). Jé Rinpoche developed tremendous respect for Rendawa's method of teaching the *Treasury of Scientific Knowledge* (*Abhidharmakosha*) and its autocommentary. Tsongkhapa asked many searching questions on certain points to the amazement of his teacher, who was sometimes unable to answer immediately. This master had innumerable spiritual qualities and Tsongkhapa later came to regard him as his principal teacher. Their relationship became such that simultaneously they were each other's master and disciple. He also received teachings on the Middle Way (*Mādhyamaka*) philosophy from Rendawa.

Tsongkhapa composed a verse in honor of Rendawa and would often recite it:

> Mañjushrī, lord of stainless omniscience,
> Avalokiteshvara, mighty treasure of unconditional love,
> O Rendawa Shönu Lodrö, crown jewel of Tibetan sages,
> at your feet I make this request,
> grant protection to me, a fly seeking liberation.

Rendawa replied that this was more applicable to Tsongkhapa than to himself, and so adapted the verse as follows. This is now regarded as Tsongkhapa's mantra:

> Avalokiteshvara, mighty treasure of unconditional love,
> Mañjushrī, lord of stainless knowledge,
> Vajrapāṇi, destroyer of all demonic forces,
> O Jé Tsongkhapa, Losang Drakpa,
> crown jewel of the sages of the Land of Snows,
> humbly I request your blessing.

During the autumn and winter, he received many teachings on the *Entrance to the Middle Way* by Chandrakīrti, who also wrote an autocommentary to it. He then returned to U-tsang, where the great translator and metaphysician Jangchup Tsemo was to give teachings in Lhasa on the five major treatises.

Upon arrival in Lhasa, Tsongkhapa went straight to him and requested teachings. However, this old lama was in delicate health and intended to leave soon for an area south of Lhasa. Tsongkhapa was not satisfied with the short discourses he received, so he returned to Nyetang to become the student of the great scholar of monastic discipline (*Vinaya*), the Abbot Kashiwa Losal, at whose feet he studied the root texts of Guṇaprabha's *Monastic Discipline Sūtra* and Vasubhandu's *Treasury of Scientific Knowledge*, as well as many related commentaries. By the time he left, his depth of understanding surpassed that of his teacher. He memorized a commentary on the extensive root text of the *Monastic Discipline Sūtra* at the daily rate of seventeen Tibetan folios, which is thirty-four pages.

While reciting prayers with the other monks, he had complete and effortless single-pointed concentration on insight meditation.

However, he remained dissatisfied and continued to search for further teachers and teachings. Surely we can derive inspiration from such rectitude, considering that he had memorized, for example, over twenty thousand verses of the extensive *Perfection of Wisdom Sūtras*.

During that winter, a troublesome back pain developed and he thought of returning to Rendawa in U-tsang, but the bitterly cold weather forced him to stay at Nenying, where he gave his first teachings. Scholars had asked for teachings on *Scientific Knowledge* (*Abhidharma*), or metaphysics, and in particular on Asaṅga's *Compendium of Scientific Knowledge*, which develops the Mahāyāna *Scientific Knowledge*. He also wished to study again the *Treasury of Scientific Knowledge* written by Vasubhandu, which is a compilation of the Hīnayāna *Scientific Knowledge*. Tsongkhapa studied the higher tenets, and although it was his initial encounter with this text, he mastered it on first reading and gave perfect teachings.

From there he went to Rendawa, who was at Sākya, and for eleven months taught the *Compendium of Scientific Knowledge*.

At this time, he himself received teachings on Dharmakīrti's *Commentary on Valid Cognition* as well as various texts such as Chandrakīrti's *Entrance to the Middle Way* and the transmission of Guṇaprabha's *Monastic Discipline Sūtra*.

While at Sākya he also received an explanation on the *Hevajra Tantra* from Dorjé Rinchen. This lama also taught him a method by which to cure his painful back.

In the company of the master Rendawa, he left for northern Tibet and spent the spring and summer at the monastery of Chödey. Here Rendawa wrote his commentary to the *Compendium of Scientific Knowledge*, which he later taught to Tsongkhapa upon the disciple's request.

At this time, many people from Tsong Kha were coming to Lhasa with gifts from Tsongkhapa's now-wealthy family and brought with them numerous letters from family and friends imploring him to come back. Reading these upon his return to Lhasa, Jé Tsongkhapa considered going back but realized that return would necessitate a break in his studies with the consequence of failure in his drive to help sentient beings. Thus he stayed back and wrote to his mother instead, enclosing a self-portrait that spoke to her when she opened it. From childhood, he had always possessed a strong sense of renunciation and, later on, even refused an invitation from the emperor of China, who had requested his services as imperial tutor.

Tsongkhapa went into retreat for a few months and in between sessions studied the *Commentary on Valid Cognition*. This text contains four chapters, and when he reached the second, he realized the profundity of the work and developed the greatest respect and admiration for Dharmakīrti while deepening his conviction in the Buddha and his teachings.

He then returned to Tsang to debate, traveling to Narthang where the Tibetan woodblocks of the Tibetan translations of the Buddha's actual teachings (the Kangyur) and of the scientific treatises (the Tengyur) were kept. Here he met the great translator Donzang, author of a critique to the *Commentary on Valid Cognition*, which he taught to Tsongkhapa. They also debated on the two sets of *Scientific Knowledge* and on the *Monastic Discipline Sūtra*. He received teachings on the technical aspects of poetry from the translator Namkha Sangpo and then returned to Rendawa for further elucidation on the five major treatises: the *Middle Way* philosophy, *Logic*, *Scientific Knowledge*, *Perfection of Wisdom*, and *Discipline*. He especially concentrated on the *Entrance to the Middle Way*, and from the Abbot of Narthang received instruction on the *Six Works on Reason* by Nāgārjuna.

Having further refined his dialectical skills, he returned, with Rendawa, to Sākya, where he took examinations on four of the five treatises, omitting the *Perfection of Wisdom Sūtras*, which he had previously covered. Tempers are sometimes short during a debate, but he always remained calm and spoke with amazing mastery.

Tsongkhapa practiced simplicity and lived without affluence or great comfort. People felt overawed before meeting him, but once in his presence were happy and relaxed. He would treat all questions with equal respect. Many of his disciples attained enlightenment in one lifetime.

By this time, people realized that Tsongkhapa was an exceptional person who had taken birth by choice in order to help all sentient beings. His pure morality gained him the greatest respect from all sides and his devotees in U-tsang were now legion. It is uncertain when he took the vows of a fully ordained mendicant monk, or bhikṣhu, for there is nothing to substantiate the commonly accepted thesis that he was twenty-one. However, at a monastery just south of Lhasa, the Abbot Tsultrim Rinchen and a group of bhikṣhus were present at the ordination ceremony. This was conducted in accordance with the tradition of the Hīnayāna, which requires the presence of ten bhikṣhus and an abbot when ordination is given in a place where the teachings are flourishing, technically called a central land. If the ordination is not held in such a place, then at least five bhikṣhus and an abbot should attend. In either case, the presence of two elders is essential. One reads from the *Monastic Discipline Sūtra* and the other questions the candidate concerning his suitability for the monastic way of life.

After ordination, he returned to the great lama at the Drikung Kagyü center, and while the two were engaged in lengthy conversation the elderly lama was overcome by tears, wishing that he too could have practiced so intensively in his youth. He later told his disciples that both he and they had merely received higher rebirths, whereas Jé Tsongkhapa received a stream of realizations even in his youth. He received many teachings from the lama on such topics as tantra, the six yogas of Naropā, the works of Jé Phakmo Drupa (who was one of the foremost disciples of Gampopa), and the teachings of the founder of the monastery.

By this time, Tsongkhapa had received from this Drikung Kagyü master all the teachings that Marpa had given to two of his four sons: Milarepa and Ngokchu Dorjé, the other two "sons" being Metön Chenpo and Tsultrim Dorjé Wang. In addition, Tsongkhapa was constantly developing spiritual qualities and reading all the texts and commentaries available.

At the age of thirty-two he traveled to Tsal Gungthang, where he commenced writing a commentary on the *Perfection of Wisdom Sūtras*. He synthesized all twenty-one Indian commentaries on the *Ornament of Realizations*, for Maitreya's text is itself a commentary to the *Perfection of Wisdom Sūtras*. He called this work *The Golden Rosary of Eloquent Teaching* (*Legshay serteng*). The translator Tagtsang, who had previously disputed many of Tsongkhapa's viewpoints, was amazed by this commentary and showered praise on the text and its author. He wrote, "As your sun of wisdom rises, my flower of arrogance disappears."

Tsongkhapa and his chief disciples traveled to Lhasa and started a fasting retreat near the statue of Avalokiteśhvara. One evening he told the disciple who was his scribe to observe his dreams that night. The acolyte did so, and dreamed that two conch shells appeared in the sky and then descended into his lap, where they merged. He blew this conch, which gave forth a deep resonance. The dream symbolized that Tsongkhapa's teaching would flourish.

After this retreat, he visited Nyethang once more and gave many discourses on the *Middle Way* and the other major treatises. He decided to study the Kālachakra literature and received the relevant teachings from Thupten Yeshé Gyaltsen, who lived near Lhasa. This teacher also imparted the relevant instructions on astrology and mandala construction.

He now started giving tantric initiations and the teachings related to its practices, especially the permission of Sarasvatī, a female deity of wisdom, whom some took to be his particular protectress. The instructions that he conferred ripened and liberated many disciples. While staying at Moenkar Tashi Dzong, just south of Lhasa, he taught the biographies of the great accomplished beings of the past. Jé Tsongkhapa was requested to teach in the tradition of Geshé Shatönpa and others who had dealt with as many as eleven volumes during the period of teaching. He promised to do so and went into retreat for twenty days to prepare. His idea was to commence the discourses on the first day of the Tibetan month, but as so many people wished to attend, he deferred until the fourth to give them time to arrive. In the interim he gave some teachings from the lineage of Marpa and Milarepa, and thereafter proceeded to teach not just eleven but seventeen texts in three months. Each day was divided into fifteen sessions between dawn and dusk and the texts covered were as follows: Dharmakīrti's *Commentary on Valid Cognition*, *Ornament of Realizations* and the other four works of Maitreya, Vasubhandu's *Treasury of Scientific Knowledge*, Asaṅga's *Compendium of Scientific Knowledge*, Guṇaprabha's *Monastic Discipline Sūtra*, the five key texts by Nāgārjuna, Chandrakīrti's *Entrance to the Middle Way*, Āryadeva's *Four Hundred Stanzas*, and Śāntideva's *Entrance to the Bodhisattva's Way of Life*.

He taught all these texts and their commentaries from memory, explaining their use of profound logical analysis and expounding on them in great depth, yet he continued concurrently with his own daily practices. For example, he carried out many self-initiations daily into the mandalas of various deities such as Yamāntaka.

From here he went to the south for a very intensive retreat in the practice of Heruka, in which he did the self-initiation each night. In the Kagyü tradition great emphasis is placed on the six yogas of Naropā and the six teachings of Nigu, both of which deal with breathing and mystic heat meditation. After tremendous practice, in which he engaged in eight hundred rounds of heat meditation daily, he developed both powers.

The summer was spent with his Sākyapa teacher Rendawa. They resided together and mutually gave many initiations on the hill where the famous Potala palace was later to be built. Rendawa then returned to Tsang and Tsongkhapa returned to Kyomo Lung, where he gave discourses on the *Kālachakra Tantra*, the *Ornament of Realizations*, and *Entrance to the Middle Way*.

He decided to concentrate on the four classes of tantra and searched once more for a teacher, even though he had been giving initiations to himself since the age of seven. He left for Tsang to discuss his plans with Rendawa, and on the way, at Rongrub Chölung, Abbot Drakpa Shenyen Rinpoche gave him many initiations. Each of the four Tibetan sects has a standard set of initiations and permissions with respect to the practice of the lower divisions of tantra, and the Rinpoche conferred part of such a set. Two of Tsongkhapa's disciples had received many discourses from Lama Umapa Pawo Dorjé, who now requested Tsongkhapa, via the disciples, to give the initiation of Sarasvatī. This lama as a young shepherd in eastern Tibet had received visions of Black Mañjuśhrī. Tsongkhapa asked him for the teaching of Mañjuśhrī Dharmachakra, but was unable to receive it at the time, since he was determined to see Rendawa.

One night Tsongkhapa dreamed of Chökyi Pal. In his dream, he asked the lama how many times he had received Kālachakra teachings from Butön Rinpoche. The reply was seventeen, which he subsequently substantiated on meeting Chökyi Pal in person. At that time, the living tradition of Kālachakra was in danger of extinction.

He arrived in Tagten, meeting Rendawa and two other teachers, Drakpa Gyaltsen and Chöjé Abacha, and together the four gave many discourses. He received teachings from Rendawa on the *Guhyasamāja Tantra*, called "the king of tantras," and Rendawa advised him to concentrate on the teachings of the three baskets (Tripiṭaka)—the *Discourses, Scientific Knowledge*, and the *Discipline*.

He returned to Lama Umapa Pawo Dorjé to receive the *Mañjuśhrī Dharmachakra* teaching and a commentary on *Entrance to the Middle Way*. Thereafter, due to military activity in the area, he practiced intensive meditation in a cave. Afterward he set off to meet Nyento, a learned scholar and practitioner of Kālachakra, who was also a disciple of Butön Rinpoche. Upon arrival, he found that this great master had already finished teaching the first chapter of the *Kālachakra Tantra*. Tsongkhapa first presented him with a yellow scarf, the color symbolizing accomplishment of the completion-stage yogas, and the next day offered blue and green brocade, the colors being auspicious regarding the development-stage yogas. In their ensuing conversations, the master told Tsongkhapa that his predispositions would enable him to reach the pinnacle of the completion stage of that practice, and proceeded to give him the external, internal, and secret Kālachakra teachings.

One night during this discourse Tsongkhapa dreamed of the Nyingma Lama Kyungpo Lhepa, seated on a great throne, a crown on his head and bell and dorjé in hand, repeating the word *karmavajra*, the Sanskrit form of Tsongkhapa's mystic name. Jé Rinpoche was overjoyed and determined to go to Zhalu, where this lama lived. Another night he dreamed of the same lama, who had at his heart many circles of mantras. The image was so vivid that Tsongkhapa could read them all individually. Consequently, he journeyed to Zhalu to meet this lama, who proved to be identical to the figure in his dreams.

From this master Jé Rinpoche received a complete set of standard initiations into the three lower classes of tantras. Later he embellished the walls of the temple where these initiations were conferred with gold leaf as an act of devotion to the master. He also received here the teachings that this lama held on the *Heruka Tantra* in accordance with the three traditions of the Mahāsiddhas—those of Luhipada, Ghaṇṭapada, and Kriśhṇapada.

Not only should the disciple have impeccable devotion for the master, as exemplified by Tsongkhapa's actions, but the master in turn should be willing to fully teach such a receptive vessel. After every initiation, in order that psychic attainment be transmitted, this lama would always say that he had received the material from such and such a teacher, who had been completely willing to instruct him.

Tsongkhapa and Lama Umapa Pawo Dorjé left for Lhasa in the year of the monkey for Gawa Dong, the seat of the Second State Oracle, located about three miles from Lhasa. In Lhasa Cathedral, they paid their respects to the large statue of Śhākyamuni Buddha, which had been made during the Buddha's lifetime and consecrated by him in person.

This sacred image had been brought to Tibet via China in the seventh century CE by the first queen of King Songtsen Gampo. They offered some prayers before the statue and then returned to Gawa Dong for intensive retreat.

During the retreat, Tsongkhapa received many tantric lineages, including the special teachings on Mañjuśhrī Dharmachakra. Although he experienced visions of Arapacana Mañjuśhrī, the most well-known of the five aspects of Mañjuśhrī, he spoke of these to no one but Khedrup Rinpoche, who was one of his chief disciples and, after Jé Rinpoche had passed away, was also his biographer. Henceforth, Mañjuśhrī and Tsongkhapa became teacher and disciple. From this time onward, Jé Rinpoche was able to question Bodhisattva Mañjuśhrī on any topic.

After this retreat, many thousands of people came for teachings. Mañjuśhrī advised him to enter another intensive retreat, but Lama Umapa felt that it would be of greater benefit for sentient beings if he gave discourses. Thus in spite of Mañjushrī's exhortations, he carried on teaching for some time out of respect to his guru. However, secretly he felt that it was vital for him to master the import of Nāgārjuna's profound view and that sutras and teachers were unable to provide him with these. What was required, he felt, was intensive meditation.

Therefore, after teaching for a short period, he announced that he would soon enter a retreat. Lama Umapa chose to go to eastern Tibet and Tsongkhapa escorted him to Lhasa, where they stayed in one of the small rooms on the upper floor of the Jokhang Cathedral and engaged in long discussions.

Tsongkhapa then returned to Kyomo Lung and taught until winter. He then left for Wolka Chölung, a few days' journey south of Lhasa, in order to enter meditation. When in the Lhasa Cathedral he had asked Mañjushrī how many disciples to take with him into retreat. The reply was eight, and he chose four from central Tibet and four from the two eastern provinces.

The retreat was to last for four years. During the first phase, both master and disciples undertook intensive generation of spiritual energy and purification of the obscurations in order to demonstrate the indispensability of such practices from the outset. Jé Rinpoche personally performed 3.5 million full-length prostrations and 1,800,000 mandala offerings. Indeed, his prostrating form wore an impression in the floor of the temple, and at the conclusion of the mandala offerings his forearm was raw and bleeding.

While the nine were engaged in prostrations, they recited the names of the thirty-five confessional buddhas, who are found in the *Sūtra on the Three Heaps of the Doctrine*—eventually they received a vision of a golden Maitreya. The next vision was that of the medicine buddha, Bhaiṣhajyaguru, and by this stage their insights and spiritual qualities had increased to an extraordinary degree. After they carried out many self-initiations into the thirteen-deity Yamāntaka mandala, they received a vision of Nāgeshvararāja, the king of nāgas buddha, who is one of the thirty-five confessional buddhas. Tsongkhapa subsequently wrote a detailed commentary describing the visions.

The first Tibetan month is known as the month of miracles, for the Buddha competed with six non-Buddhist masters in a contest of miracles from the first to the fifteenth. On the new year's day after the retreat, they went to the temple of Dzingji Ling, where there is a statue of Maitreya. They found this to be in very poor condition, and Tsongkhapa wept on seeing it thus cracked and covered with bird droppings. In order to repair it they all sold all their possessions, except their robes. However, as this was insufficient to make significant repairs, they made offerings to Vaishravaṇa, the wealth deity, and lit a lamp using butter that they had been given by a passing monk. Mañjushrī himself blessed the work, and as a result many people came and offered both financial and physical assistance. Everyone involved in the restoration took daily Mahāyāna precepts and they were all careful to ensure that their speech during the work was prayer rather than mundane chatter. This work on the Maitreya statue was the first of Tsongkhapa's four major social deeds.

Soon thereafter Tsongkhapa wrote down two prayers composed and given to him by Mañjushrī: a praise of Maitreya and a prayer for rebirth in the pure realm of Sukhāvati.[1]

Tsongkhapa and the eight disciples then traveled south of Lhasa to Nyaello Ro, where they spent five months meditating in the mountains. Here they gained many insights and Tsongkhapa gave a large number of discourses on topics such as the *Discipline*. They had a vision of Mañjushrī surrounded by a concourse of not just bodhisattvas but also great adepts (*mahāsiddha*) like Naropā and Tilopā and great scholars like Nāgārjuna and Asaṅga. Tsongkhapa made little of such experiences and did not mention them. Mañjushrī predicted that by following the teachings of these Bodhisattvas, Tsongkhapa would be able to benefit living beings immeasurably. Mañjushrī also manifested to Tsongkhapa in the aspect of Yamāntaka, and after that reappeared as the youthful Mañjushrī, his sword handle at his heart and its tip at Tsongkhapa's chest with a stream of nectar flowing down the blade. Thus Tsongkhapa experienced utter bliss.

The Nyingma Lama Lhodrak Khenchen Namkha Gyaltsen invited Tsongkhapa to his residence at the Lhodrak Drawo monastery to answer some questions for him. When they met, the lama saw Tsongkhapa as Mañjushrī and Tsongkhapa saw that lama as Vajrapāṇī. When he was seventy the Khenchen had a vision of a white goddess who had told him that he would meet a man indistinguishable from Mañjushrī and closely linked with Sarasvatī. The goddess had also noted that there was a karmic connection between Jé Tsongkhapa and the lama spanning their past fifteen lifetimes. That evening Tsongkhapa requested the Khenchen to give teachings on guru yoga, and during these he had a vision of Vajrapāṇī.[2]

The oral teachings of the Kadam tradition had been passed to Atīsha's chief disciple, the layman Dromtönpa. He in turn passed on the lineage in three distinct lines. The textual Kadam lineage was given to Geshé Potowa[3] and emphasized the need for a thorough comprehension of the Buddha's actual words in their entirety, not omitting even a single word or syllable. The Kadam *lamrim* lineage was given to Gampopa and places reliance on Atīsha's *Lamp on the Path to Enlightenment*. The guideline instruction lineage was given to Geshé Chen Ngawa, the disciple of Geshé Sharawa, and depends on the transmission of oral instructions, especially those Atīsha obtained from

Guru Suvarṇadvīpa. This included the lineage of Śhāntideva's *Entrance to the Bodhisattva's Way of Life*, which Atīśha had traveled to an island near Java in order to receive.

Only the latter two lineages were taught to Tsongkhapa by this Nyingma master, for he had already received the first one elsewhere. The Khenchen dreamed that he was told to receive Śhāntideva's *Compendium of Training* from Mañjuśhrī, so he asked Tsongkhapa for this instruction. On Tsongkhapa's head he witnessed Maitreya Buddha; on his right shoulder, White Mañjuśhrī; on his left, Sarasvatī; and he saw many Dharma protectors as well. Tsongkhapa and the Khenchen gave each other reciprocal teachings, and this kind of mutual teacher-disciple association quickly became the pattern in Tsongkhapa's relationship with his various masters.

At this time, Tsongkhapa was considering going to India to meet Nāgabodhi and the great Mahāsiddha Maitrīpa, for he desired further elucidation on Middle Way theory as well as the tantric teaching on the magic body, which is one of the highest stages in the tantric path. So he checked his dreams that night and beheld himself and his disciples, dressed in robes, sitting on Vultures Peak at Rajgir, where the Buddha had taught the *Perfection of Wisdom Sūtras*. Tsongkhapa discussed his plans with Khenchen Namkha Gyaltsen, and the lama said that he would consult Vajrapāṇī. The reply was that if Tsongkhapa went to India, he would develop great renown and probably become the abbot of one of the monasteries there, but Vajrapāṇī advised Tsongkhapa to remain in Tibet because it would be of greater benefit both to sentient beings generally and to his direct disciples, some of whom had already attained the Mahāyāna path of preparation. Furthermore, the heat in India would prove unbearable for some of the Tibetans. The present junior tutor to His Holiness the Dalai Lama, Kyapjé Trijang Dorjé Chang, has said that we have this Nyingma lama to thank for such works as Tsongkhapa's *Great Exposition on the Stages of the Enlightenment Path*, because Tsongkhapa might otherwise have gone to India and been lost to Tibet.

For six months Tsongkhapa stayed at Nyan studying the *Great Exposition of the Stages of the Teachings* by Geshé Trinlé,[4] which is a text on the stages of the path (*lamrim*). Contrary to popular belief, this literary form was neither the creation of Jé Rinpoche nor of Atīśha but originates from the Buddha himself. Tsongkhapa derived innumerable insights from this particular text and would offer incense in its honor. He also gave a variety of other teachings while in Nyan.

Tsongkhapa had now gained complete understanding of all the five paths and perceived the need to compose a text for the benefit of future practitioners. He planned to write in accordance with the works of Nāgārjuna and Atīśha, taking guru-yoga as the foundation of the path and proceeding onward to meditative quiescence and penetrative insight, the very heart of all meditation. He also planned to compose a similar graded text explaining the stages of tantra. The basis for the former project would be the *Light on the Path to Enlightenment*.

From Nyan, Tsongkhapa and thirty others went on a pilgrimage to Tsari, a sacred place of Heruka. This site is visited only once every twelve years during the year of the monkey. It is in a very primitive area inhabited by extremely wild peoples. Here Tsongkhapa had a vision of Maitreya, who told him that he was propagating the teaching in the same manner as Buddha Śhākyamuni had done. The cave in which he experienced this vision can still be seen there.

Tsongkhapa then went into retreat on the *Kālachakra Tantra*, which contains the "six-branched yoga." Again he had a vision of Kālachakra, who said that he would become a second Dharmarāja Suchandra, the famous king who received the Kālachakra system from Vajradhāra, the bodily form with which Buddha conferred the highest tantric teachings.

Tsongkhapa gave many ordinations and discourses on the *Discipline*, for he was a very strict practitioner in that respect and would never transgress even the minor rules of a monk.

He received a vision of Sarasvatī, who told him that he would live to only fifty-seven and until then he should maximize his work for the teachings and sentient beings. Because of this he offered prayers to the eight-armed Uṣhṇīṣhavijayā, a female aspect who is one of the three longlife deities. His disciple Tokden Jampal Gyatso approached Mañjuśhrī regarding the possibility of lengthening Tongkhapa's life, and the reply was affirmative.

Mañjuśhrī told Tsongkhapa in a vision that it was no longer necessary for him to ask for further advice regarding the correct view of emptiness, since he himself now had extensive insight into it. He advised Tsongkhapa to teach in accordance with the standpoints of Nāgārjuna and Atīśha. Jé Rinpoche traveled to the south of Lhasa to stay for the summer, and there he met Gyaltsap Dharma Rinchen, the great scholar and debater from the Sākya tradition. Gyaltsap Jé wanted to debate with Tsongkhapa and first encountered him while the latter was giving teachings. Gyaltsap even had the temerity to climb onto Tsongkhapa's throne, but as he listened to the discourse, all of his questions were so perfectly answered that he realized his grave error, got down from the throne, offered three prostrations and humbly sat with the listeners. Later on Gyaltsap Jé was to become renowned as one of the foremost disciples of Tsongkhapa.

Tsongkhapa then returned to Wolka Chölung, the scene of his four-year retreat, this time to undertake an intensive one-year retreat in which he concentrated on the Middle Way schools of thought in greater detail. During this period, he received a vision of Nāgārjuna with his five chief disciples known as the "holy father and sons." Buddhapālita, one of the sons and also the author of a famous composition by the same name, placed his text on Tsongkhapa's head to give him inspiration and blessings. Buddhapālita's book, *Sustaining Buddha,*[5] is the best commentary to Nāgārjuna's *Wisdom: Root Verses on the Middle Way.* The very next morning while Tsongkhapa was perusing the eighteenth chapter of this commentary, he gained complete nonconceptual understanding of emptiness. He then composed a text in praise of the Buddha's teachings on the interrelativity of all things. This text, popularly called *Essence of Good Eloquence,* or *Praise to Dependent Origination,*[6] mentions how he was unable to restrain tears whenever he thought of the Buddha's kindness in teaching the *Perfection of Wisdom Sūtras* at Vulture's Peak.

After intensive practice, many retreats, and a great deal of meditation, Tsongkhapa received visions of many deities. He also constantly sought Mañjuśrī's advice on his choice of abode and study material.

He traveled to Wolka and spent the winter and spring teaching the monks the enormity of the altruistic attitude and the profundity of emptiness. He accepted an invitation to spend the rainy season retreat in the south of Lhasa, after which he came back to Lhasa at the request of Namkha Sangpo and stayed on the Potala Peak, giving many discourses. Thereafter he traveled to Gawa Dong.

For tantric practice, extraordinary devotion to the tantric master and flawless moral discipline are necessary, especially to keep the very easily broken tantric pledges. Tsongkhapa taught the *Fifty Stanzas on the Guru,* written by Aśhvaghoṣha, who had initially been a non-Buddhist but who had changed his faith after defeat in debate by Āryadeva and thereafter was known as Āchārya Vīra or Āryaśhūra. Jé Tsongkhapa also taught a text on the root tantric vows and Asaṅga's *Bodhisattva Levels* as well as writing commentaries to them.

Rendawa had so far remained in Tsang but now came to meet Tsongkhapa at Gawa Dong, where they gave many teachings to each other. Tsongkhapa made elaborate offerings to Rendawa in connection with his practice of guru-yoga.

They both considered doing a retreat at Reting, the monastery that had been founded by Dromtonpa. The great Kadam geshés had stayed there and a special tradition of group retreats had originated at this monastery. Thus it seemed to be an ideal environment for such activity.

Reting is a place of beautiful juniper forests, located three days' journey by horse to the north of Lhasa. It was here that Tsongkhapa wrote the *Great Exposition of the Stages of the Enlightenment Path* as well as many commentaries. Just above the monastery was a large rock in the shape of a lion where Tsongkhapa sat with a scroll painting of Atīśha next to him. This painting was still in the monastery in 1959. First he made entreaties to Atīśha and received a vision of all the lineages from the Buddha to his own teachers. The vision continued for one month, giving Tsongkhapa the chance to put forth many questions. Finally, all the lineages dissolved into Atīśha, Dromtonpa, Geshé Potowa, and Geshé Sharawa. Thus Tsongkhapa was able to have prolonged discussion with these great lamas. Then the latter three masters dissolved into Atīśha, who gave Tsongkhapa a blessing by placing his hand on Tsongkhapa's head.

After this vision Jé Rinpoche completed the *Great Exposition of the Stages of the Enlightenment Path* as far as the section on penetrative insight.[7]

At this point he hesitated, feeling that in future such teachings would be beyond anyone's comprehension. However, Mañjuśhrī appeared and bade Tsongkhapa both to finish the work and to write a short and medium-length exposition on the stages of the path for those whose aptitude was not commensurate with the presentation in the *Great Exposition*. The eight great Dharma protectors also requested him to continue with this work, and it is a tribute to his humility that such great names were not included in the colophon, where it is customary to mention those who have requested the teaching. In fact he wrote only the name of one of his disciples there.

Meanwhile Rendawa had been discoursing on some of Nāgārjuna's tantric writings. Tsongkhapa gave many teachings using Asaṅga's work, the *Disciple Stages*, which includes a section on meditative quiescence, and at this time many people staying in the surrounding mountains developed samādhi. Rendawa and Tsongkhapa also clarified points of issue concerning certain tantric practices.

They were then invited by the great Lama Jamkawa to stay some time at the main Drikung Kagyü monastery. So they went there in the spring when the great translator Kyabchok Palsang was in residence. Tsongkhapa was now over forty. There he received instruction according to the Kagyü tradition on the six yogas of Naropā and a special oral teaching on the *Great Seal*.

The master Yönten Gyatso invited Tsongkhapa, Rendawa, and Kyabchok Palsang to Namtze Deng, a monastery of six hundred monks, where they spent the rainy season retreat with their host as sponsor. Tsongkhapa gave an elaborate discourse on the *Discipline* so lucidly that it is regarded as the second of his four greatest social deeds. He also gave teachings on *Validating Cognition* and the *Middle Way*.

After the retreat Rendawa left for Tsang and Tsongkhapa went to Reting, where, ensconced at the lion-shaped rock above the monastery, he completed the *Great Exposition*. Kyabchok Palsang had particularly urged the completion of this work.

Tsongkhapa now decided to teach tantra and so sent twenty-five of his disciples to Kyabchok Palsang for initiations before he started. He was concerned that many people who had taken bodhisattva vows from him and from countless other masters did not know how to guard their vows properly. Therefore he wrote a commentary on the moral discipline chapter of Asaṅga's *Bodhisattva Levels*. There are two distinct lineages with respect to taking these vows, one of which derives from the above text, whereas the more well-known one is from Shāntideva's *Entrance to the Bodhisattva's Way of Life*. In both cases the vows are identical. Jé Tsongkhapa wrote a commentary to the *Fifty Stanzas on the Guru* to reinforce the supremacy of such devotions in the Tantric Vehicle. He then taught the *Great Exposition* in its entirety to Kyabchok Palsang, who thereafter went to U-tsang with the text while Tsongkhapa stayed and gave teachings on this remarkable composition. He spent the month of miracles at Reting making offerings, after which he returned to Lhasa.

Until Tsongkhapa's time, little value was given to the study of dialectics and epistemology; but his discourses provided the necessary impetus for people to realize the enormous importance of these subjects as an indispensable tool in the quest for enlightenment. Khedrup Rinpoche noted that people were able to appreciate this because of Jé Tsongkhapa's infinite kindness, which would be difficult to repay. At the request of Miwang Drakpa Gyaltsen, Tsongkhapa spent the next rainy season retreat at Wonde Chenteng, where he gave many discourses.

At Wolka Jampa Ling he taught all the stages of the highest tantras as well as the *Great Exposition of the Stages of the Enlightenment Path*, and then entered a strict retreat with a few disciples. During this retreat, he composed a commentary to Nāgabodhi's *Twenty-Verse Rite on the Guhyasamāja Mandala*, Nāgabodhi having been a disciple of Nāgārjuna.

One of the most difficult parts of tantra is the Guhyasamāja teaching on the magic body. Here Tsongkhapa confidentially told several disciples that he had clearly understood and mastered these teachings some ten years earlier and affirmed his intention of explaining how to actualize such a body. Complete understanding of this ensures the attainment of buddhahood in one lifetime.

Following many requests, he wrote the *Great Exposition of the Secret Mantra Stages,* the sequel to his previous *Great Exposition* dealing with the path, from the point where the previous text ended, continuing up to unsurpassed enlightenment. He also composed a text on the method of attaining enlightenment as found exclusively in the practice of Yamāntaka. In all facets of the practice, his concentration was single-pointed and uninterrupted. During meditation he was completely oblivious to all disturbances around him.

South of Lhasa at Jangchup Ling he taught both *Great Expositions*, after which he went to the area near Lhasa where Sera monastery now stands. Close to the site was Chöding hermitage, where he had spent many rainy season retreats. After completing a retreat there, he taught the *Guhyasamāja* and *Heruka Tantras* and gave general discourses on the completion stage of the other tantras.

Nāgārjuna's *Wisdom: Root Verses on the Middle Way* is very difficult to understand, and Tsongkhapa, now almost fifty, was requested to write a commentary to it. During the composition, he invoked Mañjushrī and seed syllables of the twenty voidnesses appeared in the sky around him.

Once the wisdom letter *AH* appeared and descended onto a nearby rock, leaving an impression that could still be seen in 1959 in one of the Sera gardens. Jé Rinpoche prophesied that a large monastery producing many sages would be constructed at that spot. Sera monastery was duly built there by one of his disciples, Jamchen Chöjé, who was later sent to China as the imperial tutor in Tsongkhapa's stead. Tsongkhapa foresaw interruptions if he remained at Chöding, so he departed for the peace and solitude of Raka Drag. Soon afterward a party of Chinese officials and ministers arrived at Chöding, but in the absence of Tsongkhapa, they proceeded on to Lhasa. Miwang Drakpa Gyaltsen met these dignitaries, who requested his services in obtaining an audience with Tsongkhapa. So he traveled to Raka Drag to inform Tsongkhapa of the situation.

Jé Tsongkhapa came to Lhasa, where the ministers presented him with a letter from the Chinese emperor requesting his presence in China that he might teach, but Tsongkhapa replied that his advancing age and his wish to stay in retreat precluded acceptance. The officials went back to China with his reply and some images of the Buddha for the emperor while Tsongkhapa returned to Raka Drag.

Tsongkhapa then commenced writing the *Essence of True Eloquence, An Analysis of Interpretable and Definitive Meaning Teachings*, which studies different theories of how to differentiate between the interpretable and definitive teachings of the Buddha. He then went to Chöding and stayed for two years, giving teachings on his stages of the path texts.

After the rainy season retreat, Miwang Drakpa Gyaltsen invited him to spend the winter at Kyimay Drumbu Lung and he traveled there with an estimated five hundred to one thousand disciples, many of whom were great scholars. He gave many discourses on the *Stages of the Path*, the *Heruka*

Tantra, and other tantric systems during his stay. Upon leaving Chöding, he conceived the idea of and decided to inaugurate the Great Prayer Festival, asking two of his disciples to prepare many offerings for it; however, funds were lacking because he always gave away whatever he received. Henceforth he kept everything he was given solely for use in the festival.

The two disciples gathered many artists to both wash with perfumes and paint the statues and walls of the Lhasa Cathedral. In 1409 Tsongkhapa was fifty-two, and during the final evening of the year of the mouse eight thousand monks assembled for the first Great Prayer Festival, which ushered in the year of the bull. An enormous offering ceremony commenced at midnight with Tsongkhapa presenting a crown of fine gold to the statue of Śhākyamuni Buddha, which he consecrated, thus fulfilling the Buddha's prophecy. This was the third of his four major social deeds.

Tsongkhapa also presented a jeweled silver crown to the statue of Avalokiteśhvara. This statue was destroyed by the Chinese after 1959, though some Tibetans managed to salvage three of the heads, two of which are now on display in the cathedral at Dharamsāla in India. Jé Rinpoche made copious offerings, including a huge silver begging bowl, which he presented to the Buddha statue. He also robed and crowned many of the other statues in the Jokhang Cathedral.

Large amounts of food were offered and later distributed among the poor and destitute. The multifarious events of the festival, which lasted twenty-one days, would take many pages to describe even in broad outline. Each day gold was applied to the face of the Buddha statue, and on the eighth and fifteenth the bodies of all the statues were painted with gold.

During the festival, Tsongkhapa gave many teachings on both sutra and tantra, including a discourse on Āryaśhūra's *Former Birth Tales*. This teaching is still given annually in Dharamsāla on the fifteenth of the first Tibetan month by His Holiness the Fourteenth Dalai Lama. The power and clarity of Tsongkhapa's discourses wrought beneficial change in many people, who also saw visions of great accomplished beings of the past appearing in the sky. Tsongkhapa by now had become celebrated as an author and teacher of great renown.

At the close of the festival his disciples concluded that it would be unwise for him to continue his peripatetic lifestyle. Hence they offered to build him a monastery wherever he chose. He prayed in front of the Śhākyamuni statue and examined his dreams, concluding that such a monastery should indeed be built, and he chose Nomad Mountain (Drogri) as the site. This was in fact the very spot cited in the Buddha's prophecy. He decided to call the monastery Ganden—in Sanskrit, Tushita—the present abode of Maitreya, the next Buddha. Tsongkhapa went to the site with one of his disciples, Gendun Drup, who was later posthumously recognized as the First Dalai Lama, appointing two others to take charge of the construction.

Many gave donations and many volunteered their services in the building of the monastery. The main temple and over seventy other buildings were completed within a year. The monastery was built in accordance with the rules of the *Monastic Discipline Sūtra* laid down by the Buddha, so there was a preliminary survey of the site for future dangers and a check to make sure that there was no infringement of land ownership. In the following year, the year of the tiger (1410), Tsongkhapa went to Ganden and gave instruction on the *Great Exposition of the Stages of the Enlightenment Path*, discourses on the *Guhyasamāja Tantra*, on Asaṅga's *Compendium of Scientific Knowledge*, and explanations of difficult dialectical points.

Not only did he compose a host of commentaries to such texts as the *Guhyasamāja Tantra*, but on careful consideration of the list of Tsongkhapa's discourses and teachings, it would also appear that he must have spent his whole life discoursing. Yet from the point of view of his daily practice it seems that he spent his whole life in meditative retreat. But upon reading his literary output, it would seem that he could only have read and composed texts. His Holiness the Dalai Lama feels that Jé Rinpoche's greatest feat was to have done all three.

Signs now appeared suggesting the onset of considerable health problems from his fifty-seventh year onward. Therefore, when he was fifty-five, his disciples requested him to perform special practices in the extensive Yamāntaka system in order to transcend these auguries. Together with thirty disciples he went for a Yamāntaka retreat during the winter and spring, after which Khedrup Rinpoche and many other disciples performed longlife rituals for their master's well-being.

At fifty-six he taught extensively, telling his disciples not to forget such instruction, for his ability to continue teaching was uncertain. His disciples' mounting concern impelled them to offer still more prayers and mandalas, and it is said that every longevity practice possible was carried out for his benefit.

In Tsongkhapa's fifty-fifth year, the year of the dragon (1412), he and many disciples entered an intensive retreat on the seventh day of the eighth month, and during it the disciples offered fervent prayers for his long life.

During the eleventh month he felt unwell, and though no sickness manifested, he was unable to sleep. Khedrup Rinpoche and the future First Dalai Lama carried out a wide range of rituals and offerings to the Dharma protectors in order to safeguard their master's life.

He frequently entered long periods of single-pointed concentration, until one day, while out walking, he said that he felt much better. From his throne he urged his disciples never to separate themselves from total altruism or from meditation on it, and while seated there, he had a vision of the Buddha Vajraviḍaraṇa (Crusher of Interferences). The Buddha approached Tsongkhapa, then dissolved into him filling him with renewed strength and vigor. He was temporarily cured and his disciples rejoiced. In the following year he accepted Miwang Drakpa Gyaltsen's invitation to spend the rainy season retreat at Wongyi Tashi Dokar, where he gave many discourses. After this sojourn he returned to Ganden and composed a commentary to Luhipada's system of *Chakrasaṃvara* (the *Heruka Tantra*), a commentary to Chandrakīrti's logical analysis of the completion stages of the unexcelled yoga tantras, and the commentary known as the *Four Commentaries Combined* on the *Guhyasamāja Tantra.*[8]

At this juncture he decided to erect a special temple where tantric rituals could be carried out privately, since the uninitiated are not permitted to see artifacts such as the mandalas. In the year of the sheep (1415) the construction of this hall at Ganden commenced. He was fifty-eight at the time.

Two years later in the third month of the year of the bird (1417), artists and sculptors congregated at Ganden to make a statue of Buddha Śhākyamuni. This was to slightly exceed the dimensions of the one in the Lhasa Cathedral. The artists were commissioned to make gilded copper three-dimensional mandala palaces relating to the thirty-two-deity Guhyasamāja, the sixty-two-deity Heruka, and the thirteen-deity Yamāntaka practices.

During the fabrication of these, miraculous manifestation occurred, and effulgent symbols of various deities, possessing an inherent sheen and luster, came forth from the molds and were often surrounded by rainbow light. The consecration ceremonies were performed, thus completing the construction of Ganden's main hall and the various figures contained therein. This is held to be the fourth of Tsongkhapa's major social deeds.

In the year of the dog (1418), when Jé Rinpoche was sixty-one, he gave extensive discourses and wrote a commentary on *Entrance to The Middle Way*. His complete works fill eighteen large volumes.

Four of his disciples one day witnessed him losing a tooth, and each of them asked if he might have it. Jé Tsongkhapa's choice fell on Khedrup Rinpoche, whom he likened to Mount Meru surrounded by rings of golden mountains. However, the other three disciples did not relent, so Tsongkhapa elected to satisfy everyone. He took back the tooth, placed it on the altar, and then proceeded to make offerings, perform rituals, and recite prayers. The tooth transformed into the youthful Mañjuśhrī, from whose forehead came a white relic pill the size of a plover's egg, from whose throat came a red one, and from whose heart came a blue one. Thus everyone was satisfied. The manifestation became the tooth once more, which was returned to Khedrup Rinpoche.

In the year of the hog (1419) Tsongkhapa's disciples invited him to the hot springs at Tolung. From Ganden, Tsongkhapa first went to Lhasa and made offerings and prayers, then journeyed on to the hot springs, where he gave teachings to those assembled there. On a previous visit there, he had leaned against a rock and his body had left an imprint that still can be seen. Here he also received a vision of the sixteen great arhats. Thus Tolung was included on the itinerary of the Lhasa Lower Tantric College during their annual one-month stay at Ganden. Tsongkhapa then went on to Drepung at the invitation of the founder, Tashi Palden, and gave a variety of discourses on teachings such as the *Stages of the Path*, the six yogas of Naropā, and the *Entrance to the Middle Way*. Those present saw rainbows appear in a clear sky, which they took as an indication of Tsongkhapa's impending death. About two thousand of the roughly nine thousand monks present were holders of the Tripiṭaka, the three baskets of the sutra teachings. Tsongkhapa privately requested a sculptor to fashion a large silver image of Buddha Vairochana. During a teaching on the root text of the *Guhyasamāja Tantra*, which contains seventeen chapters, Tsongkhapa unexpectedly halted at the end of the ninth, saying that he would break there. This was a most unusual occurrence, and again people felt it to be an indication that he was preparing for his passing away. It is considered auspicious to leave a teaching unfinished, if departing somewhere, to ensure that master and disciples will meet again and continue the teaching in this and future lives. Before he left Drepung, there was a minor earth tremor and the appearance of more rainbows.

From there he went to the Lhasa Jokhang Cathedral to make comprehensive prayers and offerings with the wish that the teachings might endure for the benefit of all sentient beings. He prostrated before leaving the cathedral, which also was unusual because it is only done in such circumstances when return to that place will be impossible for a long time. He said that he might be unable to come again to the cathedral.

He was invited to Chöding hermitage by a disciple, whom he instructed to build a large monastery there. This came to be the famous Sera monastery, and Tsongkhapa went to the site of the future monastery to conduct a confession ceremony in order to strengthen the links between master and disciples. He also taught the root tantras of Guhyasamāja and Heruka.

From there he returned to Ganden, stopping on the way at Dechen at the invitation of a government official. He suggested that Dechen monastery should be rebuilt and that the monks should harmonize their practices of the *Discipline* and the tantras following the method introduced into Tibet by the great kindness of Atīśha. He presided at an elaborate consecration ceremony and stated that he would be unable to return to conduct another when the reconstruction was finished. In addition, he donated many things to furnish the monastery.

Back at the main hall in Ganden, he offered a massive ritual cake, then concluded the rite with many prayers from the *Stages of the Path* tradition. Together with the assembly of monks gathered in the hall, he dedicated the accumulated merit for the benefit of all sentient beings and finally recited the *Prayers for the Pure Land* and other auspicious verses. Afterward, in the room, he expressed satisfaction at being back in the monastery far removed from trivial affairs. That night he developed a back pain, so many monks gathered for prayers. It was the year of the hog and Tsongkhapa was sixty-two.

The next day he admitted he was in pain, though it was not immediately obvious. He gave his hat and robe to Gyaltsap Jé and proffered advice to his disciples, stressing the importance of not drifting away from an altruistic state of mind.

He continued to perform self-initiations and four-session yoga of many deities. On the twentieth of the tenth month, he made an extensive offering to Heruka and that night meditated on the adamantine recitation (*vajrajāpa*), a special tantric breathing exercise. Very early on the morning of the twenty-fifth, sitting in full lotus posture, he meditated on emptiness, then at dawn made a series of inner offerings, although no one present could understand why.

His breathing ceased and his body regained the vibrancy of a sixteen-year-old, similar to the generally depicted appearance of the youthful Mañjuśhrī. Many disciples present witnessed the emission of variegated light rays from his body, which substantiates the belief that Tsongkhapa entered the intermediate state as a fully enlightened being. For the following forty-nine days, an offering of one hundred thousand butter lamps and many other offerings were made at Ganden and Drepung. Many saw a rain of flowers descend from the sky. A high lama of the Kagyü tradition, Kagyü Panchen, came to Ganden fifteen days after the passing away and composed *The Eighty (Main Deeds) of Tsongkhapa*, which is regarded as the standard biography, and which contains elaborate details of his life.

The disciples consulted oracles—those who, in a state of trance, become the mediums of certain Dharma protectors—in order to divine the most appropriate treatment for the body. The oracles' prophesy was that it should be enshrined in a stupa. A special hall was built to accommodate a silver platform, on top of which was a solid-gold stupa that became very well known and was visited by many Tibetans and Mongolians. Another famous stupa associated with Tsongkhapa is the one containing the tree that grew from his afterbirth. It appeared in the middle of his parent's house in Amdo, now the site of Kumbum monastery, and this stupa still exists.

The Ganden stupa was desecrated during the Cultural Revolution of the midsixties when the whole of Ganden was demolished. However, some of Tsongkhapa's hair was recovered and there are a number of statues containing clippings in Tibetan homes in India. What is extraordinary is that the mummified body of Jé Tsongkhapa was still intact in the middle of this century. Gyaltsap Dharma Rinchen was requested by the other disciples to ascend the throne of Ganden, signifying that he was to be head of the monastery. His incumbency lasted for twelve years until his own demise. Gyaltsap Jé was a prolific writer and his works are contained in eight volumes. Khedrup Rinpoche then succeeded to his office until he passed away at the age of fifty-four. These two are always depicted flanking Jé Tsongkhapa in scroll paintings of the *Hundred Gods of Tushita*.[9]

Khedrup Jé received five visions of Tsongkhapa after his master's decease. The first occurred when Khedrup Jé had grown disheartened at being unable to give clear teachings on emptiness. Tsongkhapa appeared and advised him concerning the correct view. Later Khedrup Jé was again downhearted at his failure to fathom a difficult tantric text written by Tsongkhapa, and since he was the best scholar of the time, he could not refer to anyone. Tsongkhapa appeared on an elephant and answered many questions. Again, while reading the *Great Exposition of the Stages of the Enlightenment Path*, he was struck by the brilliance of Tsongkhapa as a master and, at that moment, his teacher appeared.

Jé Tsongkhapa, who was only sixty-two when he passed away, taught and achieved so much. This is especially true considering the much longer life spans of Asaṅga and Nāgārjuna, which were one hundred and fifty years and six hundred years, respectively.

On another occasion, Tsongkhapa appeared and fortified Khedrup Jé when he became discouraged after musing on the decline of the Buddha's doctrine. Khedrup Jé, who often thought of joining his master in the Tushita Pure Land, received the final vision when he wished to ascertain whether Tsongkhapa had been born in Tushita as had been predicted. Tsongkhapa appeared on a tiger, holding a sword and a skull-cup, and this time Khedrup Jé asked for Tsongkhapa's approval of his decision to enter parinirvāṇa, which was given. Khedrup Jé prepared to leave this life but was urged by six-armed Mahākāla, in a vision, to remain for the benefit of sentient beings. However, Khedrup Jé felt that he had done everything possible, and so went to the Land of Ḍākinīs.

His body was placed inside another stupa beside that of Tsongkhapa, and the same was done with Gyaltsap Jé's remains. However, the lineage of the throneholder of Ganden, who is also the head of the Gelug sect that Tsongkhapa founded, did not cease. The ninety-seventh successor to Tsongkhapa was the senior tutor to His Holiness the Fourteenth Dalai Lama, Kyabjé Ling Rinpoche.

Many of Tsongkhapa's disciples benefited sentient beings through the foundation of religious institutions, such as the great monasteries of Drepung, Sera, and Ganden. Furthermore, the First Dalai Lama founded Tashi Lhunpo monastery at Shigatse, about halfway between Lhasa and the Nepalese border to the south. The two tantric colleges in Lhasa were also inaugurated.

After Tsongkhapa's passing away several biographies were written by lamas from the different traditions. They all agreed that he was a teacher without parallel. The ninth Karmapa Lama praised Tsongkhapa as one "who swept away wrong views with the correct and perfect ones."

It is generally accepted that the three greatest contributors in the annals of Tibet were Guru Padmasambhava, Atīsha, and Tsongkhapa, all of whom appeared when a great teacher was needed. It was the thirty-seventh Tibetan king, Trisong Detsen, who first invited the Bodhisattva Shāntarakṣhita to Tibet. At that time, there were many evil forces in Tibet strongly resenting the appearance of the Buddha's teaching there, thus hindrances and calamities occurred. Shāntarakṣhita advised the king to invite Padmasambhava, who came and subdued these malignant forces, and then instigated the construction of the first monastery at Samye, south of Lhasa. After the repression of the Dharma by King Lang Darma, there was a period in Tibet when a very degenerate form of religion was practiced. During this time, no one could find compatibility between the systems of sutra and tantra, which were considered to be an irreconcilable dichotomy. It was Atīsha who dispelled such views and started the Kadam tradition. Later, when people could not see how learning and yogic practice were to be united, Tsongkhapa came and revealed the correct path.

Today we should strive to emulate Tsongkhapa's peerless progress along the path. To hear as many teachings as possible and never to be satisfied with less than ultimate knowledge are the most important lessons to be applied in life. It is imperative to appreciate and work toward the peerless goal of wishing to achieve enlightenment in order to help every other sentient being do exactly the same. Jé Rinpoche's example of scriptural learning and meditative application taken as a unified path show the essence of Buddha's intent and the truly quick method of achieving enlightenment.

2 Destiny Fulfilled

rTogs brjod mdun legs ma

———————————— ༺ ————————————

Tsongkhapa's Education as a Song of Realization

Om! May all be happy and well!

I bow to the feet of the kind Guru,
root of all good fortune,
and to the Holy Wisdom Treasure, Mañjuśhrī,
who is the eye to see the liberation of enlightenment
and even all ascendance in the world,
and who are the place of recuperation
from the weary wandering in the roads of life!

When one's efforts still are slight,
it is said to be best to congratulate the virtues of others
in order to gather the momentous stores (of merit and wisdom).
One feels an even greater joy, especially
when free of claims to one's own past virtues,
thinking, "increase past virtues ever more,"
in order to live up to the impact of the Victor's teaching,
also seeing many other dire necessities—
it is excellent, O my mind, when you feel such joy!

First, I sought out often extensive learning,
then all teachings dawned as transformative instructions.

Finally, I practiced all day and all night,
completely dedicated to spread the teaching!

Thinking this over, how well my destiny was fulfilled!
Thank you so very much, O Holy Wisdom Treasure![10]

Quest of Extensive Learning

If the lamp of true learning does not illuminate
the darkness that hides the ground of ethical choice,
you cannot know even the path, not to mention
entrance into the supreme city of liberation!
Therefore, not satisfied with partiality and rough ideas,
I studied closely all the books of Maitreya, Dharma Lord,
and of those (great sages) greatly renowned in India
as the Six Ornaments and the Two Superiors.[11]

Thinking this over, how well my destiny was fulfilled!
Thank you so very much, O Holy Wisdom Treasure!

Especially for an egocentric person, the sole door
for determining the precise reality of things
is the treatise on valid reasoning; so, with many efforts,
I studied its crucial points again and again.

Thinking this over, how well my destiny was fulfilled!
Thank you so very much, O Holy Wisdom Treasure!

Though I had worked hard on the treatises of sutra and tantra,
and I was practicing and teaching the impact of the profound,
when I realized that my view had not advanced far beyond
the view that learned nothing and knows nothing at all,
I then studied thoroughly all the essential keys
that bring out the authentic view, which I discovered
on the path of subtle philosophy that probes the profound,
especially opened up in the scientific treatises of Nāgārjuna—
and I fully resolved all my perplexities!

Thinking this over, how well my destiny was fulfilled!
Thank you so very much, O Holy Wisdom Treasure!

It is said that "there are two vehicles
for the journey to perfect enlightenment,
the Transcendence Vehicle and the deep Vajra Vehicle;
and the secret tantras are very much superior
to the vehicle of the transcendences!"
This is as well-known as sun and moon.
Yet there are those, pompous with pretense of wisdom,
who verbally assert the truth of that saying
yet make no inquiry into the vehicle of the profound!
If such as they are supposed to be intelligent,
how could anyone else ever be thought dumb?
Alas! It is amazing that any should repudiate
such an unexcelled path, so hard to come across!
Therefore I entered that deep treasury of twin accomplishments,
the Vajra Vehicle, the Supreme Vehicle of the Victors,
more rare even than the buddhas themselves;
and I worked hard at it and studied it afar.

Thinking this over, how well my destiny was fulfilled!
Thank you so very much, O Holy Wisdom Treasure!

Seeing clearly that if I did not understand
the methods of the paths of the three lower tantras,
my decision that the unexcelled yoga tantra is best of all
would be no more than an unsupported assertion,
so I inquired deeply into the general and specific three types
of action tantra—the *General Ritual Secret*, the *Well-Attained*,
the *Subāhu Dialogue*, and the *Meditation Ultimate*.[12]

Thinking this over, how well my destiny was fulfilled!
Thank you so very much, O Holy Wisdom Treasure!

Among the second class, the performance tantras,
I studied the main tantra, the *Vairochana Enlightenment*,
and I ascertained thoroughly the precise orientation
of all the performance tantras.
Among the third class, the yoga tantras,
I studied the main tantra, the glorious *Compendium of Principles*,
and its explanatory tantras, such as the *Vajra Summit*,
and I enjoyed the banquet of the yoga tantras!

Thinking this over, how well my destiny was fulfilled!
Thank you so very much, O Holy Wisdom Treasure!

Among the fourth class, the unexcelled yoga tantras,
I studied the root tantras and explanatory tantras
of the father tantra, the *Guhyasamāja Root Tantra*,
renowned as sun and moon among the Indian sages;
and of the yogini tantras such the *Super Bliss* and the *Hevajra*,
and of the *Kālachakra*, tantra of the champions,
whose method differs from other sutras and tantras,
along with its commentary, the *Stainless Light*.

Thinking this over, how well my destiny was fulfilled!
Thank you so very much, O Holy Wisdom Treasure!

All Teachings Dawn as Training

With a firm, intense, and enduring faith in Mañjushrī,
best banisher of darkness from the disciple's mind,
I prayed that all the teachings dawn as transformative instructions
and applied myself to all the requisite conditions.

Thinking this over, how well my destiny was fulfilled!
Thank you so very much, O Holy Wisdom Treasure!

Working in that way, I found a special certainty
in the stages of the path of enlightenment,
the tradition come down from Nāgārjuna and Asaṅga,
and the *Perfection of Wisdom*, best book on the profound,
dawned for me as a transformative instruction.

Thinking this over, how well my destiny was fulfilled!
Thank you so very much, O Holy Wisdom Treasure!

In this northern land, many speak out in unison,
whether they have studied the logical texts or not:
"There is no stage of practice of the path to enlightenment
in the *Collection* and the *Seven Branch Texts* of *Validating Cognition*."
But one should take as authoritative the direct revelation
granted by Mañjushrī to Dignāga, saying explicitly—
"This book will in the future become the eye for all beings!"

Thus seeing that the view above was absolutely wrong,
and especially investigating deeply the methods therein,
I developed a deep-seated conviction about the import
of the dedication of the *Validating Cognition Collection*:
That the Lord Buddha, as the personification of reason,
is authoritative for the seeker of liberation
because of (his unerring description) of evolution and cessation,
and that therefore His teaching is the only haven
for those who would be free. And I found a special joy
in getting clear all the keys of the paths of both vehicles
by studying them in combination on the path of reasoning.

Thinking this over, how well my destiny was fulfilled!
Thank you so very much, O Holy Wisdom Treasure!

Then through the hard, methodical work of interconnecting
the *Bodhisattva Levels* and the *Mahāyāna Sūtra Ornament*,
all the treatises of the Invincible Dharma Lord Maitreya,
and those following them, dawned as transformative instructions.

Thinking this over, how well my destiny was fulfilled!
Thank you so very much, O Holy Wisdom Treasure!

Especially depending on the *Transformative Instruction Collection*,
which grants certainty about all the essentials of the path
by arranging the profound and magnificent sutras in stages,
I saw clearly as stages of practice the many meanings
of the Nāgārjuna's precious texts, such as the *Sūtra Collection*.

Thinking this over, how well my destiny was fulfilled!
Thank you so very much, O Holy Wisdom Treasure!

Then, relying on Buddhaguhya's lucid practical instructions
on the *Meditation Ultimate* and the *Vairochana Enlightenment*,
all the keys of the path dawned well as transformative instructions.

Thinking this over, how well my destiny was fulfilled!
Thank you so very much, O Holy Wisdom Treasure!

Seeing how the essentials of the Glorious Principles
    Compendium path

are contained in the three samādhis, and realizing
how hard to fathom is the way of meditation on that deep
    import,
I relied on the great paṇḍit Buddhaguhya's correct explanation
integrating the *Root, Explanatory,* and *Combined Yoga Tantras,*
and on the *Stages of Meditation's* proper explanations
of the profound practices of the three tantra classes,
and the confusion in my mind was cleared away!

Thinking this over, how well my destiny was fulfilled!
Thank you so very much, O Holy Wisdom Treasure!

The ultimate of all the eloquent teachings of the Sage
is the glorious unexcelled yoga tantra,
and among them the most unutterably profound
is the king of tantras, the glorious *Guhyasamāja Root Tantra.*
The supreme philosopher Nāgārjuna said about it
that "the essentials of the path of the *Root Tantra*
are sealed therein by the six limits and the four procedures,[13]
and thus they must be understood following the Guru's
    instructions
in accordance with the *Explanatory Tantras.*"
Holding that fact as essential, I inquired deeply
into all the subtleties of the noble tradition of the *Community,*
their ultimate private instructions contained in the *Five Stages,*
The Lamp of Concentrated Practices, and the *Stages of
    Arrangements,* and so on.
Relying on their lamp-like illumination of the *Root Tantra,*
combining the five great *Explanatory Tantras,*
I practiced with enormous efforts.
With practice I discovered all the essentials
of the *Community's* two stages in general,
and especially the essentials of the perfection stage.

Thinking this over, how well my destiny was fulfilled!
Thank you so very much, O Holy Wisdom Treasure!

By the power of that, the essential imports of many tantras,
such as *Superbliss, Hevajra,* and *Kālachakra,*
dawned in my mind as transformative instructions.

I have explained these fully elsewhere,
this just opens the door for the discerning.

Thinking this over, how well my destiny was fulfilled!
Thank you so very much, O Holy Wisdom Treasure!

Constant Practice and Total Dedication

Thus having become filled with the treasure of instructions,
I practiced by combining the two Mahāyāna paths,
the ordinary path (of the transcendences)
and the two stages of the extraordinary path,
into a complete path of concentrated essentials.

Thinking this over, how well my destiny was fulfilled!
Thank you so very much, O Holy Wisdom Treasure!

"All the Ganges rivers of the vows of the bodhisattvas
are contained within the vow to uphold the holy Dharma,"
thus whatever base of virtue I accumulated,
all was dedicated to the spread of Buddha's teaching.

Thinking this over, how well my destiny was fulfilled!
Thank you so very much, O Holy Wisdom Treasure!

In order to extend enormously my own virtue,
and to show the entrance without error in a way appropriate
to the many fortunate persons of clear discernment,
I wrote this record of my education.
By the mass of virtues thus attained,
may all beings, through this same procedure,
maintain the unexcelled discipline of the Buddha
and enter the path that pleases all the victors!

Written by the Eastern Bhikṣhu Tsongkhapa Losang Drakpai Pal, at the Triumph of Virtue monastery on Nomad Mountain, with Kabshipa Rinchen Pal as scribe.

3 *Song of the Mystic Experiences* of Lama Jé Rinpoche

rJe rin po che'i gsang ba'i rnam thar

BY JAMYANG CHÖJÉ TASHI PALDEN (1379–1449)

O sun-like Prince of the Conqueror,
whose wisdom, vast as the heavens,
has the brilliance of knowledge
that sees what ultimately is
and what merely seems to be.[14]
O Venerable Lord of Dharma, Most Perfect Guru,
the dust of your feet I place on the crown of my head.

Even the buddhas and bodhisattvas
who fill the ten directions
cannot describe the excellence
of your body, speech, and mind,
yet out of passionate inspiration I shall sing of them;
pray, listen for but a few moments.

As a blossoming garland of flowers
to adorn the necks of the clear-minded,
and as a precious jewel
to enhance the force of faith,

this song in praise of your oceans of splendor
to delight all sages, I have composed.

Like a cloud, the merit of your superb deeds
releases a torrent of rain that swells
the virtue of those to be taught,
and proclaims with a dragon's thundering roar
the sweetness of the vast and the profound.[15]
O glorious, powerful, billowing Lama.

Foremost of tantric adepts, the mighty yogi
who mastered the many millions of samādhis,
composed faultless expositions,
and made true effort in practice;
most resplendent of lamas,
you tower over the heads of all.

At Vajrāsana[16] in a former birth,
to the Victorious One you offered
a rosary of one hundred crystal beads.
Thus you acquired the fortune
later to attain the realistic view.[17]
O Illustrious Lama, at your feet I pay homage.

At the age of seven you directly perceived
Dipaṃkara Atīsha, the great Path Clearer,
and Vajrapāṇī, Lord of Secrets.
The exhortations of both the sutras
and tantras dawned upon you.
O Illustrious Lama, at your feet I pay homage.

O Jetsun, Lord of objective existence,
you directly perceived Mañjushrī,
bodhisattva of the wisdom of emptiness,
seated in a radiant aura as blue
as the color of a perfect sapphire.
O Illustrious Lama, at your feet I pay homage.

From this time onward, O Noble One,
whenever desired, you could invoke
Mañjushrī, Treasure of Stainless Wisdom,

and constantly listen to the teachings
of both Sūtrayāna's *Transcendent Wisdom*
and Tantrayāna's *Esoteric Community*.[18]
O Illustrious Lama, at your feet I pay homage.

When practicing the seven-limbed ritual
of the thirty-five confessional buddhas,
continually and clearly you beheld them,
and all their forms, mudras, and symbols.
O Illustrious Lama, at your feet I pay homage.

Seated in the auspicious posture,
hands in the Dharma-teaching mudra,
Buddha Maitreya prophesied that,
just as the Sugatas who possess the ten powers,
you will one day perform the twelve acts
of a supreme, universal teacher.
O Illustrious Lama, at your feet I pay homage.[19]

Victorious Master of both life and death,
true visions you received
of Amitābha Buddha, the medicine buddhas,
and that teacher of humans and gods,
Śhākyamuni, Prince of the Śhākya throne,
each with a retinue vast as the oceans.
O Illustrious Lama, at your feet I pay homage.

Holy Tara, source of all siddhis,
Uṣhṇīṣha Vijaya, exalted and radiant,
Uṣhṇīṣha Sitatapatra, dispeller of obstacles,
and other such mystic female buddhas,
again and again you directly perceived.
O Illustrious Lama, at your feet I pay homage,

Bodhisattva Nāgārjuna, Āryadeva, noble Buddhapālita,
magnificent Chandrakīrti, and the mighty yogi Nāgabodhi[20]
appeared, then constantly cared for you.
O Illustrious Lama, at your feet I pay homage.

Exalted Asanga, who delights the three worlds,
the brother, Vasubandhu, a second buddha,

and Dignāga,[21] child of Mañjushrī,
appeared, then constantly looked after you.
O Illustrious Lama, at your feet I pay homage.

Dharmakīrti, a moon among teachers,
as well as Guṇaprabha, Shākyaprabha,
Shāntideva, and the glorious Abhaya
appeared, then constantly cared for you.
O Illustrious Lama, at your feet I pay homage.

All the great adepts of India and Tibet,
such as Indrabhuti, Saraha, Luhipa,
Krisnachārin, Drilbupa, Tilopā, and Naropā,[22]
appeared, then constantly looked after you.
O Illustrious Lama, at your feet I pay homage.

Clearly Mañjushrī prophesied
that, relying on these lineages,
you would produce huge spiritual benefits
for yourself and for all sentient beings.
Great Bold One who spontaneously
fulfills the wishes of the world.
O Illustrious Lama, at your feet I pay homage.

When the samādhi of the yoga combining
mental tranquility with realization of emptiness
increased like the waxing moon,
you beheld the form of the Terrifier,
Yamantaka, Terminator of the Lord of Death,[23]
complete with all gestures and expressions.
O Illustrious Lama, at your feet I pay homage.

Having touched your heart
to the wisdom sword of Mañjushrī,
a stream of undefiled ambrosia
flowed into the depth of your being,
spontaneously arousing the propitious
suffusion of supreme joy.
O Illustrious Lama, at your feet I pay homage.

The *Prayer for Rebirth in the Land of Bliss*
and the *Eulogy of the Perfect Intention
of the Dauntless Protector Maitreya Buddha*,[24]
as well as their graduated levels of meaning,
Mañjushrī lucidly conveyed to you,
who recorded and skillfully presented them.
O Illustrious Lama, at your feet I pay homage.

Whenever you consecrated a religious image,
the wisdom heroes actually entered
into the symbolic heroes.
This host of deities that you summoned
still generates fields of merit within beings.
O Illustrious Lama, at your feet I pay homage.

One night you dreamed of Nāgārjuna
and his five spiritual sons
discussing among themselves
the fabric of relational origination.
From their midst came Buddhapālita,
who touched you with a text.
The very next day within you
arose the mind of a noble one.[25]
O Illustrious Lama, at your feet I pay homage.

By focusing on the pith of the six branches
of Kālachakra, "The Wheel of Time,"
you directly perceived his buddha form.
He foretold that soon you
would equal even King Suchandra.[26]
O Illustrious Lama, at your feet I pay homage.

When for the first time you led
the Great Prayer Festival of Lhasa,
a hundred magical omens appeared.
At your making that joyous offering,
the buddhas and their heirs in the ten directions
were filled with supreme delight.[27]
O Illustrious Lama, at your feet I pay homage.

Creating the form of a great bliss deity
through the yoga of the nonduality
of profound luminosity and magical visions,
you attained the vajra yoga body.
O Illustrious Lama, at your feet I pay homage.

By practicing the mantric science of inhaling
and exhaling *om ah hum* on the lotus heart,
the vital energies entered the central nadi channel,
rested as breathing stopped, and then dissolved.
Thus you experienced the clear light, mahāmudrā,
the great seal, attaining the vajrayoga speech.
O Illustrious Lama, at your feet I pay homage.

Raising the navel chakra's mystic heat
that rests at the base of the central channel,
the letter *HAṀ* at the crown of your head
melted and fell to your heart
as simultaneously the experience
of the blisses dawned upon you;
thus you attained the vajra yoga mind.
O Illustrious Lama, at your feet I pay homage.

Having been invoked as witnesses
to your pure and perfect aspirations,
all buddhas and bodhisattvas came forth.
Only when you had summoned them
into their respective positions
did you honor them with offerings.
O Illustrious Lama, at your feet I pay homage.

While contemplating the principal mandala
of the Vajra Mañjushrī of the *Esoteric Community*,
you dreamed that Maitreya and Mañjushrī,
who were speaking of Dharma, passed down to you
a jeweled vase brimming with water,
portending that you would master all teachings.
O Illustrious Lama, at your feet I pay homage.

On a throne adorned with precious gems
sat the omniscient Kagyü Lama Butön Rinchen Drup,

who gave to you a text
of the *Guhyasamāja Root Tantra*,
exhorting you to be its keeper.
O Illustrious Lama, at your feet I pay homage.

Having accepted [the Guhyasamāja Tantra]
by being blessed with mantras and mudras three times on your
    head,
you regarded the thoughts of Marpa of Lhodrak—
the crucial points on mixing [wind with mind] and transferring
    consciousness—
to be the pith instructions of that tantra within the Ārya
    tradition.
O Illustrious Lama, at your feet I pay homage.

Accepting this responsibility,
with mudras and mantras, thrice
you touched the text to your head.
By its blessings, it became obvious
that the *Separating and Mixing Tantra* instruction,
obtained by Marpa of the Southern Hills,
is the true oral tradition of exalted Nāgārjuna.
O Illustrious Lama, at your feet I pay homage.

Your mind absorbed in the mystic circle of Heruka—
Chakra Saṃvara, the Wheel of Perfect Bliss—
myriad dakinis of the outer, inner, and secret places
made you offerings of vajra songs,
transporting you in ecstasy.
O Illustrious Lama, at your feet I pay homage.

In meditation destroying the forces of darkness,
you beheld the radiant Buddha, Mighty Demon Tamer,
having an aura as pure as burnished gold,
more brilliant than a million suns.
O Illustrious Lama, at your feet I pay homage.

Your being having become indivisible from
the body, speech, and mind of all buddhas,
the might of the power of evil was subdued.
As the Dharma protectors crushed the devil clans,

shrieks of the defeated demonic forces
resounded across the universe.
O Illustrious Lama, at your feet I pay homage.

These multitudes of Dharma protectors
that you brought under control,
in a previous eon had been commanded
by Buddha Vajradhāra to guard your doctrine;
with profound reverence they work this still.
O Illustrious Lama, at your feet I pay homage.

That you would, after entering total nirvāṇa,
sit in the presence of Dauntless Maitreya,
in Tushita, Pure Land of Joy,
and would be known as Mañjushrī Essence,[28]
was, O Lord of Life, rightly prophesied
by both Mañjushrī and Vajrapāṇī.
O Illustrious Lama, at your feet I pay homage.

By the strength of this eulogy
sung from the depths of pure love,
may the addictions of beings
limitless as the sky be extinguished.
In this and all future lives
may all be nurtured by true teachers
and embraced by the sacred Dharma.

May the innate wisdom of great bliss
rain throughout the world;
may the stains of erroneously grasping
mind and its objects be uprooted;
and may all be inspired quickly to become
like you, a jetsun lama.

May the wisdoms of learning, contemplation,
and meditation permeate the earth;
may the arts of deliberation,
debate, and composition flourish;
may the ordinary and supreme siddhis
come to each and every practitioner;

and may all be inspired quickly to become
like you, a jetsun lama.

By the limitless oceans of merit
of having presented, like Samantabhadra,
clouds of offerings spanning the skies,
of having bared every negative instinct
and downfall accumulated since infinity,
of having rejoiced in the spirituality
of those on the paths to enlightenment,
and of having beseeched the lamas
to turn the Wheel of Dharma
and not to enter total nirvāṇa.

May all beings experience peerless samādhi,
may goodness increase like the waxing moon,
and may the doctrine of omniscient Tsongkhapa
thrive until time's end.

The colophon: Written at Drepung Chökyi Dechen at the request of the two meritorious Drungtrapa Palsangpo brothers, by Lama Tashi Palden, a Buddhist monk and teacher who had searched many hundreds of thousands of sutras with the lights of his wisdom.

PART 2

STAGES OF THE PATH TO ENLIGHTENMENT

This part contains the essence of the path-to-enlightenment (*lamrim*) type of teaching—a comprehensive arrangement of the stages of practice from the beginning, in attainment of human life, up to the end, in perfect enlightenment of buddhahood.

The first chapter, "Three Principles of the Path," stems from a revelation granted by Mañjuśrī to Tsongkhapa on the roof of the Lhasa Cathedral when Tsongkhapa was bidding farewell to Lama Umapa. It is thought of as the seed of the whole path-to-enlightenment teaching. The Venerable Geshé Wangyal first published its translation in his *Door of Liberation*. Having been one of the translators who worked on it then, I am sure I still do not understand it as well as the Venerable Geshé, but my English translation varies a bit nowadays, still just approaching the crystal clarity of the original Tibetan.

The second chapter, "Lines of Experience," presents the shortest form of path teaching written by Tsongkhapa, the first stage of expansion of the *Three Principles*. Its style is expressive and communicative rather than literal, and so it is quite helpful to make the practices clear to the beginner.

The third chapter is a further expansion of the complete path, including both sutra and tantra practices, written in a letter to Konchok Tsultrim. The section concludes with a short prayer for supportive circumstances for practice. These last three selections were translated by Sherpa Tulku and Alexander Berzin based on explanations by Geshé Ngawang Dhargé.

4 Three Principles of the Path

Lam gtso rnam gsum

Reverence to the Holy Gurus!

I will explain as best I can
the essential import of all the Victor's teachings,
the path praised by all the holy bodhisattvas.
Best entrance for those fortunates who seek freedom.

Listen with clear minds, you lucky people
who aspire to the path that pleases buddhas,
strive to give meaning to leisure and opportunity,
and are not addicted to the pleasures of cyclic living.[29]
Lust for existence chains all bodied beings;
addiction to cyclic pleasures is only cured
by transcendent renunciation.[30]
So seek transcendence first of all!

Leisure and opportunity are hard to get,
and there is no time to live; keep thinking on this,
and you will turn off your fixation on this life!
Contemplate the inexorability of evolutionary effects[31]
and the sufferings of life—over and over again—
and you will turn off your fixation on future lives!
By constant meditation, your mind will not entertain
a moment's wish even for the successes of this life,

and you will aim for freedom all day and night—
then you experience transcendent renunciation!

Transcendence without the spirit of enlightenment[32]
cannot generate the supreme bliss
of unexcelled enlightenment—therefore,
the bodhisattva conceives the supreme spirit of enlightenment.

Carried away on the currents of four mighty streams,
tightly bound by the near-inescapable chains of evolution,
trapped and imprisoned in the iron cage of self-concern,
totally enveloped in the darkness of misknowledge,
born and born again and again in endless cyclic lives,
uninterruptedly tortured by the three sufferings—
such is the state of all beings, all just your mothers—
from your natural feelings, conceive the highest spirit!

Even though you experience transcendence,
and cultivate the spirit of enlightenment,
without wisdom from realizing emptiness,
you cannot cut off the root of the cyclic life—
so you should strive to understand relativity.[33]

Who sees the inexorable causality of all things,
of both cyclic life and liberation,
and destroys any sort of conviction of objectivity—
thereby enters the path pleasing to the victors.

Vision inevitably relative,
and emptiness free of all assertions—
as long as these are understood apart,
the Victor's intent is not yet known.
But when they coincide, not alternating,
just the mere seeing of inevitable relativities
is sure knowing free of objectivistic habits—
and investigation of the realistic view succeeds.

Furthermore, as vision precludes absolutism,
and emptiness precludes nihilism,
you know emptiness dawn as cause and effect—
then you will never be deprived by extremist views.

When you realize the essentials
of these three principles of the path,
rely on solitude and powerful efforts,
and swiftly achieve the eternal goal, my son!

5 Lines of Experience

Lam rim nyams mgur

Popularly known as "The Summary Points of the Graded Path"
(Lam rim bsdus don)

❦

(1)
I prostrate before you, (Buddha,) head of the Śhakya clan. Your enlightened body is born of billions of virtues and accomplishments.[34] Your enlightened speech grants the wishes of limitless beings. Your enlightened mind sees all knowables as they are.

(2)
I prostrate before you, Maitreya and Mañjuśhrī, supreme spiritual sons of this peerless teacher. Assuming responsibility (to further) all Buddha's enlightened deeds, you sport through emanations to countless worlds.

(3)
I prostrate before your feet, Nāgārjuna and Asaṅga, ornaments of our southern continent, famed throughout the three realms,[35] you have elucidated the most difficult to fathom "Mother of the Buddhas,"[36] just exactly as it was intended.

(4)
I bow to Dīpaṃkara (Atīśha), holder of a treasure of instructions, (as seen in your *Lamp on the Path to Enlightenment*),[37] which includes all the complete and unmistaken points of the paths of the profound view and the extensive activity, as transmitted intact from the two great pioneers above.

(5)
Respectfully, I prostrate before my own (two) spiritual masters.[38] You are the eyes that let us behold all the infinite sutra declarations and the best ford for those of good fortune to cross to liberation—you make all clear with your skillful deeds, moved by intense loving concern.

(6)
The stages of the path to enlightenment have been transmitted intact by the successors of both Nāgārjuna and Asaṅga, those crown jewels of all erudite masters of our southern continent, the banner of whose fame stands out above the masses. As (traveling the stages) fulfills every good aim[39] of all nine kinds of beings,[40] they are a power-granting king[41] of precious instruction. Because they collect the streams of thousands of excellent classics, they are indeed an ocean of illustrious, correct explanation.

(7)
(Atīsha's text) makes it (easy) to understand how there is nothing incompatible in all (Buddha's) teachings, and makes every scriptural statement, without exception, dawn in your mind as a personal guideline. It makes it easy to discover what Buddha intended[42] and protects you as well from the abyss of "the great mistake."[43] Because of these, what discerning person among the erudite masters of India and Tibet will not have his or her mind be completely captivated by these stages of the path, (arranged) according to three levels of motivation,[44] the supreme instructions to which many fortunate ones are devoted.

(8)
Although (there is much merit in) listening to or reciting even once this brief presentation (of Atīsha's text) in which can be included the essential points of all the scriptural statements, yet it is certain that you will amass even greater waves of beneficial stores from actually teaching and studying the sacred Dharma (contained within). Therefore you should consider the points (for doing this properly).

(9)
Then after (having taken refuge), you should see that the root cause, excellently propitious for as great a mass of good fortune as possible for this and future lives, is proper, zealous devotion in thoughts and actions to your sacred guru who shows you the path (to enlightenment). Thus you should please

him by offering your practice of exactly what he says, which you would not forsake even at the cost of your life. I, the yogi,[45] have practiced just that. If you would also seek liberation, please develop yourself in the same way.

(10)
This working basis (of a human form endowed) with liberties[46] is superior to a wish-granting gem. Moreover, such is only obtained this very one time. Hard to get and easily lost, (it passes in a flash) like lightning in the sky. Considering how (easily this can happen at any time) and realizing that all worldly activities are as (immaterial as) chaff, you must try to take advantage of its essential significance at all times, day and night. I, the yogi, have practiced in the same way. If you would also seek liberation, please cultivate yourself in the same way.

(11)
After death, there is no assurance that you will not be reborn in one of the three bad states.[47] Nevertheless, it is certain that the Three Jewels of refuge[48] have the power to protect you from their terrors. For this reason, your taking of refuge should be extremely solid and you should follow its advice without ever letting (your commitments) weaken. Moreover, (your success in) so doing depends on your considering thoroughly which are the evil or the good karmic actions, together with their results, and then living according to the guides of what is to be adopted and what rejected. I, the yogi, have practiced just that. If you would also seek liberation, please cultivate yourself in the same way.

(12)
The fullest strides (of progress) in actualizing the supreme paths will not come about unless you have attained a working basis (of an ideal human body) that is complete with (all eight, ripened, favorable) qualities.[49] Therefore you must train in the causal (virtuous actions) that will preclude (your attainment of such a form) from being incomplete. (Furthermore,) as it is extremely essential to cleanse away the stains of negative karmic debts and downfalls (from broken vows) tarnishing the three gateways (of your body, speech, and mind), and especially (to remove) your karmic obstacles (which would prevent such a rebirth), you should cherish continually devoting yourself to (applying) the complete set of four opponent powers[50] (which can purge you of them). I, the yogi, have practiced just that. If you would also seek liberation, please cultivate yourself in the same way.

(13)

If you do not make an effort to think about true sufferings and their draw-backs, you will not properly develop a keen interest to work for liberation. If you do not consider the stages whereby (true) origins of all suffering place and keep you in cyclic existence, you will not know the means for cutting the root of this vicious circle. Therefore you should cherish exuding total disgust and renunciation of such existence, while knowing which factors bind you to its wheel. I, the yogi, have practiced just that. If you would also seek liberation, please cultivate yourself in the same way.

(14)

Ever enhancing your enlightened motive of bodhicitta is the mainstay for the Supreme Vehicle's path. It is the basis and foundation for great waves of (altruistic) conduct (to bring you to enlightenment). Like a gold-making elixir, (it turns) everything (you do) into the two stores,[51] (building up) a treasure of merit gathered from infinitely collected virtues. Knowing this, the bodhisattvas have held this supreme precious mind as their innermost mental bond. I, the yogi, have practiced just that. If you would also seek liberation, please cultivate yourself in the same way.

(15)

Generosity is the wish-granting gem by which you can fulfill the hopes of sentient beings. It is the best weapon for cutting the knot of miserliness. It is the (altruistic) conduct that enhances your self-confidence and undaunted courage (to help everyone toward enlightenment). It is the basis for your good reputation to be proclaimed in the ten directions. Knowing this, the wise have devoted themselves to the excellent path of completely giving away their body, possessions, and merit. I, the yogi, have practiced just that. If you would also seek liberation, please cultivate yourself in the same way.

(16)

Moral discipline is the water to wash away the stains of faulty actions. It is the ray of moonlight to cool the scorching heat of the delusions. (It makes you) radiant like a Mount Meru in the midst of the nine kinds of beings. By its power, you are able to bend all beings (to your good influence) without (recourse to) mesmerizing glares. Knowing this, the noble ones have safe-guarded, as they would their eyes, the rules they have accepted (to keep) purely. I, the yogi, have practiced just that. If you would also seek liberation, please cultivate yourself in the same way.

(17)

Patience is the best adornment (to wear) for those with power and the perfect ascetic practice for those tormented by delusions. It is the high-soaring eagle, the enemy of the snake of anger, and the thickest armor against the weapons of abusive language. Knowing this, (the wise) have accustomed themselves in various ways and forms to the armor of supreme patience. I, the yogi, have practiced just that. If you would also seek liberation, please cultivate yourself in the same way.

(18)

Once you wear the armor of resolute and irreversible enthusiastic perseverance, your expertise in the sutras and insights will increase like the waxing moon. You will make all your actions meaningful (for attaining enlightenment) and will bring whatever you undertake to its intended conclusion. Knowing this, the bodhisattvas have exerted great waves of joyous effort, washing away all laziness. I, the yogi, have practiced just that. If you would also seek liberation, please cultivate yourself in the same way.

(19)

Meditative concentration is the king wielding power over the mind. If you fix it (on one point), it remains there immovable like a mighty Mount Meru. If you project it, it can permeate any virtuous object (at will). It leads to the great exhilarating bliss of having your body and mind be applicable (to any virtuous task). Knowing this, the yogis of (mental) control have devoted themselves continuously to single-minded concentration, which overcomes the enemies of mental wandering (and dullness). I, the yogi, have practiced just that. If you would also seek liberation, please cultivate yourself in the same way.

(20)

Discriminating awareness is the eye with which to behold profound emptiness and the path by which to uproot (ignorance) the source of cyclic existence. It is the treasure of genius praised in all the scriptural statements and is famed as the supreme lamp that eliminates the darkness of closed-mindedness. Knowing this, the wise who have wanted liberation have advanced themselves along this path with every effort. I, the yogi, have practiced just that. If you would also seek liberation, please cultivate yourself in the same way.

(21)

In (a state of) merely single-pointed meditative concentration, you do not have the insight (that gives you) the ability to cut the root of cyclic existence.

Moreover, devoid of a path of mental quiescence, discriminating awareness (by itself) cannot turn back the delusions, no matter how much you analyze them. Therefore, on the horse of unwavering mental quiescence, (the masters) have mounted the discerning awareness, totally decisive about how things exist. Then with the sharp weapon of Middle Path logic, devoid of extremes, they have used wide-ranging discriminating awareness to analyze properly and destroy all underlying supports for their (cognitions) aimed at grasping for extremes. In this way, they have expanded their intelligence that has realized emptiness. I, the yogi, have practiced just that. If you would also seek liberation, please cultivate yourself in the same way.

(22)
Once you have achieved single-minded concentration through accustoming yourself to single-pointedness of mind, your examination then of individual phenomena with proper analysis should itself enhance your single-minded concentration settled extremely firmly, without any wavering, on the actual way in which all things exist. Seeing this, the zealous have marveled at the attainment of a union of mental quiescence and penetrative insight. Is there need to mention that you should pray (to attain one as well)? I, the yogi, have practiced just that. If you would also seek liberation, please cultivate yourself in the same way.

(23)
(Having achieved such a union) you should meditate both on space-like emptiness while completely absorbed (in your meditation sessions) and on illusion-like emptiness when you subsequently arise. By doing this, you will, through your union of method and wisdom, become praised as someone perfecting the bodhisattva conduct. Realizing this, those with the good fortune (to have attained enlightenment) have made it their custom never to be content with merely partial paths. I, the yogi, have practiced just that. If you would also seek liberation, please cultivate yourself in the same way.

(24)
(Renunciation, an enlightened motive, and a correct view of emptiness) are necessary in common for (achieving) supreme paths through either of the two Mahāyāna Vehicles of (practicing) causes (for enlightenment) or (simulating now) the results (you will achieve).[52] Therefore, once you have properly developed these (three principal) paths, you should rely on the skillful captain (of a fully qualified tantric master) as your protector and set out (on this latter, speedier vehicle) across the vast ocean of the (four) classes of tantra.

Those who have (done so and) devoted themselves to his or her guideline instructions have made their attainment of (a human body with all) liberties and endowments have its full meaning (by achieving enlightenment in their very lives). I, the yogi, have practiced just that. If you would also seek liberation, please cultivate yourself in the same way.

(25)

In order to accustom my own mind to this and also to benefit others as well who have the good fortune (to meet with a true guru and be able to practice what he or she teaches), I have explained here in easily understandable words the complete path pleasing to the buddhas. I pray that the merit from this may cause all sentient beings never to be parted from these pure and excellent paths. I, the yogi, have offered prayers for just that. If you would also seek liberation, please offer prayers in the same way.

This concludes "The Summary Points of the Graded Path to Enlightenment," compiled in brief so that they may not be forgotten. It was written at Ganden Nampar Gyalwai monastery on Drog Riwoché Mountain, Tibet, by the Buddhist monk Losang Drakpa, a meditator who has heard many teachings.

6 A Letter of Practical Advice on Sutra and Tantra

A Brief Indication of the "Graded Stages of the Path" (Lam gyi rim-pa mdo tsam du bstan pa)

━━━━━━━━━━━━━━━━━━❧━━━━━━━━━━━━━━━━━━

Homage to Guru Mañjughoṣha.

May I always be cared for by you, the foremost of the peerless (Dharma) expounders. Your flawless wisdom is unimpeded even concerning the subtlest points. This is due to your acquaintance with the ways of widespread (altruistic actions) and the profound (insight of emptiness that you developed) over many years with many magnificent skillful methods.

O my excellent spiritual mentor and friend, first you strove to hear and study many scriptural statements. Then you spread the teachings with your good explanations. In the end, it was over a long period of time that you made such great effort to realize them in practice. May your feet be firm throughout a long life!

I have received the perfectly delightful tree of your letter together with the tasteful fruit of your presents, which you have sent, my undying dear friend, out of your affectionate thoughts for me. Not being quenched by the well-explained accounts (already available), as an ocean (cannot be satisfied) by a great cloud full of rain, you have requested that I write and send you in a letter further (practical advice on) how to apply yourself to the two stages (of the unexcelled class of tantras). (A mind of) little intelligence can easily be filled by hearing (merely a few teachings), as a small pond (can readily be replenished) by a babbling brook. Thus it is awe inspiring that minds of superior intelligence (such as your own) are so vast they cannot be satisfied by these wonderful accounts.

However, granted that this may be so, it is quite preposterous for there to be any call for someone like myself to appease the mind of a great man like you. I have heard and studied few (teachings). My intelligence is low; my Dharma actions are meager. Although I may have a few words (in my mind), I have been very lax in living up to their meaning. Nevertheless, dandelion seeds, animated by the wind, can soar to compete with the eagles, though they lack the power to do so on their own. Similarly uplifted by your ennobling words, I shall try to offer you something in brief.

Well then, (as for lowly people like myself), we have in fact found the excellent working basis (of a human rebirth complete) with all the liberties (for Dharma study and practice). We have in fact met with the precious teachings of the victorious (buddhas), and have in fact been cared for by superb gurus. With such an opportunity, and when we do have the power of mind to discriminate between what should be adopted and what rejected, we must strive definitely to take advantage of such an excellent working basis. This, of course, depends solely on our becoming involved in the buddhas' teachings. But to do so merely by having kind thoughts is not enough. Either we ourselves must know, without any confusion, the (proper) stages for entering the teachings, or we must definitely rely for guidance on someone who does.

Moreover, (not any teacher will do). He or she must be a skillful one who knows the nature of the paths, the definite count (or their details), as well as their graded order and the disciples' level of understanding. He must be like this because if he mistakes wrong paths for right ones, or right for wrong ones, then even if we were to realize and achieve such (mistaken) paths as he has taught us, we will not accomplish any of our aims. Similar to having been wrongly prescribed some medicine, (in the end) we will have received no benefit and nothing but harm.

But even if the teacher knows the nature of the paths well, the teaching will still be ineffective if he (adds) extra unnecessary (stages) or leaves them incomplete. Thus if he does not know the definite count (of the detailed points of the stages), then even while on the course of these (paths) we will be unable to progress in the most direct fashion. This is because we will proceed while having omitted certain recognized essentials and will sidetrack onto the superfluous practice of what is unnecessary.

But then even if the teacher does know the nature and the definite count (of the specific details of the paths), still if he does not know which (points) to apply at each stage of our mental development as he leads us from the beginning to the middle to the end, (he will be acting as in the following example). Suppose (a doctor) thought, "Here is a medicine, and since it is the best of all medicines it is proper to prescribe it to (any) patient for (any) disease." If, thinking (like this), he was actually to give it (to someone it did not suit), then because it was such a powerful drug, not only might it not help (this patient), but it might actually cause him great harm by taking his life. Likewise, suppose he thought, "Here is a sacred Dharma teaching, and since it is the most profound Dharma what wrong could there possibly be in teaching it?" If, thinking like this, he were to lead us by means of it, then if he accords it with our level of understanding (and follows the graded order from there) it will bring only benefit. But if he does not accord it with our level, then not only will he not benefit us, but he might actually cause us (by our own confusion) to kill our opportunity to attain a fortunate rebirth or liberation. Therefore it is especially important for him to know the graded order (of the stages of the teachings and the disciples' level of understanding).

Furthermore, even though the teacher may be skilled in these important practical points, nevertheless he must also be someone whose certainty gained about the complete stages of the path has come from his own (experience of) having been set straight himself and led by a holy being through not a cursory, nor a sporadic, but a thorough (study) of the great classics themselves, as composed by the standard, valid authors. (For you see,) the abbreviated guideline instructions for how to lead (disciples) through these (paths) are in fact only what have been condensed from these great classics. Actually, the very meaning of a guideline instruction is that it gives us certainty more easily about the classics, which themselves are very extensive, the meanings of which are extremely difficult to comprehend, and which, for necessary (reasons), scramble the graded order of understanding (and practice) in their showing of the teachings. Because these (guidelines) have been compiled (with this purpose in mind), then to take the great classics as Dharma for lecturing and the brief guideline instructions as Dharma for practicing, and thereby to hold these two as disharmonious, is not to understand the point of the teachings at all. This is so because Buddha's scriptural pronouncements as well as their (Indian) commentaries are in fact—like we recite, "hearing, debating, and eagerly practicing"[53]—only for eager practice and aimed at such practice.

This being so, (how should we begin our practice? As Nāgārjuna) has said in *The Friendly Letter*, "O you who are free from fears, it is not necessary (for me) to tell you much. But this is an essential and beneficial piece of advice, 'Tame your mind!' As Buddha has said, 'The mind is the root of Dharma (practice).'"[54] Also, as (Āryadeva) has said in his *Four Hundred Stanzas*, "Because we cannot see (any action), such as going and so on, (becoming) meritorious and so on, except through the thought (that immediately motivates it), the mind therefore is said to be first (before) all karmic actions."[55]

Thus, as these noble ones, father and spiritual son, have said, the root of everything right or wrong is but the mind. This is because it is definite that the channels for acting wrongly or engaging in what is right are in fact (only) three, and (of these) the body and speech themselves are controlled by the mind.

Therefore, first of all (before any Dharma practice), it is extremely important for our motivating thought to be one that we have (properly) worked ourselves up to and not one that has (simply) come from mere words. Although the stages for working ourselves up (to a proper motivation) have been explained in many (different ways), the most commonly helpful scheme for minds of superior, middling, and all (scopes of capacity is as follows).

First (on an initial level) we should make ourselves continually mindful of our (forthcoming) death and not staying long in this world. We should also familiarize ourselves a great deal with the two ways in which we can go to our next life (either up to a fortunate rebirth or down to an unfortunate one), together with their causes (our virtuous or nonvirtuous acts). In this way, we should turn our mind from working with keen interest for this life (alone) and thereby develop as much as possible the attitude to work with keen interest for the happiness of future lives beyond.

Then (on an intermediate level) we should exert much effort in thinking about the faults of all the various (rebirth states) of cyclic existence and the advantages of the peaceful (attainment of liberation). In this way, we should turn our mind from working with keen interest for the (so-called) good things of cyclic existence and thereby develop the strong and continuing attitude to work with keen interest for liberation.

Then (progressing to an advanced-level motivation) we should see that just as we ourselves are benefited by happiness and harmed by suffering, so too are all sentient beings. Thereby we should thoroughly familiarize ourselves with love, compassion, and the enlightened motive of bodhicitta. If we do this, we will turn our motivating intentions completely away from eagerly endeavoring for only our own aims, not caring at all about bringing happiness to sentient beings and eliminating their suffering. Thereby we will see the aims of others as actually the (only) aims we strongly wish (to work for). By doing this and also by being certain that the supreme method for accomplishing these (aims) is in fact only if we become a buddha ourselves and that alone, we will then develop the very firm motivating intention of wishing to attain (the state of) a buddha because of these reasons. (These then are the actual stages for working ourselves up to having such an enlightened motive of bodhicitta for our Dharma practice.)

But suppose we were to take as the foundation (for our practice) the self-deception of having only a partial, merely intellectual understanding of the verbal formulations of these (stages for building up our motivation) and then were to engage in hearing, thinking, and meditating (on a certain Dharma practice). We might then say with many sweet-sounding words that "I am doing these for the sake of my future lives" or "I am doing these for liberation" or "I am doing these for the benefit of sentient beings." But despite (such noble claims), I think the way our mind probably has been working will have been nothing other than aiming for the sake of either (benefits in) this lifetime, or for certain pleasurable fruits of cyclic existence to which we have given the name "liberation," or for a partial (ultimate) aim for ourselves (and not enlightenment at all). Therefore, to develop these motivating thoughts nonartificially, it is not sufficient to have merely an intellectual understanding (of them). We must meditate (in order to build them up as a natural, instinctive habit).

As for how to meditate, we need to actualize and achieve (these motivations) by acquainting ourselves over and again with the analytic meditation with which we meditate by examining, in many aspects, (the situations that are) the causes pertinent for (developing) each of these kinds (of motivations). (For instance, by examining many aspects of the suffering of others, we can develop compassion.)

In this regard, even though cultivating (repeatedly meditating with the proper) aspects and focal objects for these (motivations) is the main cause (for actually developing them, such as focusing on the suffering of others with the wish that they be parted from it as the way to develop compassion), just (to do) this much is not enough. In between sessions we should make (our understanding of how to develop them) firm and certain by looking at the stainless expositions (of the Buddha), the (Indian) treatises, and also the guideline instructions that have been composed around (the themes of) these (motivations). Thus we should read, for example, the accounts of how Buddha developed renunciation, compassion, and bodhicitta in his previous lives. In addition, we must reach the heart (of our problems preventing us from developing them) by doing a great deal of collecting (of merit) and cleansing (of obstacles) in order to eliminate the contrary factors (such as our selfishness) and bring about conducive conditions (such as a kind heart) for (developing) these motivating thoughts (like compassion). Thus to eliminate our negative karmic debts we should openly admit our past wrongs and apply the four opponent powers of regretting them, promising never to commit them again, invoking the Three Jewels of refuge and a bodhicitta motivation as our basis, and amassing as much counteracting virtue as we can. This might include the accumulation of a hundred thousand prostrations, mandala offerings, and recitations of the hundred-syllable Vajrasattva mantra and our guru's name mantra and so forth.

Like this, then, we need to make the causal factors (for developing these motivations) be never partial but complete and thus fully effective. In addition, we need to meditate and examine well with discriminating awareness and in detail (to differentiate) for each individual (type of motivating thought) what is detrimental for it (such as self-cherishing that would hinder developing compassion) and what is beneficial (such as an attitude of cherishing others). When we have (done both of these), we will then understand deeply (how to assure that if we meditate over and again) by having such and such a focal object, such and such an aspect, and such and such a manner in which we work ourselves up (to having this feeling), we will develop on our mindstream such and such an uncommon imprint as a result. In doing this we will thereby come to gain confidence in (our ability to actualize) even the subtlest points of these practices.

At such a time, we should also be aware of the special functions of each (of these motivations) to bring about what is beneficial and end what is detrimental, for in fact we must be certain of what is to be abandoned and adopted for any and all (of the paths. Thus, for instance, compassion makes us cherish others, which brings about happiness, and also blocks our self-cherishing, which has been causing us unhappiness.) By (knowing this) and also by thinking that (developing) just (some of) these (motivating thoughts) is not enough (for in fact we must generate the entire progression), then for certain it will come about that we will never abandon any of the sacred Dharma (stages for building up our motivation).

(Although) we must indeed generate these motivating thoughts before (any actual session of meditation or offering), yet just to develop them is not sufficient. (We must maintain them) steadily and continuously (throughout). Not only that, we must also try to increase them as much as possible. Therefore (it is a mistake) to think that, since they are preliminary practices, it is unnecessary to have continual familiarity with them (throughout our session) or that it is unnecessary to work at all times for them not to degenerate (because) it is enough just to send (these motivations) ahead once (at the start of our session. Or it is also a mistake) to think, on the other hand, that as these are yogas that are like crusts or chaff, it is all right to leave them (aside) and, not taking them into consideration, to think to familiarize ourselves (only) with the actual practices.

(To think in any of these mistaken ways) is not to understand the essential point of the paths at all. This is because meditations in which we have acted out Dharma practices, but devoid of these previously explained motivating thoughts, and especially (if devoid of) bodhicitta in the manner explained above, turn out in fact to be just seemingly Dharma (practices that do not bring about their intended result). And furthermore, even if we meditate perfectly with single-minded concentration on emptiness, it is not at all fit (to be considered) a Mahāyāna (practice if we lack a bodhicitta motivation), and this has been said not once.

Meditating on bodhicitta at the beginning of a session and directing (the merit toward our enlightenment) with great waves of prayer at the session's end are in fact great skillful means for causing the merit cultivated during the main part of the session to hit the mark (of our intended aim) and become inexhaustible. Therefore, as this is the case, we must be certain to integrate them with our mind, never allowing ourselves sometimes to act (negligently) in just any fashion.

If we cherish enhancing motivating thoughts like these, holding them without ever letting them degenerate, and then, on top of this as our foundation, practice the two stages of the secret tantra path, (we should do so as follows). In general, when we enter the doorway of whatever (Buddhist) vehicle it may be, we must set as the basis (for our practice) our own specific moral discipline (of whatever set of lay or ordination vows we hold). And especially when we enter the Tantra (Vehicle) it is very important to have (as our basis) a stable (development of the enlightened motive). This is because bodhicitta, as explained before, is the ultimate essential point of all the Mahāyāna paths. In addition, there are the (tantra) vows and close bonds (to the buddha families) that we will have received when we have taken a pure empowerment (into any of the higher deity systems) from a fully qualified guru. It will be best if we then (also) have, (as our foundation, these in a state of) their never having been forsaken by giving them up and never having been degenerated by violating them. Otherwise, (if we have forsaken or caused them to weaken, then to continue to have a firm basis for practice) we need to have restored or revitalized them, having taken (another) empowerment and purified and cleansed ourselves of these former faulty actions and downfalls.

And further, having recognized well and with certainty the faulty actions (that violate) our root and branch (vows), we need to restrain ourselves definitely to stop (ever breaking them) again. Thus we should make a strong effort never to be stained by the downfall (of transgressing any) of our root (vows). And further, if we happen to commit any faulty actions (of breaking some) of the rest (of our branch vows), we must, having recognized this, carefully expiate (the consequences by applying the appropriate antidotes).

Thus, as I see it, (the facts of the matter are these). We must enter into the meditations of the two (unexcelled yoga tantra) stages with these (tantric vows and close bonds) indispensably (set) as our foundation. Furthermore, even if we do not meditate on the two stages, still, if we have received an empowerment, we are required to keep them by all means. As these are the case, we must therefore strive to develop great certainty in this (matter concerning vows). This is because (of two points Buddha has made). He has said that, having received an empowerment, if we keep our close commitments and vows purely, then even if we have not meditated on the two stages during this lifetime, we can still reach the supreme attainment (of buddhahood) in seven or sixteen lifetimes and so on (of consecutively keeping them). And also, he has said that if, treating them lightly, we give up the commitments and vows we have promised to keep, then even having done seemingly meditation on the two stages, we will fall to an unfortunate rebirth and thereby not attain (enlightenment).

(Another point can be seen from two more of Buddha's statements.) He has said that if our working basis for practicing tantra is as a householder, we must practice while continually maintaining the five (vows of lay) discipline, or, if as ordained, then while maintaining either the two or three sets (of novice or full vows). Further, he has said that for upholding (and practicing) tantra it is best to be fully ordained, next best a novice, and at minimum someone with lay vows. Therefore it follows (from these statements) that (Buddha's) presentation (of this ranking) is by means of the number of vows that are (actually safeguarded) and not merely by the (number that are) promised to be kept. This is why (Kamalashīla) has said in his *Illumination of the Middle Way* that if someone maintaining both individual liberation and bodhisattva vows practices tantra, he or she will actualize results more quickly.[56]

(In stating this) he is asserting that the actualizations gained by having taken the tantric vows while already safeguarding bodhisattva and ordination vows are (gained) much more quickly than those from having safeguarded only the tantra vows themselves.

It is similar also in the case of actualizing paths on the (nontantric Mahāyāna Vehicle of the perfections). The actualizations gained by having taken bodhisattva vows while having already been ordained (on one of the levels) according to the discipline (rule) are best (compared) to those gained by having maintained only bodhisattva vows alone. This is what (Buddha) meant when he said in many sutras that if there were two bodhisattvas equal in all respects, (except that) one was a layperson (with no vows of individual liberation) and the other ordained, the latter would be more praiseworthy. (Buddha has clearly set forth all these points) in his presentation of these (vows). But despite this, although people frequently appear who can explain them by expounding forth merely their verbal formulations, and partial ones at that, yet when it comes time to apply these to personal practice, those who do so appear ever so rarely. This falls in the category of something very difficult to understand.

Be that as it may, (Nāgārjuna) has said (in *The Five Stages*), "Those who wish for the completion stage should (first) abide well on the creation stage, for the method to complete buddhahood is said to be like (climbing) rungs of a ladder."

(This means) that just as we must depend on climbing the lower rungs of a ladder in order to proceed to the higher ones, (likewise) we must travel (the path to enlightenment) by meditating on the creation and completion stages in their (proper) order. It will not do to (practice them) in just any order of understanding or to leave out the creation stage. As (this is what Nāgārjuna) has said, we must meditate on the creation stage.

Even though there is no certainty that (while on the creation stage) its (practice) will smooth away the undesirable occurrences that occasionally befall us (such as sicknesses) or bring us the subtle actual attainments we desire (such as clairvoyance), yet it is a fact that the creation stage can bring us to the attainment of peerless enlightenment. This point has been established clearly from the tantric texts with scriptural authority and well-attested to by learned masters who themselves are valid sources. Therefore we must please practice (this creation stage) in the circle of a mandala.

Also on this stage we must perform the actions for accumulating the collections (of merit and insight, such as the yogas for eating, sleeping, and waking), and in between sessions be mindful of (viewing everything in a) pure (form, such as ourselves and all others as meditational deities, our surroundings as a mandala palace, and so forth, and we must first meditate. Likewise we must) recite the (pertinent) mantras, make offerings, and perform the rituals of the torma offering cake. Since we must build up (the impressions of) all these on our mindstream at their appropriate occasions while remaining ever mindful of the meanings of this (point) and that, without letting ourselves just merely recite the words (of the ritual texts and mantras mindlessly), why shouldn't we please take pleasure (in so doing)?

Then, as it is very important to know how to meditate with single-minded concentration on (ourselves as) the meditational deities during the actual main body (of our sessions), let me say a little about how to do this. It will be easier to develop certainty about how to meditate on this, in fact, if we know (beforehand) what the single-minded concentration is like that we need to have developed when we have finished accustoming ourselves to meditating on the creation stage. Therefore, if we ask what do we need to have developed, (it is like this). By meditating now on (ourselves as having) the bodily colors, hand implements, jewelery, and garb (of all the deity figures) of the supported as well as of the supporting (mandala of the palace and its surroundings), in short, on (our having all) the aspects of their colors and shapes, then at the conclusion (of our training) we need to have actualized being able to visualize ourselves appearing clearly as all of these, in toto and simultaneously, in one state of single-minded concentration. We should meditate (aspiring for this scope of attainment).

Therefore we must train by focusing first on one focal object (out of this entire visualization). If we train by focusing (first), for instance, on (visualizing ourselves as) the main central figure (of the mandala) and ask how we should train, (it is like this).

Actually, two traditions for doing this appear (in the literature). One is to train from fine details upward by focusing (first) on one of the finest details of the body, thereby actualizing its clear appearance, (and then building up from there by progressively adding more and more details). The second is to train from the rough stage downward (by visualizing) the entire body (roughly from the start and then progressively filling in the details one by one. Of these) the former is fit for only a few special individuals, while the more commonly beneficial (method) is in fact the latter because it is easier to develop. Therefore, for instance, of the two aspects of the main figure, namely, the rough whole and its fine details, we should (first) visualize (ourselves) as the complete (deity), from the head to the feet, in merely the roughest form. When this appears clearly, we must hold (our attention) on just this without letting our mind wander. If the general form of the body is clear, we should hold this, and if the general is unclear but a few of its parts are lucid, we should hold (our attention) on whatever is clear. If these fade as well, we should visualize the (entire) general (rough form once more) and hold that. If some aspect arises that is totally extraneous to what we should be meditating on, we should hold our mind (only) on the main focal object without following out (any spurious ones).

For beginners in these (visualization practices), it has been said that if the meditation sessions are too long, we will not progress in the most direct fashion at all. This has appeared to be so (from experience as well). Therefore, if we meditate holding as many extremely short sessions as possible, our development of single-minded concentration will proceed without fault.

Furthermore, in the beginning we must also keep our faculty of discernment alert and hold on to it tightly. This is because if we do not meditate while carefully checking whether or not we have come under the power of mental dullness or agitation, we might meditate passing a great deal of time in a muddled state, holding ourselves to our meditation with (only) the roughest discernment. In so doing we will never develop in our entire lifetime any single-minded concentration as we had wished. Therefore we must keep a careful check (with discernment for any meditational faults).

(In this way) we will come to gain a single-minded concentration having four defining characteristics and (focused) on the general form of, for instance, the main figure. (These four are,) we must be able to have (the visualization) appear (clearly) whether the effort required is strong or easy. Further, we must be able to extend (this concentration on the visualization) throughout our session. During it, we must never come under the power of either mental dullness or agitation, and (lastly) we must come in contact with an exhilarating joy and bliss of both body and mind. (Such a concentration, then) is a similar equivalent (for what is developed by training) in the direction of mental quiescence meditation.

Once we have (gained concentration with these four characteristics) and our mind has both maintained (its attention) firmly on this (rough, general form of ourselves as the main figure of the mandala) as well as held (the clarity of) its fine details, we must then extend our focus to (include visualizing ourselves as) the other deities (around the mandala as well). But when we do so, we must expand our focus on top of (the foundation of) still maintaining it on the deity on which we had been previously focusing and not forsake this. If we hold our attention focused on these latter (deities around the mandala) while having given up (our focus on the main, central figure), how will it ever come about that we can (visualize) ourselves appearing as all these deities simultaneously?

Therefore, since the generation stage (as explained) like this is in fact an indispensable (part) of the subject matter of the precious tantric texts, and is both very important and widely praised as one of the essentials of the tantric paths, it is extremely crucial for us to do its meditations.

The completion stage was known to the earlier (masters) in terms of having two (parts): the nonprofound and the profound completion stages. The first of these appears (in their literature) to be constituted by meditations on the energy channels, winds, and vital drops, and are to be sought in their individual guideline instructions. The latter appears as consisting of meditations on emptiness. Whether or not these two form (distinct categories for a valid division scheme) for the completion stage (and whether or not they are exclusive to that stage) needs to be investigated. But no matter which way it turns out to be, they (both) are similar to what is practiced on the completion stage. Concerning this, (Buddha) has spoken about the view of emptiness in exactly the same fashion (and as having the same significance) in both the Tantra and the Perfection (Vehicles). The learned masters have also spelled this out (explicitly). Because of this, then even though differences do exist, such as in the Perfection (Vehicle), the methods for generating single-pointed concentration on (emptiness) are less well-known, while they are more abundant and easier in the Tantra Vehicle. Still there is in fact nothing better than the Perfection (Vehicle's teachings) for methods for initially seeking an understanding of it. Since quotations and lines of reasoning (for establishing emptiness) are clearer on the side of the sutras, we must come to have a decisive understanding (of its correct view) by hearing, studying, and thinking about (teachings) that accord with what derives from (Buddha's) scriptural pronouncements in the Perfection (Vehicle) as well as from their commentaries. (More specifically,) the foundation for this on which we should base our hearing, studying, and thinking should be in fact (Buddha's) scriptural pronouncements about the profound meaning of emptiness and such (Indian) treatises of sound reasoning as the (six) logical works (of Nāgārjuna)[57] and so forth. (Such texts as these latter) can dispel all our doubts concerning extreme (positions) extraneous (to what Buddha intended), and which would lead us to some meaning of (emptiness) other than (the correct one). Thereby in not allowing us to be misled by any aspects (of understanding) other than (the truth), they can bring us certainty (about emptiness) in accordance with reality.

There do exist some special persons who have trained themselves thoroughly (by studying and thinking) like this in past (lifetimes). As a result, then even though they may not train for long in this life, they gain a deep understanding of the meaning of profound (emptiness because of their instincts). But even so, such cases as these are extremely difficult (to come by). Therefore, for all of us who are other than that, we should seek (our understanding) through (studying and thinking about) such lines of reasoning as "neither one nor many." (This is the line that a person, for instance, is empty of existing inherently as something findable from his own side, because he does not exist so as either one or many with his basis for imputation.) Even though we might claim something else as the gateway for entering into a quick and easy (realization of emptiness) by ascribing this name to (a method that) cuts off fantasies in general (without such reliance on sound lines of reasoning), we will not be able to please the intelligent (masters with such a claim).

When we seek (our understanding of emptiness) by training like this in (studying and thinking about) scriptural quotations and lines of reasoning, there are two ways in which such an understanding can be generated—a deviant and a nondeviant one. Of these, the first might be (as follows). Suppose we had analyzed from the viewpoint of many lines of reasoning the arisal, cessation, and so forth of phenomena. When (we had done so), the entire presentation of conventional things had fallen apart (for us) and thereby we could not find (any way of) taking anything as being conventionally "this." (Thus we felt there was nothing conventionally true or real.) Because (of that), we might come (to the wrong conclusion) that all bondages and liberations (from cyclic existence) are in fact like only so many bondages in and liberations of children of barren women. Then we would go on (to wrongly imagine) that the occurrence of happiness and suffering from virtuous and nonvirtuous actions was in fact no different than the arisal of horns from a rabbit's head. Thereby we would come to a (completely false) understanding of all conventional objects as being distorted conventional phenomena and all conceptual cognitions as being distorted cognitions deceived with respect to the objects about which they conceptualize. If we see the meaning of the Madhyamaka middle path in this (mistaken manner), there are two (further wrong conclusions we could draw). Of these, the first (would be as follows). If this were the case (that if all things lacked inherent, findable existence, then all conventional phenomena would be distorted), then since the entire presentation (of conventional reality) would be improper, (we would feel that) the view of all phenomena as lacking inherent existence was in fact a view of nihilism and therefore not Buddha's intention. In so thinking, we would be abandoning (the teachings of) the perfection of wisdom (by denying that the lack of inherent existence was what Buddha meant by emptiness). Even karmic obstacles that are completely ineradicable by other (means) can be purified away by relying on a (realistic) view of emptiness. But even though (that is the case), with this (incorrect view) we become like what (Buddha) said, "He who abandons (emptiness), and thereby comes to lack any refuge, goes in fact to the (Avīchi Hell of) Uninterrupted Pain." In other words, since there are no other refuges nor anything else to rely on (once we have rejected the true meaning of emptiness), we must remain in the Hell of Uninterrupted Pain for a very long time. This was said (by Buddha) in the chapter on hell beings (from the *Close Contemplations Sūtra*).[58]

The other (wrong conclusion from this misunderstanding would be like this). We might accept the position of emptiness with the highest (meaning as the lack of inherent, findable existence). And (we might also accept that) all mental trainings on the side of extensive actions, such as going for refuge, training to have an enlightened motive, meditating on the generation stage, and so on, as well as all actions of hearing and thinking (about teachings), are (only) what can be imputed by conceptual thoughts. But by (incorrectly) regarding all conceptual thoughts as (distorted and thus) functioning to bind us in cyclic existence, we would repudiate, ignore, and cast away all (such) excellent (and virtuous) karmic actions (as these). In so doing, we would only be opening the door for (us to fall to) an unfortunate rebirth.

These two (mistaken positions) are similar in that both are deep misunderstandings of emptiness, (bringing) nothing but the false pride (of inflatedly feeling we have understood something when in reality we have not). But (there is one big difference). With the former (by totally denying that emptiness means the lack of inherent existence) we are in fact divorced from any causes for having fervent regard for (the true meaning of) emptiness, (and thus incentive to study it further and correct our view). With the latter (on the other hand) we have actually still retained the causes for such fervent regard (by at least accepting emptiness as the lack of inherent existence, although misunderstanding its implications).

If, by taking emptiness mistakenly (as not meaning the lack of inherent existence) like this (while still accepting it but with another, more limited meaning), our fervent regard (for correcting our understanding) is burned away, then what need to mention those who, in taking the totally distorted position (of denying any type of emptiness whatsoever), are thereby hostile (to this view)? This is (the point Nāgārjuna was making when he) said in *The Precious Garland*, "(Consider) someone who has faith (in something but misunderstands it) by his misconception and another who despises (that same thing and totally rejects it) out of (closed-minded) hostility. If it has been explained that even someone with faith can burn away (his incentive to search for a correct understanding of what in theory he accepts), what need be said about someone with his back turned in hostility?"[59] (Nāgārjuna) has also said (in this same work), "This doctrine (of emptiness) when wrongly understood can cause the unlearned to become ruined, in fact, for by their (misunderstanding) like this they sink into a mire of nihilism (denying everything). Moreover, because of their having taken (emptiness) incorrectly, these fools with the pride of (thinking they are) clever go headfirst to the Hell of Uninterrupted Pain as they have a nature unfit (now for buddhahood) because of their rejection (of the correct view of emptiness)."[60] As for the way to develop an unmistaken understanding, (Nāgārjuna has said in *Disclosure of the Spirit of Enlightenment*, "Anyone who, from understanding this emptiness of phenomena, can thereby adhere to (the conventional existence of) karmic actions and their effects is more amazing than amazing and more wondrous than wondrous."

Also (Aśhvaghoṣa) has said in *Praises Extolling the Praiseworthy*, "You do not act while ignoring emptiness (as irrelevant), but harmonize it in fact with the conventional (world)."

Thus, as has been said (in these two quotations), we must see that no matter what (conventionally existent object) we take as the focal aim for our grasping for truly (findable) existence, what is conceptualized (by that mind, namely, the appearance of this object as being truly findable) has not even an atom (existing as inherently findable). Then, taking the fact of this emptiness as a (causal) condition, we must thereby find the deepest conviction that (conventionally) "this comes about from that" with respect to everything such as bondage and liberation, karmic actions and their effects, and so on. When we have taken to be on the side of what is reasonable the first part (of this realization, namely, the fact of the ultimate unfindability of everything), we need not (make excuses) about the latter (concerning the functioning of conventional appearances), feeling uncomfortable with it in our own system and therefore ascribing it (to be true only) to the face of others or on the face of deception. When it comes about that we can see how both (parts of this realization) are reasonable in our own (Dialecticist-Centrist) system, then something truly amazing and wondrous has occurred. This is because we will have achieved the skillful method of understanding deeply how what appears as contradictory to ordinary persons is (in fact) noncontradictory.

Therefore, with a (correct) understanding of emptiness, we must come to (the conclusion) that the presentations of cyclic existence and the nirvana beyond sorrow are reasonable (and function). But suppose, while not understanding what this (emptiness of inherent, findable existence actually means), we came to (the conclusion) that if we were to understand it as being reasonable, then these presentations would not function. If (we were to reason falsely like that), then with (our position) no different from the way of understanding of those who assert truly existent phenomena, we would be formulating lines of reasoning (about emptiness) without understanding at all what emptiness meant. (Thus we would be asserting absurd consequences that follow only from our own mistaken notion of emptiness and not from emptiness as correctly understood.)

(An example would be, for instance, what Nāgārjuna) has said in *Wisdom: Root Verses on the Middle Way*, "(You might argue with us debating that) if all these things were empty, then the absurd conclusion would follow for you that nothing could arise, nothing could cease, and there would be no such thing as the four noble truths."[61]

This (verse) presents the charge (based on the misconstruction that the Dialecticist view of emptiness is tantamount to nihilism) that if everything were void of inherent, findable existence, then the presentations of cyclic existence and the nirvana beyond sorrow would be improper. In answer to this (Nāgārjuna) has said (it is just the opposite), "If all these things were not empty, then the absurd conclusion would follow for you that nothing could arise, nothing could cease, and there would be no such thing as the four noble truths."[62]

In other words, with such lines (Nāgārjuna) has said that these things are improper in terms of nonemptiness (namely, if phenomena either inherently existed as ultimately findable or totally did not exist at all, then they could never arise or fall), but in terms of the (correct) position of emptiness, these are completely reasonable. He has said this even more clearly in the same work through a statement of an implication and its converse, "Everything becomes proper for those to whom emptiness is proper and everything becomes improper for those to whom emptiness is improper."[63]

Therefore, if the finding of a (correct) view of emptiness were to entail merely developing the understanding that if phenomena were divested of their spatial and temporal contexts there would be no way for them to be apprehended as anything, then it would be pointless (for the masters to have said that the understanding of emptiness) is difficult (to gain). This is because even extremely dull-witted persons who have not trained (their minds) at all can understand (this point that nothing can exist independent of its context). Thus merely this much (insight) is not enough. It will only be sufficient when for ultimate truth we have the total stillness (or absence) of any underlying support (for any cognition's being) aimed (at the inherent existence of anything, in other words, we understand for ultimate truth the emptiness of inherent findable existence) and for conventional truth, which is like an illusion, we accept the entire presentation of cyclic existence and the nirvana beyond sorrow. What makes the understanding of emptiness so difficult, then, is that it is difficult to hold (the realization of) these two (truths) jointly (without feeling there is any contradiction). Since it is necessary to have both, it has been said that if we do not know the classification scheme of the two levels of truth, we do not know emptiness as taught (by Buddha), whereas if we do know it, we are not muddled about what Buddha intended. And also, by accumulating the two collections (of insight and merit) in reliance of the ultimate and conventional (levels of truth) we can go to (a buddhahood that is) the total completion of what is supreme. (These are the points made in the following two quotations. Nāgārjuna) has said in *Wisdom: The Root* (*Verses of the Middle Way*), "Those who do not understand the division scheme of the two aspects of truth do not understand the profound fact (of emptiness found) in Buddha's teachings."[64]

And (Jñānagarbha) has said in *Distinguishing the Two Realities*, "Those who understand the division scheme of the two truths are not muddled about the words of the Sage (Buddha). By accumulating the complete collections (of merit and insight), they travel to the far shore of perfection."

It is said that this was difficult to understand even for the circle (of Buddha's direct disciples) at the time when the blessed Buddha was alive. As has been stated in *The Verse Summary of the Perfection of Wisdom*, "This teaching (on emptiness) of the guiding (buddhas) is profound and difficult to see. No one has understood it and no one has attained (its realization without the help of a guru and extensive study, meditation and a vast accumulation of merit). Therefore, after (Śhākyamuni Buddha), who always had the loving compassion to benefit others, attained his enlightenment, he taxed his mind to think who among the masses of sentient beings could come to know it."[65]

Concerning the impossibility of our mind to penetrate into emptiness quickly and easily, including an example of this, and concerning the meaning of the (just-quoted) sutra, (Nāgārjuna) has said in *The Precious Garland*, "The uncleanness of our body for its own part is something gross, an object (knowable) by bare perception that can be seen all the time. Yet if this perception does not stay in our mind, how can the sacred teaching of noninherent abiding (in other words, the emptiness of phenomena) quickly and easily penetrate our mind when it is so subtle, nonobvious to bare perception, and profound? Therefore, realizing that this teaching, because it is so profound, is difficult for ordinary people to comprehend, the Sage Buddha turned away (at first) from showing this teaching."

Therefore, since in general a (fully qualified) teacher and student of this (emptiness), and in particular (such) a teacher and student of the techniques for developing in our mindstream single-minded concentration on this (emptiness), are extremely difficult to find, I think that (these accomplishments) will not come about if we have approached them in just any haphazard manner. (We must study and train in them properly.)[66]

An actual finding (of a realization) of the perfect view of emptiness, through faultless hearing, studying, and thinking, is of course completely necessary and indispensable for developing perfect single-minded concentration on emptiness. Otherwise, if we have not deeply understood the emptiness of all phenomena, then on what shall we focus in order to develop (such concentration on emptiness)? Not only that, but we must also definitely seek either an actual state of mental quiescence realized through the unmistaken methods for achieving one, or a state of single-minded concentration having the four characteristics as previously explained, and which would be a similar equivalent for mental quiescence. Once we have provided ourselves with these two, we must then actualize the single-minded concentration of a joint mental quiescence and penetrative insight settled single-pointedly on the meaning (of emptiness) devoid of all mentally fabricated (modes of existence).

In other words, if we lack a (correct) view (of emptiness) as explained above, then even if we have achieved a single-pointed settling (of our mind), it will not be settled on the meaning (of emptiness) devoid of all mental fabrications (or fantasies). Because of that, then except for its being a state of mental quiescence, (our achievement) will not be what penetrative insight means. Likewise, even if we have found an understanding of the unmistaken view, yet lack a stable state of mental quiescence, our mind will waver a great deal about its object. Then no matter how much we might analyze with individuating wisdom, we will be unable to conjoin mental quiescence with penetrative insight. Therefore this is the point (being made) when most standard classics discuss the necessity for having both.

If I were to have written only in brief about the way to cut off all mistaken deviations and thereby develop an unmistaken view (of emptiness), it seemed I would not satisfy your wishes. Yet if I were to have been very extensive, it seemed that this would have become extremely overburdening with words. Therefore today I have tried not to write (in either of these ways) in this letter.

In general, even if I were to present the (sutra and tantra) paths like this (in a letter form), it did not seem as though it would be of much benefit. Therefore, whether those who have requested me to do so have been lofty or humble, I have never in the past consented (to write such a letter). But you, my holy (teacher), are not like the other. Since you have requested me so earnestly to discuss (this topic) and since other pressing reasons appeared as well from your noble letter, I have offered you these brief (words), having dispensed with much correlation with scriptural quotations and elaborate arguments to cut off extreme positions with logical reasoning. After examining over and again (what I have written), if it seems to accord with reason, I humbly request you please to implement this in your lofty practice. (In a previous life) when you were the master translator Loden Sherab, you traveled with countless difficulties to the noble land (of India) and served there many learned spiritual masters. By so doing, you found an exact (realization) of the total and complete points of the victorious Buddha's teachings. Because of this, whatever marvelous (works and translations) you prepared eliminated the darkness of ignorance and brought clarity to this land (Tibet). The banner of your fame still waves on among all beings, including the gods, for, as an eye of the world who had a heart of compassionately cherishing others more than himself, you attained the enlightened state of a successor to the victorious Buddha.

(Now you have taken birth as) Könchok Tsultrim, someone who keeps vows strictly, is learned, vastly intelligent, and who (as your name indicates) has respect for the Supreme Jewels of refuge and excellent moral discipline. In order to fulfill your wishes, I, Losang Drakpa, a follower of learned masters who have exactly realized all the points they have heard and studied from many faultless scriptural classics, and who am (now) a renunciant meditator favoring quiet places, have exhausted (my meager knowledge and insight in trying to satisfy you) in this way. By the good force of the virtue obtained from this (humble attempt), may all beings understand the classics exactly as (Buddha,) the Guru of the three realms, has well explained and thereby spread a festive array of realizations perfect to the rule.

You with a virtuous and confident mind and I are like (Buddha's disciples, the close friends) Maudgalyāyana and Śhāriputra. I pray that whichever of us receives the nectar (of buddhahood) first will be able to share it with the other.

Ah, isn't it wonderful to have had the excellent fortune of obtaining (a human rebirth with full) liberty (to study and practice the Dharma) and to have met with the teachings of the victorious (buddhas)! Now the (only thing) reasonable is to work day and night to make our body, with which we can accomplish great purposes, have its full meaning. This is because (Buddha) has said that those who make a partial (effort) gain partial results, whereas those who make a complete (effort) gain a complete result. And what sensible person would be satisfied with something partial?

(In the past) there has never been any living being who has escaped being gobbled up by the cannibal of impermanence. As this is still the only case, mind, how can you sit and relax? Therefore we must give up meaningless activities that, even though we might exert ourselves, we will have to discard anyway (when we die). Instead we should always think about our two kinds of karmic actions (virtuous or nonvirtuous, the effects of) which will follow us no matter where we go. Having thought like this, then with a sense of shame and decency and consideration, as well as with mindfulness, alertness, and conscientious care, we will be able to tame our mind well, which is so difficult to subdue. May this thereby spread joy to our mind at the time of our death.

May the (buddhas') teachings, the basis of all happiness and excellence, abide (forever). May no harm come to those who practice the sacred Dharma. May all beings' hopes be fulfilled in accordance with the Dharma, and may they never be parted from the heart of loving one another. This *Summary Points of the Graded Path to Enlightenment* has been in response to a letter of request from the holy personage of Könchok Tsultrim, a great renunciant meditator who has exactly realized all the points he has heard and studied so extensively and thus become a sacred close friend of the precious teachings and a guide for many beings. It has been composed by the Buddhist monk Losang Drakpa in the (Tibetan) district of E at the Teura monastery.[67]

7 The Prayer of the Virtuous Beginning, Middle, and End

Thog ma dang bar dang tha mar dge ba'i smon lam

---

(1)

May the boundless prayers I have offered with a pure, extraordinary wish to be able to free countless beings from cyclic existence be fulfilled as true words by the might of the nondeceptive Three Jewels of refuge and the powerful sagely masters.

(2)

In all my lives, one after the next, may I never be born in any rebirth state in which I have reverted to being a miserable creature in an unfortunate realm. But rather, may I (always) attain a human body with complete liberty and endowments (for Dharma study and practice).

(3)

From the moment I am born, may I never be attached to worldly pleasures. In order to attain liberation, may I, by my thoughts of renunciation, involve myself with unrelenting joyous effort in seeking to live a pure moral life.

(4)

In order that I might take robes, may none of my circle or possessions cause me any interference. But rather, may all favorable conditions come about as I have wished.

(5)
Once I am ordained, then as long as I live, may I never be stained by the fault of (committing any) proscribed or naturally unspeakable negative actions, just as I promised before the eyes of my abbot and spiritual master.

(6)
By relying on pure moral conduct, may I, for the sake of all my mothers, be able to actualize over countless eons, with the myriad difficulties (involved), every profound and vast Mahāyāna teaching that exists.

(7)
May I be continually cared for by a holy spiritual master whose mindstream abounds with good qualities of scriptural knowledge and insight, whose senses are calmed, who has self-control, a heart of loving compassion, and the courage of mind to accomplish undauntedly the purposes of others.

(8)
Just as Sadāprarudita devoted himself to Dharmodgata,[68] may I also totally please my holy spiritual master unpretentiously with my body, life, and all my possessions, thereby never causing him displeasure for even a moment.

(9)
May the meaning of perfected discriminating awareness in all its profundity, stilled (of extremes) and devoid of mentally fabricated (ways of being), be shown to me always as it was taught to Sadāprarudita, unpolluted by the fouling waters of distorted conceptions.

(10)
May I never fall under the influence of misleading friends or wrong-minded gurus who are teachers of either nihilist or eternalist views that transgress the meaning of what Sage (Buddha) intended.

(11)
By securing myself to the boat of listening (to teachings), thinking about and meditating on them, and by flying the mainsail of a pure, extraordinary wish, being propelled by the wind of unrelenting joyous effort, may I free all beings from the ocean of cyclic existence.

(12)
However much I might improve my mind by listening (to teachings), being especially generous, keeping pure moral discipline, and developing analytical discriminating awareness, may I be free to the same extent from all consequent feelings of haughty conceit.

(13)
Without being satisfied, may I hear endless (teachings on Buddha's) scriptural pronouncements close at the side of a learned master who opens up the exact meaning of these texts by relying on nothing but the force of pure logic.

(14)
Having analyzed fully and correctly with the four types of reasoning,[69] day and night, the meaning of (the teachings) I have heard, may I cut off all doubts with the critical awareness I have gained from having thought about the points to be contemplated.

(15)
When, through an awareness that has come from having thought about the extremely profound ways of the teachings, I have found certain conviction (in what they actually mean), may I devote myself to solitude with the joyous effort that severs all entanglements with this life and thereby actualize (the insights) with proper (meditation).

(16)
When, by having listened (to the teachings), thought about and meditated on them, I have developed in my mindstream (the insights of) the essential points of the Victorious (Buddha's) intentions, may I never have any attitudes arise of longing for my own happiness or for the sights of this lifetime that would just cause me attachment to worldly existence.

(17)
When, with an attitude of detachment from all objects of wealth, I have overcome miserliness, may I first gather beings into my circle by material generosity and then satisfy them completely by teaching the Dharma.

(18)
Having thought well about renunciation, may I always uphold the victory banner of liberation for which I would never forsake until my attainment of enlightenment even the most minor (moral) training I have assumed, though my life be at stake.

(19)
Whenever I see, hear, or recall any beings who would beat, tease, or humiliate me, may I be free of anger and in response address myself to their good qualities and thus meditate on patience.

(20)
Having completely abandoned the three types of laziness[70] that prevent me from gaining virtues not yet attained and from improving further on those that I have, may I exert joyous effort (in virtuous practices).

(21)
Having forsaken the mental quiescent states that would practically propel me into cyclic rebirth by their missing the power of penetrative insight to deflate the extreme of worldly existence and by their lacking the moisture of compassion to soften away the extreme of tranquil passivity, may I meditate instead on a joint achievement (of both quiescence and insight).

(22)
Having fully abandoned the endless variety of wrong, distorted views that take as supreme a partial idea of emptiness that the mind has made up from having become frightened at the true meaning of the profound nature of reality, may I gain the insight that all phenomena are primally empty (of inherently findable existence).

(23)
May I yoke to the flawless rules of discipline those (monks) who, with an inconsiderate attitude, discard the pure moral trainings, never fearing the actions despised by the holy, and who, in breaking their precepts, are in fact trainees in virtue in outward appearance alone.

(24)
May I quickly and easily lead to the path praised by the victorious (buddhas) anyone who has missed the right path and is on a distorted, wrong trail, having come under the influence of a wrong-minded guru or a misleading friend.

(25)
When I have captivated the bold masses of foxes of misinformed speech with my lion-like roar of (correct) explanation, debate, and written exposition, may I then care for them with whatever means might be skilled for their taming and thus uphold the victory banner of the underlined teachings.

(26)
Each time I am born and can drink of the nectar of the Sage (Buddha's) words, may I be endowed with a good family, body, wealth, power, wisdom, a long life, no sickness, and great happiness (so that I might be best equipped to help others).

(27)
Toward those who continually harbor thoughts of harming my body, life, or possessions, and also toward those who speak unpleasantly to me, may I especially develop love as if I were their mother.

(28)
By developing in my mindstream a pure, extraordinary wish and an enlightened motive of bodhicitta through meditating on cherishing others more than myself, may I thereby confer on those (who would harm me) the peerless attainment of enlightenment without any delay.

(29)
May everyone who sees, hears, or recalls these prayers be undaunted in realizing (the aim of) all the great waves of the bodhisattvas' prayers (that they become enlightened).

(30)
By the force of offering these extensive prayers that have come into being by the power of my pure, extraordinary wish, may I fully complete the perfection of prayer and thereby fulfill the hopes of all living beings.

This "Prayer of the Virtuous Beginning, Middle, and End" has been composed at the holy Drikung Thil monastery in the Zhotaw district by the itinerant (monk) Losang Drakpa, who has heard many teachings.

Part 3

Middle Way Critical Philosophy: Insight Meditation

When Jé Rinpoche Tsongkhapa was forty, he was already famous throughout central Tibet as a scholar and a teacher of exceptional greatness. He himself, however, was still dissatisfied with his own inner realization of the ultimate reality of emptiness, and so he felt he needed still more intensive study and meditation on the profound teachings of the Middle Way. So in 1397 he withdrew from his active teaching program in the Nyal area to spend a year at the Olkha hermitage known as Oede Gungyal. He threw himself into intensive studies of the Middle Way, particularly rereading those sections of Chandrakīrti's *Lucid Exposition*, Buddhapālita's *Middle Way Commentary*, and Bhāvaviveka's *Blaze of Reason* that concern the utmost subtleties of the differences between the Dialecticist (*Prāsaṅgika*) Mādhyamakas and the Dogmaticist (*Svātantrika*) Mādhyamakas.[71]

After many months of study and meditation he still could not generate a complete certitude free of all anxiety concerning the ultimate. He then dreamed one night that he was present at a discussion of these points among Nāgārjuna himself and his spiritual sons, Āryadeva, Buddhapālita, Bhāvaviveka, Chandrakīrti, Nāgabodhi, and so on, and Buddhapālita rose from the assembly and blessed Tsongkhapa with a copy of his own commentary. He awoke feeling great bliss, and, characteristically, turned to that very commentary to reread a section in the eighteenth chapter.

While he was reading the words "the self is not the same as the aggregates, nor is it anything other than the aggregates," he effortlessly experienced the ultimate realization of absolute reality, along with perfect understanding of all the Dialecticist Mādhyamaka subtleties concerning the realistic view. On that very morning of his triumphal joy at clearly and nonconceptually experiencing the actual nature of absolute reality, he overflowed with faith in the Buddha Śhākyamuni, since after all, it was he who first had understood the absolute relativity of all things, mundane and transcendental, and had flawlessly taught this reality to his disciples then and in future generations. This poem, *In Praise to Dependent Origination*, so directly born of Tsongkhapa's own enlightenment experience, is what we have translated here as the first chapter. The translation is my own, although it is totally indebted to the teaching I originally received from the Venerable Geshé Ngawang Wangyal. My wording and interpretation here differ somewhat from the version that appeared in the *Door of Liberation*, translated under his supervision.

After his enlightenment experience of that morning, Jé Rinpoche went on to write five main works on Middle Way philosophy: the *Greater Transcendent Insight* (the last section of his *Stages of the Path to Enlightenment*), the larger *Essence of True Eloquence*, the *Ocean of Reasoning*, the brilliant *Elucidation of the Middle Way Intention,* and finally, the herein-presented *Middle-Length Transcendent Insight*, the final section of his medium *Path to Enlightenment*. All of these works are extremely difficult for the depth of their thought and the subtlety and precision of their expression. They conclusively disprove the popular misconception that Buddhism has no philosophy, no refined conceptual thinking, since its goal is nonconceptual realization. The fact is that truly insightful conceptual thought brings the philosophical meditator to the ultimate confrontation with reality where even conceptuality is transcended. In the present translation, I have restrained myself from elaborating scholarly detail in footnotes, as the argument refers to a vast philosophical literature produced by a tradition almost two thousand years old by Jé Rinpoche's time. However, in keeping with the spirit of this anthology, the translation is for the philosophical yogi who seeks to follow the thought and realize the gist, temporarily bracketing information such as names, dates, places, and so on. It is to be read as a formulation of a "simulated transcendent insight practice," in that the pattern of critical analysis contained here is a systematic warm-up for the actual practice of transcendent insight, which ensues when it is combined with one-pointed mental quiescence.

A final point is that actual transcendent insight must occur in integration with actual mental quiescence. It would therefore have been better to present this chapter together with the preceding section of the original work on mental quiescence. It is hoped that this will be possible in a later edition, until when we beg the readers' indulgence for our present inability. The chapter begins with a short section from the quiescence and insight section of the path work, then skips the quiescence section and translates the entire insight section.

8 Praise of Buddha Śhākyamuni for His Teaching of Relativity

I bow down to the Guru, Mañjughoṣha!

Homage to that perfect Buddha,
the supreme philosopher,
who taught us relativity
free of destruction and creation,
without annihilation and permanence,
with no coming and no going,
neither unity nor plurality;
the quieting of fabrications,
the ultimate bliss!

I bow down to Him whose vision and speech
made Him unexcelled as sage and teacher,
the Victor, who realized the ultimate truth,
then taught us it as relativity![72]

Misknowledge[73] itself is the very root
of all the troubles in this fleeting world;
who understood that, then reversed it,
taught universal relativity.

Thereupon, how could it be possible
that the geniuses[74] would not understand

this very path of absolute relativity
as the vital essence of Your teaching?

Such being the case, who could discover
anything even still more wonderful
to sing Your praises for, O Savior,
than this Your teaching of relativity?

"Whatever depends on conditions,
that is empty of intrinsic reality!"[75]
What excellent instruction could there be,
more marvelous than this discovery.

Although the naive can seize on it
as just confirming their extremist chains,
the wise use that very same (relativity)
to cut their way out of fabrication's trap.
This teaching is not seen elsewhere,
so You alone may be entitled "Teacher,"
merely a word of flattery for fundamentalists,[76]
as when you call a fox a lion.

Wondrous Teacher! Wondrous Refuge!
Wondrous top Philosopher! Wondrous Savior!
I pay full homage to that Teacher
who proclaimed universal relativity!

O Benefactor, to heal all beings
You proclaimed (deep relativity),
the peerless reason to ascertain
emptiness, the essence of the teaching!

How can such a one who sees
the process of relativity
as contradictory, or unestablished,
ever understand Your art?

Your position is that when one sees
emptiness as meaning relativity,
emptiness of intrinsic reality does not preclude

the viability of purposeful activity;
whereas when one sees the opposite,
activity becomes impossible in emptiness,
emptiness cannot be there during activity,
and one falls into the abyss of anxiety!

Therefore, the experience of relativity
is highly recommended in Your teaching,
and not as utter nonexistence,
nor as intrinsically real existence.

The nonrelative is like a sky-flower,
so there is nothing nonrelational.
And things' existence with objective status
would preclude reliance on cause and condition.

Thus You proclaimed that just because
nothing at all exists outside of relativity,
so nothing at all exists outside of
emptiness of intrinsic reality.

If things had any intrinsic reality,
since such could never be reversed, You said,
nirvana would become impossible,
since fabrications could not be reversed.

Dauntless, often in the assemblies of the wise,
You clearly proclaimed in Your lion's roar,
"Let there be freedom from identity!"
Who would ever presume to challenge this?

All systems are completely viable
since lack of intrinsic reality
and relativity do not conflict;
never mind they complement each other.

"By the reason of relativity,
there are no grounds to hold extremist views!"
For this excellent statement, You, Savior,
are unexcelled among philosophers!

"All this, objectively, is emptiness!"
And "This effect occurs from this cause!"
These two facts are mutually nonexclusive,
certainties, they reinforce each other.

Than this, what could ever be more wondrous?
Than this, what could ever inspire more awe?
If You are praised for this one principle,
it is real praise, and otherwise not so.

Those held in the thrall of delusions
react angrily to challenge You;
is it any wonder they should find unbearable
Your word on lack of self-identity?

But those who formally accept relativity,
the precious treasury of Your speech,
when they cannot bear the roar of emptiness,
that really does amaze me!

The unexcelled relativity,
doorway to identitylessness—
they hold it as a nominal identity!
How they do deceive themselves!

These should be led by whatever method
into that good path which pleases You,
the matchless haven well-frequented
by all the supreme noble ones.

Intrinsic reality is uncreated and nonrelative,
relativities are created and relational;
how can these two facts come together
in a single instance without contradiction?

Thus what is relationally occurrent,
though ever free of intrinsic reality,
still seems to be intrinsically real,
so You said, "All this is like illusion!"

From this very fact, one deeply understands
(Nāgārjuna's) statement that, the way You taught
those who strive to challenge this, Your teaching
rationally can find no fallacy.

Why? Because Your exposition of relativity
makes utterly remote any tendencies
to reify or repudiate things[77]
empirical and hypothetical.

This very path of relativity,
the proof that Your speech is matchless,
also creates a total confidence
in the validity of Your other statements.

You speak from Your experience of reality,
and those who train themselves under You
go far beyond every kind of trouble,
having abandoned the root of all evil.

But those who turn their backs on Your teaching,
though they have struggled for a very long time,
decry many faults once outside again,
because of their firm conviction about the self.

O wonder! Wise ones understand the difference
between following Your teaching or not—
then how could they fail to feel most deeply
great respect for both You (and Your teaching)?

What need to mention Your many teachings?
To find even a rough, general certainty
in the precise meaning of a tiny part
confers, even that, supreme happiness!

Alas! My mind conquered by delusions,
though I came from afar to seek refuge
in the profusion of Your excellence,
I could not embody even a fraction,

Yet when I stand before the Lord of Death,
And the stream of life has not quite ended,
I will consider myself most fortunate
to have even the slightest faith in You!

Among teachers, the teacher of relativity,
Among wisdoms, the wisdom of relativity;
these are like imperial victors in the world,
making You world champion of wisdom, over all.

Whatever You ever taught is realized
by means of relativity itself,
and since that brings one back unto nirvana,
no deed of Yours does not deliver peace.

O wonder! Whoever hears Your teaching
Knows liberating peace in everything—
so who is there who does not respect
the upholders of such a teaching?

My delight ever grows for this system,
which overcomes all sorts of opposition,
is free from internal contradictions,
and fulfills both main goals of human beings.

For the sake of this, You gave away,
again and again for countless eons,
sometimes Your body, other times Your life,
your loved ones, and great wealth of possessions.

When 1 behold such excellence of Yours,
I see how Your great heart reveals the teaching,
and, just as the fishhook drags out the fish,
I feel my sad fate not to hear it from You!

But even with the force of such sorrow,
I will not allow my mind to waver,
as the loving mind of the mother
always goes after her beloved child.

And even when I think on Your speech,
"That Teacher, completely surrounded
with nets of light rays, blazing with the glory
of all of the auspicious signs and marks,
spoke just in this way with his Brahmā voice!"
Then the image of great Śhākyamuni,
dawning in my mind, heals me just as well
as the moon's rays heal the pains of fever.

Though Your good system is thus marvelous,
inexpert persons get totally confused
in every respect, as if they were
all entangled up in jungle grasses.

Having understood this problem, I then
schooled myself in the writings of skilled sages,
studying with manifold exertions,
seeking Your intent again and again.

And I studied numerous treatises
of both the Buddhist and non-Buddhist schools,
yet, unremittingly, still outside, my mind
remained tormented in the trap of doubts.

So I went to the night-lily garden
of the treatises of Nāgārjuna.
Prophesied to elucidate correctly
the art of Your unexcelled vehicle,
free of the extremes of being and nothing.

And there I saw, by the kindness of the Lama,
all illuminated by garlands of white light
of the eloquence of the glorious Moon (Chandrakīrti),
whose expanding orb of taintless wisdom
courses freely in the sky of sutra,

clearing the gloom of the extremist heart,
eclipsing constellations of false teachings;
and then and there,
my mind attained relief at last![78]

Of all [Your] deeds, speech is supreme.
And for this very reason, true sages
commemorate the perfect Buddha
for this (teaching of relativity).

I renounced the world on the example of that Teacher,
my study of the Victor's speech is not inferior,
I am a Buddhist monk, energetic in yoga practice;
and such is my respect for that great Seer!

By the Guru's kindness, I was able thus to meet
the teaching of the Unexcelled Teacher.
And I dedicate this virtue as a cause of all beings'
being looked after by the holy spiritual teachers.

May the teaching of that Benefactor, till world's end,
be undisturbed by the winds of wrong prejudices,
and, finding faith in the Teacher by understanding
the natural way of the teaching, may it ever increase!

May I uphold the good system of the Muni
that illumines the actual fact of relativity
through all my lives, though I give up body and even life!
And may I never let go of it even for an instant!

May I spend all day and night reflecting
on the methods to propagate this (teaching),
achieved by that best Leader through boundless hardships,
by making strenuous efforts the essence (of His lives!)

As I strive in this way with pure high resolve,
may Brahmā, Indra, and the world protectors,
and Mahākāla and the other Dharma protectors,
always befriend me without fail!

This "Essence of Eloquent Teaching," a praise of the Unexcelled Teacher Lord Buddha, the unsolicited best friend of all peoples, from the perspective of his teaching of profound relativity, was composed by the learned monk Losang Drakpa Pal at the royal mountain retreat of Tibet, the heavenly retreat of Öde Gungyal, otherwise known as Victory monastery. The scribe was Namkha Pal.

9 The Middle Length Transcendent Insight

From Jé Tsongkhapa's Middle[79] *Stages of the Path of Enlightenment*

Benefits of Meditating on Quiescence and Insight

The Buddha stated in the *Elucidation of Intent Sūtra* that all mundane and transcendent excellences of Individual (Hīnayāna) and Universal (Mahāyāna) Vehicles are the effects of mental quiescence and transcendent insight.

One might object, "Well, aren't quiescence and insight themselves excellences of the character of one who has already attained the fruits of meditation? In that case, how is it correct for all those excellences to be the effects of those two?"

Since actual quiescence and insight, as will be explained, are indeed excellences of the character of one accomplished in the fruits of meditation, it is granted that all excellences of Individual and Universal Vehicles are not their effects. However, there is no contradiction, since all samādhis beyond one-pointedness toward virtuous objectives are classified under the heading of "quiescence," and all virtuous wisdoms that analytically discriminate phenomenal and noumenal objects are classified under the heading of "insight." With this in mind, the Lord said that all excellences of the three vehicles are the effects of quiescence and insight.

He further states in the *Elucidation of the Intention*: "If a person practices quiescence and insight, he will become liberated from bad conditioning and signifying bondages." Ratnākaraśhānti explains in the *Instruction in Transcendent Wisdom* that this means that "bad conditioning" (bondages), which are the instincts lying in the mental processes capable of generating ever-increasing distorted subjectivities, and "signifying" (bondages), which create

103

those instincts in the form of prior and posterior attachment to distorted objects, are abandoned by insight and quiescence, respectively. Now those are the benefits of what are designated as "quiescence" and "insight," and the meaning is the same even if you do not so designate them, as when you designate them the benefits of "meditation" and "wisdom." They still are to be known as the benefits of these two, quiescence and insight.

Quiescence and Insight Contain All Samādhis

The Buddha also stated in the *Elucidation* that all samādhis of Individual and Universal Vehicles that he ever mentioned are included in quiescence and insight. Therefore, since those eager for samādhi cannot possibly explore all separate categories of samādhis, they should explore thoroughly the method of cultivation of quiescence and insight, which provide a general framework for all samādhis.

The Identification of Mental Quiescence

Buddha states in the *Elucidation*: "One sits alone in isolation, one absorbs oneself within, one impresses in the mind the well-considered teachings, and one goes on impressing this within the mind continuously, the very mind that is doing the impressing. Entering in this way and repeatedly abiding therein, when physical and mental adeptness emerge, it is called "mental quiescence." This means that when the mind no longer vacillates but works continuously, naturally abiding with its chosen object, and when the joyous ease of mental and physical adeptness is produced, then that samādhi becomes (actual) mental quiescence. This is produced just from holding the mind within, without wavering from its chosen object, and does not require any realization of the thatness of things.

The Identification of Transcendent Insight

The Buddha said in the *Elucidation*: "Then, after attaining the physical and mental adeptness, one abandons the mode of keeping the mind focused on one thing, and one individually investigates the well-considered things arising as internal images in the realm of the samādhi; one confronts each one of them. Thus, with regard to those objects of knowledge that arise as images in the objective sphere of samādhi—their discernment, investigation, examination, thorough analysis, tolerance, acceptance, differentiation, viewing, and discrimination—all these are called 'transcendent insight.' And in this way, the bodhisattva becomes expert in transcendent insight."

Here "discernment" refers to differentiation of the phenomenological content of reality and "investigation" to penetrating its ontological condition. "Examination" refers to a crude consideration and "thorough analysis" refers to a fine analysis.

Buddha also states in the *Jewel Cloud Sūtra*, "Quiescence is one-pointed mind. Insight is individual consideration." And Maitreya states, "This concentration on all named teachings should be recognized as the path of quiescence. And the path of insight should be recognized as the analysis of their imports." And, "Quiescence and insight are so called because, respectively, the one is a focus of mind in mind based on authentic stability, and the other is the analytic discrimination of phenomena."[80]

Thus quiescence is said to be the focus of the mind based on authentic samādhi, and insight is said to be the wisdom that analytically discerns all things. Asaṅga agrees with this in *Bodhisattva Levels*, while Kamalaśhīla adds from the second *Stages of Meditation*,[81] "It is called 'quiescent stability' because all distractions toward external objects are quieted, and then one stabilizes the mind itself, endowed with joy in continuous focus on the inner object, as well as special adeptness. And 'insight' is the analysis of ultimate reality while staying in that very quiescence." Ratnākaraśhānti explains in the same way in his *Instruction in Transcendent Wisdom*.

So, according to Ratnākaraśhānti and Asaṅga, quiescence and insight are not differentiated according to their chosen objects, since each of them can take either ultimate or relative as their object. There is such a thing as a quiescence that realizes emptiness, and there is such a thing as an insight that does not realize emptiness.

Therefore one is called "quiescent stability" because it is a quieting of the mind's attraction toward external objects and a stabilizing of the mind on the inner object. And the other is called "transcendent insight" because there is an "excessive" or "distinctive" experience.

Now there are some who assert that quiescence is the lack of the sharp clarity of the intellect through keeping the mind thought-free, and insight is the presence of such sharp clarity. But they are mistaken, since such contradicts all the above explanations, and since that difference is merely the difference between samādhi afflicted by depression and samādhi without depression. All quiescence samādhis must definitely be cleared of depression, and all samādhis free of depression definitely arrive at sharp clarity of mind. Therefore we must recognize whether a samādhi or wisdom is or is not oriented toward emptiness by whether or not the intellect involved understands either of the two selflessnesses or not, since there are innumerable samādhis that have bliss, clarity, and thoughtfulness without having any interest in the objective ultimate reality. It is established by experience that it is enough (to generate quiescence) to hold the mind completely free of thought without discovering the view that understands the real situation. Failure to understand emptiness in no way precludes the generation of nondiscursive samādhi. By the power of holding the mind (thought-free) for a long time, one produces fitness of neural wind-energies.[82]

This production is marked as the arisal of joy and bliss in body and mind, so (lack of realization of emptiness) does not preclude the generation of bliss. Once that has been generated, by the power of the vividness of feeling of bliss, clarity dawns in the mind. Therefore one cannot represent all blissful, clear, thought-free samādhis as realizing thatness. Thus while it does happen that nondiscursive bliss and clarity occur in samādhi realizing emptiness, it also often happens in samādhis not at all oriented toward emptiness. So it is necessary to distinguish the difference between the two.

Reason for the Necessity to Meditate on Both Quiescence and Insight

Why is it not sufficient to meditate on quiescence and insight one by one, but rather both must be meditated on?

For example, if one is in a temple at night and wishes to view the wall paintings and so lights a lamp, one can see the painted deities quite clearly if one has both a bright lamp and its light is undisturbed by the wind. If the lamp is not bright, or if its brightness is too agitated by the breeze, one cannot see them clearly. Similarly, to view the impact of the profound, one can see thatness clearly if one has both the wisdom that ascertains unerringly the import of thatness and also the unwavering concentration that stays focused on its chosen object.

Even though you might have the nondiscursive samādhi that stays put without being distracted elsewhere, if you do not have the wisdom to be aware of the real situation, however much you may cultivate that samādhi, it will be impossible for you to realize the real situation. And, even if you have the view that understands selflessness, if you do not have the stable samādhi where the mind stays put on one point, it will be impossible for you to see clearly the impact of the real situation. Therefore both quiescence and insight are necessary.

Kamalaśhīla supports this from the second *Stages of Meditation*: "Practicing insight exclusively apart from quiescence, the yogi's mind will be distracted soon by external objects and will not achieve stability, like a lamp caught in the wind. And then the clear illumination of intuition will not occur. Thus both must be equally practiced." And further, he states, "By the strength of quiescence the mind will not be disturbed by the winds of discursive thought, like a lamp protected from the wind. Then insight can abandon the whole network of wrong views, which cannot be opened up by anything else." As the Buddha stated in the *King of Samādhi Sūtra*, "One becomes unmoved on the strength of quiescence. Through insight, one becomes like a mountain."

Thus intending that one can come to understand the import of reality by investigating with wisdom combined with the equipoise of quiescence wherein the mind is not imbalanced through excitement or depression, it is stated in the *Dharma Encyclopedia*, "When the mind is equipoised, you will correctly understand reality." And Kamalashīla adds in the first *Stages of Meditation*, "Since the mind moves just like so much water, it cannot stay put without the ground of quiescence. And the unbalanced mind cannot understand reality correctly. The Lord proclaimed that through equipoise, reality is correctly understood!"

If you achieve quiescent stability, not only will you get rid of the faults of distraction of wisdom that correctly analyzes selflessness, but all meditation practices using individually discriminating wisdom, such as cultivations of impermanence, effects of evolution (karma), the evils of the cyclic life (samsara), love, compassion, and the spirit of enlightenment (bodhicitta), all these will eliminate the fault of distraction from their objects and will engage their objects without wandering away to anything else. Then all your virtuous actions will become very powerful. Before attaining quiescence, all virtuous practices are weak in impact because usually you become distracted to other objects. As Shāntideva says in the *Entrance to the Bodhisattva's Way of Life*, "The person of wavering mind is caught between the fangs of passions," and "The Reality-Knower said that if your mind still gets distracted, even if you practice for a long time reciting mantras, austerities, and so on, it is all to no avail."

Determination of the Proper Order of Meditating on Quiescence and Insight

According to Shāntideva in his *Entrance*, "It is acknowledged that the transcendent insight combined with firm quiescence conquers the passions. So first seek quiescent stability." Thus you should first achieve quiescence and then practice insight on that basis.

Here one may wonder, "Why should I first seek quiescence and only then practice insight? Kamalashīla says in his first *Stages* that there is no fixed object, that the object of quiescence is not determined. Further, it was already explained that the object of quiescence has both objectivity and character.[83] If I first understand the impact of selflessness and then meditate taking that as my object, then the quiescence without mental wavering to other objects and the insight oriented toward emptiness would be generated simultaneously, so that would seem to be perfectly all right."

Now, as for the way in which quiescence must precede insight, it is not that quiescence must precede the generation of understanding of the view that realizes selflessness, since it does happen that some generate the view without having quiescence. It is also not that quiescence must precede the generation of transformative experience regarding the view, since the lack of quiescence does not preclude the arisal of spiritual transformation through the repeated practice of critical analysis by means of individually discriminative wisdom. If it did preclude such transformation, then the absurd consequence would follow that spiritual transformation through the practice of impermanence, revulsion from the life cycle, and (the conception of) the spirit of enlightenment and so forth would depend also on quiescence, for the reasons are the same (in all these cases).

Then what is the way in which quiescence must precede insight? Here the generation of insight is in the context of the common individual who has not previously generated meditative realization and must newly do so. In that context, except for the exceptional way to be explained below, in which a distinctive subjectivity for the realization of emptiness meditates on selflessness,[84] in the (usual) context of the Transcendence Vehicle and the three lower tantra divisions, analytic meditation is necessary, since without practicing analytical meditation that cultivates the discriminating wisdom's analysis of the import of selflessness, meditative realization will not emerge. Now in that case, before one has achieved quiescence, one seeks the understanding of selflessness repeatedly analyzing its meaning. Now, if quiescence has not been achieved already, it is impossible to achieve it based on that (sort of analytic meditation). And while quiescence is achieved by the practice of focusing meditation apart from analysis, there is no method of practice of insight apart from the method of practice of quiescence. Therefore insight must be sought subsequently. And therefore, ultimately, you cannot get around the order that quiescence is first sought and then insight is meditated based on the achieved quiescence.

Therefore, on this interpretation, if the process of generating insight is not understood as being the generation of adeptness by means of discriminating analytic meditation, there is no genuine reason why the meditation of insight must be based on the prior quest of quiescence.[85] And it is extremely wrong not to meditate according to that order.

The Buddha said in the *Elucidation* that one meditates insight relying on the attainment of quiescence, as mentioned already. And the order of the "meditation" and "wisdom" in the six transcendences, as well as the order of the generation of the exceptional wisdom training based on the exceptional samādhi training, namely, that "the latter is generated based on the former," these are the very same as the order of meditating insight after already having meditated quiescence. Asaṅga affirms in the *Bodhisattva Levels* and in the *Śrāvaka Levels* that insight is meditated based on quiescence. And Bhāvaviveka, in his *Essence of the Middle Way*,[86] Śhāntideva, in his *Entrance*, Kamalaśhīla in all three *Stages of Meditation*, Jñānakīrti,[87] and Ratnākaraśhānti, all of them affirm that first you seek quiescence and then you meditate transcendent insight. Therefore, just because some Indian masters prescribe that you should not seek quiescence separately but should generate insight by analyzing with discriminating wisdom from the beginning, intelligent persons should not rely on that, since it contradicts the treatises of the great champions.[88]

Of course, this order of quiescence and insight is in terms of their initial generation. Once attained, there is no fixed order, since sometimes one will first meditate insight and later quiescence. Here one objects, "Well, what about Asaṅga's statement in the *Compendium of Scientific Knowledge* that "some achieve insight, and do not achieve quiescence, so they should strive to achieve quiescence dying on their insight"?

This statement does not refer to a failure to attain the quiescence included in the threshold state of the first realm of meditative trance but only to the failure to attain the quiescences from the actual state of the first realm of meditative trance on up. And in that case, one achieves the quiescences from the actual first realm of meditative trance on up by relying on one's direct realization of the four holy truths. As Asaṅga says in the *Actuality of the Stages*, "Further, while one understands thoroughly and correctly (the four noble truths) from the truth of suffering to the truth of the path, one has not attained the first meditative trance and beyond. Immediately, one should focus the mind and refrain from investigating the mind. Then, depending on that very same exceptional wisdom, one applies oneself to the exceptional mind."

In general, in loose usage of the terms, there are statements wherein the nine stations of the mind are referred to as "quiescence" and the four mental functions—"discernment," "investigation," "appraisal," and "thorough examination"—are referred to as "insight." Nevertheless, actual quiescent stability and transcendent insight can only be presented beyond the generation of the special (mental and physical) adeptness, as will be explained below.

Skipping from Tashi Lhunpo, pha, 137b2 to 164b5.

10 Conditions Necessary for Transcendent Insight

General Setup of Conditions (APS)

(Kamalashila), in his second *Stages of Meditation*, states the three conditions for transcendent insight to be reliance on a holy person, eagerness to hear the teachings from him, and suitable reflection on them. More (explicitly), the reliance on an expert who knows unerringly the essentials of the (Buddha's) sutras, the study of the flawless scientific treatises, and the generation of the view of awareness of reality by the wisdoms of learning and reflection—these constitute the indispensable preconditions for transcendent insight. If there is no penetrating certainty about the import of actual reality, it is impossible to generate the realization that is the transcendent insight into the nature of reality.

One must seek such a view by relying on (teachings) of definitive meaning, and not on (those of) interpretable meaning. And one comes to understand the impact of the definitive discourses by knowing the difference between interpretable and definitive (discourses). Further, if one does not rely on the philosophical treatises that elucidate the (Buddha's) inner thought, written by one of the great champions who personified living reason itself, one is like a blind person wandering in a dangerous wilderness without any guide. Thus one should rely on the flawless scientific treatises.

On what sort of person should one rely?

The holy Nāgārjuna was renowned throughout the three realms and was very clearly predicted by the Lord himself in many sutras and tantras as the elucidator of the essence of the doctrine, the profound import free of all extremes of being and nothingness. So one should seek the view that

111

realizes emptiness by relying on his treatises. Āryadeva also was taken as equal in authority to the master by the great Mādhyamakas such as the masters Buddhapālita, Bhāvaviveka, Chandrakīrti, and Shāntarakṣhita.[89]

Hence, since both father (Nāgārjuna) and son (Āryadeva) were the sources for the other Mādhyamakas, the old-time scholars called these two sages the grandmother-treatise Mādhyamakas, and the others who came after were called the partisan Mādhyamakas.[90]

A certain old-time geshé maintained that there are two types of Mādhyamakas, when designated according to their presentation of conventional reality, namely, the Sautrāntika-Mādhyamakas,[91] who assert the conventional existence of external objects, and the Idealist-Mādhyamakas,[92] who assert the conventional lack of external objects.

(He) also (maintained that) there are two types when designated according to their acceptance of ultimate reality, namely, the Illusionists,[93] who assert that ultimate reality is the coincidence of truthless appearance and things such as sprouts, and the Dissolutionists,[94] who assert that ultimate reality is that isolated by the exclusion of all fabrications involving appearance. He maintained that the masters Shāntarakṣhita and Kamalashīla were exemplars of the former class. (He was supported by the fact that) certain Indian scholars also accept the names "Illusionist" and "Dissolutionist." However, the Great Translator (Ngog Lo)[95] said that the twofold classification according to position on the ultimate is foolish, an astonishing idea. Concerning this, Master Jñānasena said that the noble father and son were not explicit in their Centrist[96] treatises about the existence and nonexistence of external things, but subsequently Master Bhāvaviveka refuted the Idealist school and founded the school that held external things to be conventionally existent. Later, Master Shāntarakṣhita founded still another distinctive Centrist methodology, teaching the conventional nonexistence of external things and the ultimate realitylessness of the mind. Thus, two kinds of Centrists (*mādhyamaka*) arose, the former called Scripturalist Centrist and the latter, Idealist Centrist. Thus, (Jñānasena) was quite clear about the historical sequence in which the great treatises elucidated (the profound meaning).

Which one of these masters should one follow to seek the ultimate intention of the noble father and son?

The eminent former gurus in the line of (my) oral tradition followed the practice of the Great Lord (Atīsha)[97] in holding the system of Chandrakīrti as the supreme one. Master Chandrakīrti perceived that, among the commentators on the *Wisdom*,[98] it was Master Buddhapālita who most completely elucidated the intention of the noble ones. He took the latter's system as his basis, and while he used many of the good statements, when he worked out his own elucidation of the noble intention he refuted points that seemed slightly incorrect in the work of Master Bhāvaviveka. Therefore, since I see the analysis of these two masters (Buddhapālita and Chandrakīrti) as extremely superior in explaining the treatises of the noble father and son, I will follow them here in determining the intention of the noble father and son.

Now, while Master Chandrakīrti asserts the conventional existence of external objects, his system does not agree with any other philosophers, it not being proper to call him a Sautrāntika and incorrect to assert him to agree with the Vaibhāṣhika.[99]

(Thus) the expert of the later dissemination in the Land of Snows used the appellations "dialecticist" and "dogmaticist" for the Mādhyamakas, following the *Lucid Exposition*.[100] Thus, while there are two kinds of Mādhyamakas according to their position on the conventional existence of external objects (namely, Sautrāntika and Idealist), it is also certain that there are two kinds if one classifies them according to their respective methods of generating in awareness the definite view about emptiness, namely, the Dialecticist and the Dogmaticist.

The Method to Determine the View: Identification of Addictive Misknowledge

Misknowledge is the basis of all ills and faults, since all the Victor's teachings against other addictions such as attachment are only partial medicine and His teaching against misknowledge is the only comprehensive medicine. As Chandrakīrti says in *Lucid Exposition*: "Buddhas are renowned in this world as regulating the activities of people, by their nine modes of teaching, such as sutras, based on the two realities. Therein, teachings dispelling lust will not bring hatred to an end. Teachings dispelling hatred will not bring lust to an end. Teachings dispelling pride and so on will not conquer the other taints. Thus those teachings are not all-pervasive and do not bear the great import. But teachings dispelling delusion conquer all addictions—for Victors declare that all addictions truly depend on delusion."

That being so, the meditation on suchness is necessary as the medicine for misknowledge, and since one does not know how to cultivate the medicine without identifying the misknowledge itself, it is very important to identify misknowledge.

Misknowledge is the opposite of knowledge, and knowledge here should not be taken as whatever type (of common knowledge) but as the wisdom of the knowledge of the suchness of selflessness. The opposite of that, again, is not properly (understood) as the mere absence of that wisdom or as merely something else than that but as its very antithesis. That is (precisely) the reification of a self, and, as there are reifications of two selves, of things and of persons, the personal self-habit and the objective self-habit together constitute misknowledge. As for the manner of that reification, it is the habitual sense that things have intrinsically objective, intrinsically identifiable, or intrinsically real status.[101]

(The Buddha) states that things are established by force of mental construction, in the *Questions of Upāli Sūtra*: "The varied delights of blossoming flowers, the pleasure of the glitter of a golden palace—these (things) have no (intrinsic) function, but are there on the strength of our constructs. The whole cosmos is constructed by force of thought . . ."[102]

(Nāgārjuna) states in his *Sixty Reasonings*,[103] "The perfect buddhas do declare misknowledge is the condition for the world, so why should it be wrong to say 'This world is a mental construct'?" And (Chandrakīrti) comments that this means that worlds are not objectively established but are merely constructed by conceptual thought.

(Again, Āryadeva) states in his *Four Hundred Stanzas*, "Since there is nothing existent in desires and so on without mental constructs, what intelligent person adheres to 'true objects' and 'constructs'?" (Chandrakīrti) comments that desires and so on are like a snake imagined in a rope, insofar as they are mentally constructed while not existing objectively; as existence itself goes only with mental construction, and not without it, hence it is doubtless sure that there is no objective status (in things), just like a snake imagined in a striped rope. He does not mean that (rope-snake) and desires and so on have the same conventional existential status.

These reasons (bring out) the mode of the habitual sense of truth-status, the negatee,[104] which is the habitual notion that it is not merely imposed by force of beginningless mental construction but is established on objects as their own objectivity. The presumed conceptual object of that (habit pattern) is called "self" or "intrinsic reality." Its absence in the designated "person" is called "personal selflessness," and its absence in things such as eyes, ears, and so on is called "selflessness of things" (or "objective selflessness"). It is thus understandable by implication that the habitual notions of the existence of that intrinsic reality in persons and things are the two "self-habits." As (Chandrakīrti says) in his *Commentary to the Four Hundred Stanzas*: "The 'self' is the 'intrinsic reality,' which is that (seeming) objectivity in things independent of anything else. Its absence is selflessness. It is understood as twofold by division into persons and things, called 'personal selflessness' and 'objective selflessness.'"

As for the objective condition of personal self-habits, (Chandrakīrti) explains in the *Entrance to the Middle Way* that certain Sammitīyas assert all five aggregates, and certain others only the mind, to be the objective condition or support of self-convictions. As for that mind, the Idealists[105] and certain Idealist Mādhyamakas assert it to be the fundamental consciousness; other Dogmaticist Mādhyamakas such as Bhāvaviveka and the majority of the Individual Vehicle scholars do not accept that but assert it to be the mental consciousness. In regard to the systems of all of these schools, it is both necessary to know that the referent for the designation "person" is merely the (pronoun) "I," and also necessary to be familiar with the methods of positing a substantive basis for that "I," such as the fundamental consciousness and so on.

With regard to the subconscious egoistic view[106] that is the self-habit, in *Entrance to the Middle Way* (Chandrakīrti) refutes (the position) that its object is the aggregates and comments that its object is the dependently designated self. He also states that the conventional self is not the mere conglomerate of the aggregates. Thus, as its object is neither the conglomerate of the aggregates at any one time nor the conglomerate of the temporal continuum of the aggregates, one must take the mere "person" and the mere "I" as the objective basis of the mere thought "I." Thus one should not put either the separate or the conglomerate aggregates as the substance of that "I." This is the unexcelled distinctive specialty of this Dialecticist system, and has been explained extensively elsewhere.[107]

In regard to the objective basis of subconscious egoistic views, it must generate internally the cognition that thinks "I," and therefore the subconscious habit that holds other persons to be intrinsically identifiable is the subconscious personal self-habit but is not the subconscious egoistic view of that (same person). The object of the innate egoistic view that is the property-habit[108] is the actual "mine" object of the innate cognition that thinks "mine," and is not held to be objects such as one's eye and so on. The mode (of this habit) is the habitual holding of the objects perceived as "mine" as if they were intrinsically identifiably so.

As for the subconscious objective self-habit, its objects are the material aggregate and so on, the eyes, ears, and so on of both self and others, and the impersonal inanimate objects and so on; and its mode is as explained above.

In the *Entrance to the Middle Way Commentary*, (Chandrakīrti) affirms that "delusion is misknowledge, which functions as the reification of the intrinsic objectivity of nonobjectively existent things. It is superficial, with a nature of obscuration—seeing intrinsic realities in things." He states further (equates it with addictions) that "thus, by the force of the addictive misknowledge[109] included in the 'existence' member (of the twelve links of dependent origination) . . ." He thus accepts that misknowledge that is the truth-habit[110] about objects is the same as addictive misknowledge. Thus, while there are two systems of classification of objective self-habits either as addictive or as cognitive obscurations,[111] this system chooses the former one.

This is also the statement of the noble father and son, as in Nāgārjuna's *Seventy Stanzas on Emptiness*: "Reification of the reality in things born of conditions—the Teacher called it 'misknowledge'; therefrom twelve members arise. Seeing truly and knowing well the emptiness of objects, misknowledge does not occur, is ceased; thereby the twelve members cease." Here "reification of the reality in things" indicates the habitual perception of "truth" or "reality status" in those things.

In the *Precious Garland* (Nāgārjuna) also states in the same vein that "as long as there is the aggregate habit, so long will there be the 'I'-habit . . ." That is, that egoistic views will not be reversed as long as the truth-habit about the aggregates is not.

In the *Four Hundred Stanzas* (Āryadeva) states, "Just as the body-sense is to the body so delusion adheres to everything—and thus, when delusion is conquered, all addictions will be conquered. Seeing relativistic origination, delusion will not occur. Thus here, with all one's efforts, one should teach just that message."

The context here is the identification of that "delusion" that is one of the three poisons and hence equivalent to addictive misknowledge. To get rid of that misknowledge, he declares it necessary to understand the import of the profound relativity, which happens when the import of emptiness arises as the import of relativity. Therefore one must interpret addictive delusion according to (Chandrakīrti's) explanation in the *Commentary to the Four Hundred Stanzas* as the reification of reality in things.

This system was lucidly proclaimed by Chandrapada, following Buddhapālita's elucidation of the intention of the noble ones.

Now that just-explained misknowledge, which is thus habituated to the two selves, is not the holding of persons and things hypothesized by the distinctive beliefs of Buddhist and non-Buddhist philosophers, such as unique, permanent, and independent person; are not objects that are external yet are the aggregates of indivisible atoms without east and so on directional facets; are not subjects that are internal cognitions yet are consciousness-continua composed of indivisible instantaneous consciousnesses without any temporal prior and posterior components, such as a true nondual apperception[112] devoid of any such subjects and objects. Misknowledge rather consists of the two unconscious self-habits, which exist commonly both for those affected by theories and for those unaffected by theories, and which has persisted from time immemorial without having depended on any theoretical seduction of the intellect. Therefore it is that very (unconscious self-habit) that is here held as the root of the samsaric life cycle.

Chandrakīrti states in the *Entrance to the Middle Way* that "those who fall into bestial existence for many eons do not see this thus-unproduced, permanent (self), and yet the 'I'-habit is seen to function in them."

This reason (reveals) that all living beings are bound in the life cycle by the subconscious misknowledge. Further, since the intellectual misknowledge only exists for those philosophers, it is not properly considered to be the root of the samsaric life cycle.

It is extremely important to come to an exceptional certitude about this point. If one does not know this, at the time of determining the view, one will not know how to hold as principal the determination of the nonexistence of the hypothetical object held by subconscious misknowledge, while keeping the refuting of the intellectually held objects subordinate. And if one refutes the two selves and neglects the negation of the habit-pattern of subconscious misknowledge, then one will have determined a selflessness that is merely a rejection of those "selves" hypothesized by the philosophers, as explained above. And even at the time of meditation, one's meditation will only be the same, since the "determination of the view" also means meditation. Thus even in meditation only the manifest habits will be involved in the final analysis, and one will experience (only) the absence of two selves that are merely those hypothesized by the intellectual habits. To think this will eliminate the subconscious addictions is a great exaggeration.

(Chandrakīrti) states in the *Entrance to the Middle Way*: "When selflessness is understood, the 'permanent self' is eliminated, but this is not acceptable, even as the support of the 'I'-habit. Therefore, to say 'by knowing selflessness the self-conviction is totally wiped out'—this is extremely amazing."

In the commentary he adds: "In order to illustrate this point of mutual unconnectedness with an example, it is like when one sees a snake hole in the wall of one's house and one removes one's worry by saying, 'There is no elephant here!' and if this were to remove the fear of the snake, alas, how ridiculous it would seem to others!"

This was stated in connection with personal selflessness, but is similarly applied to objective selflessness. Again, he states in the *Entrance to the Middle Way*, "When one understands selflessness, and abandons the intellectual self, this is not accepted as even the support of misknowledge. Thus it is very strange to say that knowing selflessness will totally wipe out misknowledge."

Some may object that there is a contradiction in the fact that (Nāgārjuna) states, in the *Precious Garland*, that the objective self-habit, the truth-habit about the aggregates, is the root of cyclic life: "As long as there is the aggregate-habit so long will there be the 'I'-habit; when there is the 'I'-habit, there is action, and from actions there is birth"; while (Chandrakīrti) states in the *Entrance to the Middle Way* that the egoistic views are the root of cyclic life: "The intelligent see absolutely all of the faults of the addictions as coming from the egoistic views," because it is incorrect for there to be two different roots of the samsaric life cycle.

There is no problem here. According to this Dialecticist system, the two self-habits are differentiated according to their objects and not according to any different aspects of their habit-patterns. This is because both of them have the mode of adhering to intrinsic identifiability and because for there to be two contradictory roots of cyclic existence, these roots would have to be taken as two different habit-patterns applied to objects. Thus, when objective selflessness is shown to be the cause of the egoistic views, these two different categories of misknowledge are shown to be cause and effect, and when both are shown to be the root of addictions, they are shown to be the root of all other addictions that have different habit-patterns from them. Since such a process exists in both of them, there is no contradiction between them, just as there is no contradiction in former and later instants of homogeneous misknowledge being equally roots of the samsaric life cycle.

Although Chandrapada did not explicitly explain the egoistic views as misknowledge, without distinguishing between person and object, he declared in general that the truth-habit about things is addictive misknowledge, and he asserted that the personal self-habit is the adherence to the intrinsic identifiability of the person. Thus, since he often states that the subconscious egoistic views are the root of cyclic life, if he thought them to be something other than the misknowledge of the truth-habits, he would be contradicting himself by setting up two different habit-patterns as the root of cyclic life. (Since this is not the case) one must construe both as misknowledge.

Since it is on the very object projected by the above-explained subconscious misknowledge that all the other subconscious and intellectual addictions function, each holding that object in its own special way, it is like the eye, and the other faculties depending on the body faculty and not adhering independently to any objects. So all other addictions function depending on subconscious misknowledge, and hence it is stated that delusion is the principal addiction (as here by Āryadeva, in his *Four Hundred Stanzas*), "Just as the body-sense adheres to the body, so delusion adheres to everything." And

(Chandrakīrti) comments in the *Commentary to the Four Hundred Stanzas*: "Desires and so on function through projecting qualities such as beauty and ugliness on precisely the objective nature constructed in things by delusion; hence they cannot function apart from delusion, and become dependent on it, since delusion is the principal (addiction)."

Therefore, once delusion holds on to intrinsic identifiability in objects, if the held object is agreeable to the mind, it is perceived with desire, and if it is disagreeable to the mind, then aversion arises toward it. And if it appears neither agreeable nor disagreeable, and ordinary indifference remains in regard to it, then it is perceived without other addictions but with a homogeneous continuation of delusion. As (Nāgārjuna) states in the *Sixty Reasonings*, "Why should not the great poison of addiction arise for those whose minds have room for it? Even those who remain at ease (temporarily) will eventually be seized by the snake of addictions." And the commentary here explains as above.

It also seems necessary, from the *Precious Garland* statement, that the egoistic views (be considered to) arise from the truth-habit about the aggregates. As for the mode of arisal of the other addictions, this should be understood by extrapolation from the explanations given in the context of the mediocre person.[113]

One should also understand, according to the statement (of Dharmakīrti) in the *Commentary on Valid Cognition*: "Who sees a self always reifies an 'I' there. Supposing he identifies with that; identifying, he becomes obscured with faults. Seeing qualities, he desires them, he grasps their attainment as 'mine.' Thus, as long as one is attached to the self, so long will he revolve in the cyclic life."

Although the system explained above and this system (Dharmakīrti) are different in interpretation, they both can be understood using this sequence in the process of arisal of addictions. First, once one holds to intrinsic identifiability in the objective basis of the thought "I," attachment to the self arises. Therefrom, craving for the happiness of the self arises. Then, since the self's happiness cannot arise without dependence on one's property, craving arises for property (the "mine"). Then, being obscured by such faults, one begins to see the good qualities in those things. Then, one grasps onto the property (the "mines") as the means of accomplishing the happiness of the self. Through the addictions thus produced, conceptually motivated action occurs, and from such action, the cyclic life itself is constantly held together. As (Nāgārjuna says) in *Seventy Stanzas on Emptiness*, "Action has its cause in addictions: construction's nature is from addictions, the body has its cause in actions, and all three are empty of intrinsic reality." By such a method, one must practice finding certainty in the sequence involved in the evolution of the samsaric life cycle.

Reason for the Need to Seek the View That Understands Selflessness, Wishing to Abandon Addictive Misknowledge

It appears extremely necessary to will to abandon utterly the above misknowledge, the twofold self-habit, so one should intensely cultivate such a will. Even so, having such a desire, not to strive to understand how self-habits become the root of the life cycle, and, having seen a part of that, not to strive to generate in mind a pure view of selflessness, having properly negated the objects held by self-habits with the help of the definitive sutras and reasoning, such a person has to have extremely dull faculties, since he thinks nothing at all of completely losing the life of the path leading to liberation and omniscience. Therefore the glorious Dharmakīrti said, "Without rejecting this object one cannot abandon that (habit). For abandoning attraction and aversion according to (an object's) good points and faults is accomplished by not seeing the object (itself) and not by external methods."

That is, one does not abandon objects in the inner mind in the way that one extracts external things such as thorns by using a needle and digging them out, without having to abandon one's way of perceiving that object, but rather one must abandon such self-habits by seeing the nonexistence of the objects they purport to hold. As the glorious Chandrakīrti said, seeing that addictions such as desire and faults such as birth and old age all arise from self-habits, the yogi feels a desire to cease and abandon them, and he negates rationally the personal self, the object presupposed by the personal self-habit. He clearly states in *Entrance to the Middle Way*, "When he logically sees that addictions and faults entirely arise from the egoistic views—and he understands the self as the object of his habit, the yogi accomplishes the negation of the self." Here he calls the meditator on suchness "yogi." This method is the holy inner thought of the Savior Nāgārjuna, as in the *Sixty Reasonings*: "That is the cause of all views. Without that, addictions do not arise. Therefore, when that is truly understood, views and addictions are completely ceased. Whereby is that understood? From the fact that dependent birth is nonbirth, as the supreme Knower of suchness says."

Thus he teaches that the truth-habit positing things is the cause of all addictive views. And all other addictions are abandoned by the realization of the real condition of things as not intrinsically really produced, by reason of their relativity. For the vision of their intrinsic realitylessness will not arise without negation of the object held as the intrinsically real status of things. Although we have already quoted Āryadeva in agreement with that, further, from the *Four Hundred Stanzas*, he says, "When you see selflessness in objects, the seeds of existence will be ceased."

That is, by seeing the selflessness of the perceived object of the self-habits, misknowledge, the root of cyclic life, is cut. Reverend Śhāntideva also states, "Thus personal emptiness is very well established. Thus by cutting the root, all addictions will not arise. As stated in the *Secret of the Tathāgatas Sūtra*: "Śhāntamati, it is like this: for example, when a tree is cut from the root, boughs, leaves, and new shoots will all wither away. Śhāntamati, likewise, when egoistic views are eliminated, primary and subsidiary addictions will all be removed.' "

That is, he states that by cultivating the understanding of emptiness as emptiness of the intrinsically real status of things, the egoistic views are eliminated, and by eliminating them all other addictions are eliminated, since it is impossible to understand selflessness without negating the object of the personal self-habit. That scriptural reference shows the egoistic views to be the root of all other addictions; and they should be understood to constitute misknowledge, since otherwise if they were something different, there would be two different roots of cyclic life.

In short, the many supreme experts in elucidating the meaning of the profound discourses investigate with many references and reasonings when they determine the import of suchness. And, seeing that selflessness and emptiness cannot be understood without seeing that the self, as held by the false habits, is not existent and empty, they spoke thus (as above) because it is crucially important to find certitude about this.

If one does not meditate on the import of this negating of the object of the error fundamental to cyclic bondage, even if one meditates on any other would-be profound import, it will not disturb the self-habits at all because it is impossible to eliminate self-habits without applying the intelligence to the suchness of selflessness and emptiness, and because, even though without negating the object of self-habits one can at least withdraw the mental gravitation toward that object, that is not acceptable as applying (the mind) to selflessness. The reason is that when the mind is applied to an object, there are three habits: one holding that object in truth, one holding it as truthless, and one holding it without either qualification. So, just as the nonholding of truthlessness is not necessarily the truth-habit, so the disconnection from the two selves is not necessarily the application to the two selflessnesses, because there are limitless states of mind included in the third option.[114]

The two self-habits, further, function through perceiving things chiefly as persons and objects, and therefore it is necessary to determine right on the very basis of error the nonexistence of that person or object so held; otherwise it is like searching for footprints in the house of a thief already gone into the forest.

Therefore, since errors will be terminated by meditating on the import thus determined, such an emptiness is the supreme import of suchness. And if some other false import of suchness is determined, it is no more than wishful thinking, and you should consider it outside the meaning of the sutras.

Thus the misknowledge of truth-habits about fabrications of persons such as males and females and things such as material forms and sensations is eliminated by finding and meditating on the view that understands that emptiness that is selflessness. When it is eliminated, the conceptual thoughts that are improper attitudes that reify the signs of beauty and ugliness and so on by perceiving the objects of truth-habits are eliminated. When they are eliminated, all the other addictions, desire and so on, which have egoistic views as their root, are eliminated. When they are eliminated, actions motivated by them are eliminated. When they are eliminated, involuntary birth in cyclic life as propelled by evolutionary actions is eliminated.

(Considering this process,) the firm determination "I will attain liberation!" is generated, and thence one seeks the utterly incisive view of suchness. As Nāgārjuna said in *Wisdom: Root Verses of the Middle Way*: "Liberation comes from terminating actions and addictions. Actions and addictions come from imaginations. From their fabricating come fabrications, which will be ceased by emptiness."

Thus understanding the sequence of the origin and cessation of cyclic life, one must actively cherish the understanding of the import of suchness; and this will not happen by making oneself dizzy (in meditation) without a clear discernment of the objective.

Methods to Generate the View Realizing Selflessness: Sequence of Generating the Two Views of Selflessness

In regard to the sequence of generation of the two self-habits, it is the objective self-habit that generates the personal (or subjective) self-habit. Nevertheless, in entering the truth of selflessness, it is by first generating the view of personal selflessness that one must later generate the view of objective selflessness. As (Nāgārjuna states) in the *Precious Garland*: "A creature is not earth, water, fire, wind, space, or consciousness—if it is none of these things, what else might a creature be? Since the creature as collocation of elements is not real in itself, so each element, itself a collocation, is not really real either." Thus he first declares the nonreality of the person and then the nonreality of its designative bases, the elements earth and so on.

(Chandrakīrti) in *Lucid Exposition* and (Buddhapālita) in his *Middle Way Commentary* explain that the first entrance into the reality of suchness is through personal selflessness, and Śhāntideva also agrees. As for the reason why one must understand it that way, while there is no variation of degree of subtlety in the selflessness to be ascertained in the basic person or in the basic object because of the essentiality of the subject of concern, it is easier to ascertain (selflessness) in the person and harder to ascertain it in the object. For example, it is difficult to ascertain objective selflessness in the eye, ear, and so on, but easy to ascertain it in things such as images and so on, and this can be used as an example of the varying case of determining selflessness with regard to the former objects.

It was with this in mind that (the Buddha said) in the *King of Samādhi Sūtra*, "Use your intellect to apply to all else your understanding of the self-concept—all things have an utterly pure nature just like the sky. By a single (insight), all things are known—by one (vision), all things are seen." That is, if one knows well the real condition of the "I" that anchors the concept of self that thinks "I," and one applies the reasoning about it to internal things such as eye and nose and external things such as vases and so on, one should come to understand them in just the same way. Then, knowing the nature and seeing the reality of one thing, one is able to know and see the natures of all other things.

The Actual Generation of the Two Views in Order to Determine Personal Selflessness—Identification of the Person

The "person" is (a term used in contexts such as) the six species of persons, such as gods, or the types of persons, such as individual persons or noble persons, and also in referring to the accumulator of evil and good action, the experiencer of their effects, the traveler in cyclic life, the practitioner of the path for the sake of liberation, and the attainer of liberation. (Chandrakīrti) in his *Entrance to the Middle Way Commentary* quotes a standard sutra: "You come to adopt a view of the demon-mind 'self.' This heap of emotions is empty, therein no sentient being. Just as one says 'chariot' depending on its aggregate of components, so depending on the aggregates, one says 'superficial sentient being.'"

The first verse teaches the personal selflessness that is the ultimate absence of "person." The first phrase calls the personal self-habit the "demon-mind," the second phrase shows the holder of that habit to be the victim of evil views, and the third and fourth state that the aggregates are devoid of any personal self. The second verse teaches the conventional existence of the self, the first two phrases giving the example and the last two applying it to the meaning.

It teaches that the "person" is a mere designation based on the aggregates: this sutra states the aggregate-conglomerate to be the designative base of the person, and the designative base cannot properly be the designation itself. The aggregate-conglomerate must be understood as either the simultaneous conglomerate of aggregates or their sequential conglomerate. Thus neither the (spatial) conglomerate nor the temporal continuum of the aggregates can be posited as the "person." When the (spatial) conglomerate is put as the designative base, the (temporal) conglomerate is also included as a designative base, so it is illogical for either to be the "person."

As Chandrakīrti says in *Entrance to the Middle Way*, "In the sutra He said it depends on the aggregates; thus the self is not the mere aggregate-conglomerate. If you assert that the aggregates are the self because the Teacher said 'The aggregate is the "self"'" (you are wrong). In fact, here He is (merely) refuting the self's being other than the aggregates, since in other sutras He says, 'Form is not "self,"' and so on. Thus, as when the Buddha says, "Any ascetic or priest is viewing just these five aggregates when he holds the views of 'I' and 'mine,'" he is refuting with the word "just" that any self other than the aggregates exists as the object of the subconscious "I"-habit. Such refutation (by itself) does not indicate that the aggregates are (themselves) the object of the "I"-habit. Otherwise it would contradict the statements in other sutras that refute the self's being the five aggregates, since if, among the object and aspect of the "I"-habit, the aggregates were the objective object, then they would have to be put as the self.

Therefore the meaning of the statement in the sutra about looking to the aggregates must be explained as urging the attempt to apprehend the self that is designated on the aggregates. Therefore one must differentiate between statements about the conventionally existent self, intending the mere "I," and statements about the intrinsically real person, not existent even conventionally, and one should not maintain that this system accepts the conventional existence of the personal self. Such an identification of the person is the unexcelled distinctive specialty of this system, and the thorough ascertainment of this is the excellent method to realize the extraordinary personal selflessness.

Determination of the Nonreality of That (Personal Self)— Determination of the Nonreality of "I"

Here (one uses) the first of the four keys, analyzing one's own mental process in order to identify one's own way of habitual adherence to a personal self. This has been previously explained.[115]

The second key (is as follows): if that person has intrinsically real status, it must be established as actually the same or actually different from the aggregates, and thus one decides that there is no way for it to be established in any other way. In general, in regard to such things as pots and pillars, if one determines them on one side as matching, one excludes them on the other side from differing; or such a thing as a pot, if determined here as differing, is excluded on the other side from matching—as this is established by experience, there is no third option other than sameness or difference. Therefore one must become certain that it is impossible (for a self to exist and) to be neither the same nor different (from the aggregates).

The third (key is to) see the faults in (the hypothesis that the person and the aggregates are intrinsically really the same. The fourth (key is to) see well the faults in (the hypothesis that) the person and the aggregates are really different. Thus, when these four keys are complete, then the pure view realizing the suchness of personal selflessness is generated.

Thus, if self and aggregates were a single entity with intrinsically real status, three faults would accrue. The first is that there would be no point in asserting a self, since if the two were intrinsically really established as a single entity they would never be at all differentiable, since the two being absolutely established as a single entity could necessarily never appear as different to a cognition that perceived them. The reason is that while there is no contradiction for a false, superficial thing's appearance being different from its real mode of existence, such a difference does preclude any truth-status in that thing, since a true thing must really exist in just the way it appears to any cognition.

Thus the postulation of an intrinsically objective self is (only) for the sake of establishing an agent for the appropriation and discarding of the aggregates, and this is not plausible when the self and the aggregates have become the same. As (Nāgārjuna) states in *Wisdom*, "When it is asserted that there is no self but for appropriation, and then that the appropriation itself is the self, then that self of yours is nonexistent."

The second fault is that the self would become a plurality. If the self and the aggregates were really the same, then just as one person has many aggregates, so he or she would come to have many selves. Or else, just as the self would become many, so (if self and aggregates were the same) the aggregates would become one; as (Chandrakīrti) says in *Entrance to the Middle Way*, "If the aggregates were the self, as they are many, so the self would become many."

The third fault is that the self would become endowed with production and destruction. As (Nāgārjuna) says in *Wisdom*: "If the aggregates were the self, then it would become endowed with production and destruction." That is, just as the aggregates are endowed with production and destruction, so the self would become endowed with production and destruction, since the two are a single entity.

Now if one thinks this is merely an acceptance of the momentary production and destruction of the self or the person each instant, while it is admitted that there is no fault in accepting this merely conventionally, the opposition here asserts the intrinsic identifiability of the person, and so must assert the intrinsically objective production and destruction of that person, which assertion has three faults.

(Chandrakīrti) states the first of these faults in *Entrance to the Middle Way* and its *Commentary*: "It is incorrect for that which is intrinsically identifiably different to be included in a single continuum." Thus it is illogical for things that are objectively established as different, in being former and later, to relate with the later depending on the former, because the former and later things are self-sufficiently and independently established and cannot logically relate to one another.

Thus, since it is incorrect to include them in one continuum, the "I" cannot rightly remember its former life—"At that time I was like that"—just as two different persons such as Devadatta and Yajña cannot remember each other's lives. In our system, although things are destroyed in every instant, there is no contradiction for former and later instants to be included in a single continuum (conventionally), so it is possible for former lives to be remembered. Those who do not understand this point generate the first wrong view of the four wrong views mentioned in sutra as relating to a former limit. When the Buddha often says, "I was this former person," they think that the person at the time of buddhahood and the person of this former life are the same, or that, since created things are instantaneously destroyed, they cannot be the same, so both of them must be permanent, and so forth. In order not to fall into such (views), one must understand properly the way, at the time of remembering former lives, in which the general "I" is remembered without specifically qualifying it as to country, time, and nature.

The second fault is the fault of the evolutionary effect of action being lost. For (if they are identifiably different), it is impossible to bring the agent of the action and the experiencer of the evolutionary effect together on a single basis, the mere "I."

The (third) fault is that of receiving the evolutionary effect of actions not performed, and it is an absurd consequence that a single personal continuum would experience all evolutionary effects of all actions performed and accumulated by other different personal continua. These two faults, as explained above in *Entrance to the Middle Way,* accrue through the key point that if the person has objectively (real) status, it is impossible for his or her former and later instants to be included in a single continuum. As (Nāgārjuna) says in *Wisdom*, "If the god and the human are different, they cannot logically belong to one continuum."

Here one may object, "What is the fault if one asserts the intrinsically real difference of person and aggregates, (this not being a problem of two different persons)?" Nāgārjuna gives the fault in *Wisdom*: "If it were different from the aggregates, it would become devoid of the nature of the aggregates." If the self were objectively different from the aggregates, it would become devoid of the created nature of the aggregates and would have no production, duration, and destruction, just as a horse does not have the nature of an ox, being established as a different thing. But the objector here thinks, "Well, isn't that how it is, after all?" But then it would not be logical for the subconscious mental habit to perceive (such an absolutely different isolated and permanent self) as the object that is the basis of the conventional designation of "self" because it is not a created thing (that is, not subject to ordinary relations), just like a sky flower or nirvana. Furthermore, if it were really different from the nature of the aggregates and so on, which is "formful" and so on, it would have to be perceived as such, just as matter and mind are perceived as different. But since it is not perceived in any such manner, the self is not a thing different (from the aggregates). As Nāgārjuna says in *Wisdom*, "It is not correct for the self to be something different from appropriation; if it were different, it should be perceived apart from appropriation, logically, but it is not so perceived." And Chandrakīrti in *Entrance to the Middle Way* says, "Thus the self does not exist apart from the aggregates, since its perception beyond them is not established."

By means of such reasonings, one should cultivate a firm certainty that sees the faults of the self being objectively different from the aggregates. If you do not derive a correct certainty about the faults of these two positions of sameness and difference, your decision that the person is intrinsically reality-less will merely be a premise and you will not discover the authentic view.

Determination of the Nonreality of "Mine"

Thus, having inquired rationally into the existence or absence of an intrinsically real status in the self, when you negate its intrinsic reality by not finding (any self) either the same or different (from the aggregates), that same rationality analytic of "thatness" will not discover any intrinsic reality in one's property. If you cannot perceive the son of a barren woman, his property, such as eyes and so on, will also not be perceived. Nāgārjuna says in *Wisdom*, "If the self itself does not exist, how can its property exist?" And Chandrakīrti says in *Entrance to the Middle Way*, "When there is no agent, there is no action, and thus without the self there is no property. That yogi who sees the emptiness of self and property will reach liberation." Thus the rationality that determines the lack of an intrinsically objective status of one's own

"I," or "self," or "person" should realize the entire import of the "thatness" of personal selflessness: that all persons and their property, from hell-beings up to buddhas, have no intrinsic reality as the same or as different from their designative bases, whether they be contaminated or uncontaminated aggregates. And thereby one should also understand the method of establishing the lack of intrinsic reality of all those beings' property.

How the Person Arises as Illusion—Meaning of the Statement of Illusoriness, Unerring Meaning of Arising as Illusion

The Buddha stated in the *King of Samādhi Sūtra*, "Meditate all signs as like mirages, fairy cities, illusory, and dreamlike—all objectively empty; you should understand all things in the same way." And in the *Mother of All Victors*,[116] "All things from form to omniscience are like illusions and like dreams." Now there are two meanings in such statements of illusoriness: ultimate reality's illusoriness in that it merely exists but its truth is negated, and the appearance of an appearance that is actually empty. Here it is the latter (we are concerned with). For this, two things are required: that (something) appears, and that it is empty of its apparent objectivity. The meaning of "illusory" will not arise in the mind from something's utter nonexistence, its mere appearance being like a rabbit's horn or the son of a barren woman (appearing merely conceptually), or from (something's) appearing and not turning out to be devoid of its apparent objectivity.

Therefore the method of understanding other things as like the example of illusion is as follows: for example, when a magician manifests an illusion, although there never was any horse or ox there, the appearance of horse and ox undeniably arises. In the same way, things such as persons, although they were always empty of any objectively established intrinsic reality as objects, are understood as undeniably appearing to have that status. Thus the appearances of gods and humans are represented as persons, and the appearances of forms and sounds and so on are represented as objects, and although not even an atom in persons and objects has intrinsically identifiable intrinsic reality, all the functions of relativities, such as accumulation of evolutionary actions and seeing and hearing and so on, are viable. It is not a nihilistic emptiness, since all functions are viable, and since one simply comes to be aware of emptiness, things having always and ever been empty, neither is it a mentally made-up emptiness. Since all things knowable are accepted in that way, it is not a partial emptiness, and when one meditates on it, it serves as the remedy for all the habitual reifications of the truth-habits.

That profound import is not at all objectively inaccessible to any sort of cognition, but can be determined by the realistic view and can be taken as object by meditation on the meaning of reality, so it is not an emptiness that cannot be cultivated in the context of the path and that cannot be known and cannot be realized, a complete nothingness.[117]

Here one may object, "If this certainty that reflections and so on are empty of what they appear to have is the realization of intrinsic realitylessness, it would follow that a common individual's direct perception would realize intrinsic realitylessness, and he or she would become a holy person. If it is not so, then how can these examples be suitable for intrinsic realitylessness?"

Āryadeva states in the *Four Hundred Stanzas*, "The witness of a single thing is said to be the witness of everything. The emptiness of one thing is the emptiness of everything." Thus he explains that the witness or realizer of the emptiness of one thing can realize the emptiness of all other things as well. By understanding that a mirror-image of an object is empty of that object, no damage will be done to the object of the truth-habit that holds the mirror-image to have objectively real status, and one will not understand the emptiness that is the mirror image's voidness of intrinsic reality without refuting the object (of that truth-habit). Therefore that cognition does not understand the reality of the mirror-image.

This type of cognition, although it understands that the illusion is empty of horse and ox and that the dream-appearance is empty of what appears there, does not discover the Middle Way view that realizes illusoriness and dreamlikeness. However, these are used as examples for the reason that their intrinsic realitylessness is easier to understand than that of other things such as forms and sounds. As for their emptiness of objectively established intrinsic reality, it is established, since if an object is truly established, it is impossible for it to appear to cognition in some other way than it really is itself, by showing the contradiction between those two facts, (truth-status and false appearance).

So these examples of well-known falsities in the world first introduce one to the understanding of nonreality, but from there it is necessary to generate understanding of other things not well known as falsities to the world. These two steps have a necessary temporal sequence, and therefore it is not intended here that when one realizes the emptiness of one thing one (simultaneously) realizes directly the emptiness of all other things; it only means that one becomes capable of understanding that, since one's mind becomes oriented toward the lack of true existence of other things. Thus the two statements—one, that knowing one is in a dream, one understands that appearances therein of males and females and so on are empty, and two, in the *Ornament of Realizations*, that "even in a dream one sees all things as dreamlike"—these two are different in meaning (that is, one being the dreamer's understanding of being in a dream, the other referring to an advanced state where one's waking insight carries over into the dream).

Thus, to the perception of one experienced in meditating in samādhi, there is an understanding that apparent things such as pots and cloths are empty of what they appear to have, but this is not the same as the understanding of their illusoriness and dreamlikeness, which is their lack of intrinsically real status. Therefore one must investigate thoroughly the distinctive mode of arisal as illusory, as stated in the definitive meaning sutras and the scientific treatises in order to generate realization of illusoriness and dreamlikeness.

The cases are similar when uneducated children hold a mirror-image as the object reflected, or when an audience inexperienced in magic perceives a magical illusion as a horse or an ox, or when a person in a dream perceives as real the apparent mountains, houses, rooms, and so on. And the cases are likewise similar for the older, educated person, or the magician himself, or the person who knows he is dreaming, all these know that the appearances are untrue. But none of these types of persons have discovered the view of reality.

False Way of Arising as Illusory

When one has not properly identified the measure of the negatee as explained above, when one's analysis of the object cools down, one first begins to imagine that the object does not exist, then one comes to experience the analyzer also as likewise (nonexistent), then even the ascertainer of the nonexistence ceases to have existence, and one comes into a state wherein there is no ground of ascertaining anything at all as "this is it" or "this is not it." There then arises perception of a fuzzy, foggy appearance, occurring from the failure to distinguish between intrinsically real existence/nonexistence and mere existence/nonexistence. Such an emptiness is the kind of emptiness that destroys relativity, and therefore the arisal of such a fuzzy, foggy appearance derived from such a realization is definitely not the meaning of illusoriness.

Therefore when one analyzes rationally and one comes to consider that such a person is not present even in the slightest on its intrinsically established object, depending on which (consideration) these appearances arise in a fuzzy, foggy manner—just this is not very difficult. Such experiences occur for all those who admire the Centrist theories and have a casual learning of the teachings that demonstrate intrinsic realitylessness. But the real difficulty is to completely negate any objectively established intrinsic reality and yet develop a deep certainty about the representation of how that intrinsically unreal person himself is the accumulator of evolutionary actions and the experiencer of evolutionary effects and so on. When the combination of those two facts (realitylessness and) the ability to represent those things, is carried to the extreme limit of existence, that is the view of the Middle Way, so extremely difficult to discover. Therefore, when one investigates with the rational cognition analytic of reality, (one must understand that) the failure to discover any sort of production and so on negates intrinsically real production and so on, and does not negate every sort of production and cessation. Otherwise, if one negates (every form of production and so on) (reality) becomes like a rabbit's horn and the son of a barren woman, devoid of all functional efficiency, and there is the fault that in the remaining merely illusory appearance the functions of relativity are no longer viable. Chandrakīrti discusses this in his *Four Hundred Stanzas Commentary*, commenting on the words "That being so, how is existence not like an illusion?" (as follows):

"When you experience relativity rightly, it is like an illusory creation, and it is not like the son of a barren woman. If you should negate all forms of production through this analytic investigation, and assert that this is what is taught as the nonproduction of creations, then this is not illusoriness, but rather corresponds to the son of a barren woman and so forth. So, from fear of getting stuck in the extreme consequence of the nonexistence of relativity, do not act like that, but treat (reality) as illusory, without contradicting that (function of relativity)." And further: "Therefore, when you investigate analytically, since things will fail to maintain (their seeming) intrinsically real status, still each individual thing will remain in an illusory manner." Therefore the holding of appearance as precisely illusory yet existent relativity is not the faulty holding of illusoriness, although if you hold that illusory appearance as having objective status or truth status, it is a fault.

Buddha stated in the *King of Samādhi Sūtra*, "The states of existence are like a dream; herein there is no birth nor any death. Living beings, humans, or even life are not discovered. These things are like foam, like a plantain tree, like an illusion, like a flash of lightning, like the reflection of the moon in water, like a mirage. Although no person dies from this world and goes through transmigration into any other (ultimately), still actions committed never lose their evolutionary effect, and good and bad evolutionary effects mature in this cyclic life." When one investigates with the rationality analytic of ultimate reality, nothing whatever is discovered that can withstand analysis, such as a person who is born, dies, and transmigrates. Nevertheless, illusory things occur as the evolutionary effects of good and bad (actions). One must develop one's understanding according to this statement (of the Buddha).

Furthermore, when one does not practice in equipoise by concentrating on the view that has decisively penetrated into reality but merely finds stability in one-pointedness on not holding anything at all in one's mind, then, when one arises, from the power of that (samādhi), appearances such as mountains and so on no longer appear solid and substantial but appear indistinct like fine smoke or like a rainbow. But this is not the arisal of illusoriness explained in the sutras: because this is an appearance in emptiness with respect to a coarse substantiality, and is not an appearance in emptiness of the intrinsically real status of those apparent things, and also because the absence of solid substantiality is definitely not the meaning of emptiness, which is intrinsic realitylessness. Otherwise there would be the faults that it would be impossible for the truth-habit to arise when perceiving a rainbow as qualified object, and there would be no possibility of generating the wisdom realizing truthlessness when considering substantiality as the qualified object.

The Method Employed for the Arisal of Illusoriness

Well, what should be done for the unerring arisal of the meaning of illusion? For example, when the visual consciousness sees an illusory horse or ox, one depends on the certainty in mental consciousness that the apparent horse or ox does not exist, and one generates a certainty that that horse or ox appearance does not exist. In the same way, one depends on both the undeniable experience of person and so on in conventional cognition and the certainty through rational cognition[118] that that very thing is devoid of an objectively established intrinsic reality,[119] and thereby one generates the certainty that that person is an illusory or false appearance. By that key, one reaches the essence of the meditation on emptiness as like space wherein one's concentration allows not even an iota of the mental orientations that are intrinsic-reality-status sign-habits.[120]

When one arises from that (concentration) and one regards the arisal of apparent objects, the aftermath illusory emptiness arises. In that manner when one investigates repeatedly with the rationality analytic of the presence or absence of intrinsically objective status in things, after one has generated an intense certitude about intrinsic realitylessness, one's observation of the arisal of appearances is the arisal in illusoriness, and there is no separate method of determination of the emptiness that is illusoriness. Thereupon, when one engages in activities such as prostrations and circumambulations and so on, the certitude from the above analysis is (automatically) taken into account, and the engagement in those activities becomes the training in the arisal of illusoriness. From within the actuality of that, one should perform those (activities).

When one purifies that, the mere remembrance of the view causes those things to arise in illusoriness.

To express the method of seeking that certainty in an easily understandable way: having initiated the proper arisal in general of the above-explained rational negatee, one should identify it by considering thoroughly how one's own misknowledge reifies intrinsic realities. Then, considering specifically the pattern wherein if such intrinsic reality exists it will not go beyond sameness or difference (with its basis of designation), and the process wherein devastating refutations accrue to the acceptance of either alternative, one should derive the certainty that is aware of the refutations. Finally, one should confirm the certitude that considers that there is not even the slightest intrinsically real status in the person. And one should cultivate repeatedly such (a thus-derived certainty) in the emptiness orientation. Then one should become involved in the experiences of the conventional "person" undeniably arising as objects of cognition, and one should cultivate the attitude oriented toward relativity, wherein that (conventional person) is represented as the accumulator of evolutionary actions and the experiencer of evolutionary effects, and one should discover the certitude about the systems wherein relativity is viable within freedom from any intrinsic reality. When those two facts (that is, the viability of relativity and the absence of intrinsic reality) seem contradictory, one should consider the pattern of their noncontradiction by using the examples of mirror images and so on. Thus the mirror image of an object (such as a face), although it is empty of the eyes and ears and so on that appear in it, is still produced depending on the object and the mirror and is destroyed when either of those conditions are removed. Those two facts (its emptiness of the objects and its being produced depending on them) are undeniably coincident in the same phenomenon. Like that, there is not even an atom of intrinsic reality status in the person, and yet this does not contradict its being the accumulator of evolutionary actions, the experiencer of evolutionary effects, and its being produced depending on the evolutionary actions and addictions of previous (lives). One should cultivate this consideration. And so, one should understand (illusoriness) in this way in every such occasion.

Determination of the Objective Selflessness

"Objects" are the five aggregates that are the person's designative base, the six elements such as earth, and the six media such as eye, and so forth. Their emptiness of objectively established intrinsic reality is the selflessness of those things. There are two parts to the way of determining this: one negating (objective self) by the reasonings mentioned above and the other negating it by other reasonings not yet mentioned.

Negating the (Objective) Self Using the Above Reasonings

There are two kinds of things among the aggregates, elements, and media, (the physical and the mental). (Their selves) are refuted as above through the analysis of objectively real sameness and difference of parts and wholes, (the parts being) directional, eastern sector, and so on, in the case of physical things, and temporal, former, and later moments, and so on, in the case of mental things. And this is the meaning of the above-cited sutra: "Just as you understand the self-concept, you should use intellect to apply it to everything."

Refuting the Objective Self with Other New Reasons—Demonstrating the Reason of Relativity

The reason of relativity is clearly stated in the *Questions of Sagaramati Sūtra*, as logically refuting the intrinsic reality status of things: "Things that occur relativistically do not exist with intrinsic objectivity." In *Questions of Nāga King Anavatapta Sūtra*, the Buddha also clearly states, "What is produced from conditions is unproduced, it is not produced through any intrinsic objectivity. I declare that everything conditional is empty. One who knows emptiness is consciously aware." This (kind of statement) is extremely common in the precious sutras.

In the latter quotation, the "unproduced" in the first line is explained by the "not produced through any intrinsic objectivity," which thus qualifies the negatee in the negation of production. Chandrakīrti, in the *Lucid Exposition*, cites the *Visit to Lanka Sūtra*, "intending the lack of intrinsically real production, I say all things are unproduced!" Thus the Teacher himself explicates his own inner intent in the sutra, explaining—for those who worry that perhaps the unqualified statements of productionlessness mean that all things produced do not exist at all—that it means rather that there is no production through any intrinsic reality.

In the third line, the Buddha states that the conditionality of dependence on conditions is equivalent to emptiness of intrinsic objectivity, which is tantamount to the equation of emptiness of intrinsic reality with relativity, and shows that the Buddha does not intend any voiding of functional efficacy, which would be the negation of mere production.

Nāgārjuna also states, in *Wisdom*, "Whatever is relatively occurrent is peace in its objectivity." That is, (things are) peaceful, or empty, with respect to intrinsic objectivity, by the reason of their relativity. Thus one should understand that these statements clear away the darkness of erroneous opinions, such as that the Centrist system must advocate nonproduction with respect to (even) relative production.

Such a reason of relativity is extremely praiseworthy. The Buddha states in the *Questions of Nāga King Anavatapta Sūtra*, "Wise persons will realize the relativity of things and will no longer entertain any extremist views." That is, one no longer entertains extremist views once one realizes relativity. Furthermore, Chandrakīrti declares in *Entrance to the Middle Way*, "Since things are occurrent in relativity, such reifications cannot be attached to them. Hence this reasoning of relativity cuts open the whole network of bad ideas." This is the unexcelled distinctive specialty of the eminent beings Nāgārjuna and sons. Therefore here among (all) reasonings we should celebrate the reason of relativity.

Here there are two chief points of resistance that obstruct the realistic view. One is the reificatory view or absolutist view that has a fixed orientation toward truth-habits that hold to the truth-status in things. The other is the repudiative view or nihilistic view that goes too far by not appraising the measure of the negatee and becomes unable to incorporate in its system the certitude about cause and effect within relativity, losing all ground of recognition about anything such as "this is it" and "this isn't it." These two views are completely eliminated by the negation of intrinsic reality based on the reason that brings certitude that from such and such a causal condition such and such an effect occurs. For the ascertainment of the import of the thesis radically refutes absolutism, and the ascertainment of the reason radically refutes nihilism.[121]

Therefore all things—"inner" such as mental creations and so on and "outer" such as sprouts and so on—that occur in dependence on misknowledge and so on (and seeds and so on, respectively), being thus (relative,) are not correctly established as intrinsically identifiable. For if they were to be intrinsically objectively established, it would be necessary for each to have an independent, self-sufficient reality status, which would preclude their dependence on causes and conditions. As Āryadeva says in his *Four Hundred Stanzas*, "What exists relativistically will never become independent. All this is without independence, hence the self does not exist."

By this, one should realize that persons and (things) such as pots have no intrinsically real status, since they are designated in dependence on their own aggregation (of components), this is the second formulation of the reason of relativity. Since (things) are dependently produced and dependently designated, they are not objectively the same as what they depend on; for if they were the same all actions and agents would become the same. Neither are those two objectively different; for if they were, any connection could be refuted and that would preclude any dependence.

As Nāgārjuna said in *Wisdom*, "When one thing depends on another, they are not (objectively) the same, and neither are they (objectively) different; therefore there is no cessation and no permanence." He also said in *Transcendental Praise*, "The sophists believe that suffering is self-created, other-created, created by both, or causelessly created; you declared it is relatively occurrent! Whatever occurs relativistically you proclaim to be empty—'things have no independence!' This is your matchless lion's roar." That is, the reason of relativity refutes the holding to sameness and difference, the entertaining of the absolutist and nihilist extremisms, and the holding to the four extreme modes of production.

Thus, having derived certitude about emptiness that is the emptiness of all the objectifying attitudes of substantivism, it is extremely praiseworthy to assume responsibility for ethical choice by not abandoning certitude about the relevance of the evolutionary effects of actions. As Nāgārjuna states in *Disclosure of the Spirit of Enlightenment*, "While knowing this emptiness of things, one who still assumes responsibility for evolutionary actions and effects, this one is even more wondrous than wonder, even more miraculous than miracles!" To achieve this, one must distinguish between intrinsically real existence and mere existence, and between lack of intrinsically identifiable existence and nonexistence. As Chandrakīrti states in the *Entrance to the Middle Way Commentary*, "While understanding how to represent the intrinsically unreal cause and effect of a mirror-image, what intelligent person, perceiving the mere existence of forms and feelings and so on, things going not beyond causality, would attribute intrinsic reality to them? Therefore, while existence is perceived, there is no intrinsically real production."

If you do not distinguish these (existences and nonexistences), you will not get beyond the two extremisms of reification and repudiation, since as soon as something exists it will have objective existence, and once something lacks objective existence it will become utterly nonexistent. As Chandrakīrti says in his *Commentary to the Four Hundred Stanzas*, "According to those who advocate the substantial existence of things, as long as something is actually existent, it must be intrinsically objectively existent. If it ever loses its intrinsic objectivity, it becomes completely nonexistent, like the horn of a rabbit. These persons thus never get beyond dualistic positions, and hence they have a difficult time making their various claims consistent."

Therefore, (in our system), we are freed from all absolutisms by the absence of intrinsic objectivity, and we are freed from all nihilisms by our ability to present an intrinsically unreal causality in that very actuality (of emptiness of objectivity). As for "extreme," Vasubandhu defines it in his *Methodology of Elucidation*: "extreme" means terminus, conclusion, proximity, direction, and contempt. Granted that these "extremes" are even accepted in our own system, nevertheless, the "extreme" that is a resistance to the view that is called "extreme free" (is something different). Now Kamalashīla, in his *Illumination of the Middle Way*, (criticizes an exaggerated notion of extremism), saying, "If there is some sort of existence in the ultimate of something whose objective nature is purely mental, then, just because it existed, how would adherence to its permanence or impermanence become an extremism? It is not logical to consider a proper attitude that accords with the true nature of things a downfall." What he says here is correct, that a correct mental attitude according with reality is not a downfall, hence not extremism. Rather it is as in common parlance, where the edge of a cliff is called the "extreme," and falling off it "falling into an extreme." Just so holding things to have truth-status and holding them to have no status at all or not to exist at all: these are falling to extremes of permanence and annihilation that are the precise opposite of actual reality. Holding things not to exist ultimately and holding evolutionary causality to exist conventionally are not extremisms, since the objects so held do in fact exist as they are held, and since Nāgārjuna says in *Rebuttal of Objections* that things that are ultimately nonexistent do exist (conventionally): "If you get rid of what is actually realityless, what is actual reality will be established," and in *Seventy Stanzas on Emptiness*, "we do not negate this way of the world, that 'this occurs relative to this.'"

Therefore to differentiate between saying something "is not existent" and "exists" and saying it "does not exist" and "is not nonexistent" is merely to discern a difference in the mode of expression, for there is not the slightest difference in the meanings that arise in the mind, no matter how much you analyze them. So to say that such difference in expressions constitutes the difference between extremism and nonextremism is just to prattle nonsense about mere words.

How the Above Reasonings Prove the Truthlessness of the Uncreated

Nāgārjuna, thinking that the truthlessness of uncreated things such as space, calculated cessation, uncalculated cessation, and suchness could be easily proved once the truthlessness of persons and created things was proved by the above-explained reasonings, stated in *Wisdom*, "If created things are utterly unestablished, how can uncreated things be established?"

As for the way in which it is easy to prove: once intrinsic reality in created things is negated as above, their (intrinsic) nonreality is established as sufficient for the presentation of all (relational) functions such as bondage and liberation, cause and effect, and objects and means of knowledge. That being established, then uncreated things also, such as (ultimate) reality and calculated cessation, even though also lacking truth-status, can still be well represented as the goals of the paths, objects of knowledge, and as the Dharma Jewel, refuge of disciples. It is never said that "if one does not maintain these things as truths, the systems that must present those things are invalid." Therefore there is no point in maintaining the truth-status of these (uncreated) things, (since truth-status is not compatible with conventional viability).

Even if one did claim their truth-status, one would still be required to maintain their presentability as demonstrated by such and such characteristics, as (their being) disconnected causes and disconnected effects, and as their being recognized by such and such validating cognitions. And in that case, if they are (claimed to be) not connected with their own means of attainment, characteristics, and means of cognition, then one cannot avoid the faults of all unconnected things being characteristic and characterized (to one another), and so forth. And if it is claimed that they are connected, then, since it is impossible for a true, intrinsically real thing to depend on anything else, the claim of connection cannot be sustained.

Thus one should negate (truth-status) through the analysis of sameness and difference. If this rational analysis cannot refute the truth-status of these (uncreated things), then one cannot refute even in the slightest the truth-status of anything, since created things are completely similar.

Here some may imagine that, since the meaning of created things' emptiness of intrinsically real objectivity is that there is no objective reality in that kind of thing, it is a nihilistic emptiness, whereas suchness has its own intrinsic objectivity and thus truly exists. This is the view that repudiates the relativity of created things, the ultimate resistance that misconceives the determination of created things' emptiness of intrinsic reality. And the latter (idea that the uncreated absolute) has intrinsic objectivity amounts to the intolerable absolutism that reifies truth-status (in the absolute), and is a misunderstanding of the realistic import of emptiness.

Now there are some people who insist that there must be something with truth-status, since a thing's being empty of intrinsically real objectivity means that it does not exist in itself, and once not existent in itself it is impossible for it to exist anywhere else. They then carry on and present a theory that something must have truth-status, since if everything were truthless, the reasons and references proving that (truthlessness) themselves would be devoid of intrinsically real objectivity, and the proofs would have an unestablished subject. But these are just irresponsible statements arising from a failure of investigation.

If the logical implications of this are thoroughly understood, it becomes apparent that the Indian Buddhist schools, once they assert the truth-status of things, definitely maintain the truth-status of all things, even calling themselves "philosophical realists," and once they assert truthlessness, they no longer assert anything at all to have truth-status; this fact is a sign of their utterly distinctive superiority to the babbling philosophers of the area around here![122]

Here those who say two inconsistent things about suchness, agreeing about the above pattern of emptiness of intrinsically real objectivity of superficial things yet getting into various ways of argument about whether or not the ultimate is ultimately established or not—these persons should be clearly recognized from the above explanations. For the nonassertion of the truth of all things through the logical negation of the truth in things and the advocacy of the truthlessness of all things based on a nihilistic emptiness from a flawed grasp of emptiness are two absolutely dissimilar positions.

Here one may object that if the meaning of Nāgārjuna's statement "If created things are utterly unestablished, then how can uncreated things be established" is as explained above, then how does this not contradict his statement from the Sixty Reasonings, "The Victors declare that nirvana is the only truth, thus what wise person would imagine that therein some residue is not eliminated," that is, that only nirvana is truth and others are not true and also his statement from the Praise for the Dharmadhātu, "All of the Victor's sutras wherein he teaches emptiness are for the sake of eliminating addictions and not to cause the destruction of this realm," that is, that the sutras teaching emptiness that is intrinsic nonreality are for the sake of eliminating addictions and do not show that there is no realm whose nature is purity. These (assertions) actually refute the meaning of the references.

The meaning of the first reference is the same as that of the passage, "The Lord (said): Monks! This supreme truth is unique. It has a nondeceptive nature. It is nirvana. All creations are deceptive and false in nature." This sutra teaches that nirvana is truth and all creations are false. It clearly shows that the meaning of "truth" here is "nondeceptive" and the meaning of "falsehood" is "deceptive." Now since "nirvana" here means "ultimate reality" according to Chandrakīrti's Sixty Reasonings Commentary, the cognition that directly experiences it is undeceived by any appearance of intrinsic objectivity where there actually is none. On the other hand, the remaining creations are deceptive in that they appear intrinsically real to cognitions perceiving them when they actually are not intrinsically real. Hence the "truth" here is not a truth-status that withstands analysis by the rationality analyzing for ultimate truth-status or its lack. Still, what can one do when people do not carefully think over the meaning but merely fasten on the name?

Furthermore, Nāgārjuna explains in his *Sixty Reasonings* that " 'existence' and 'nirvana,' these two do not exist; the very knowledge of existence itself is that which is called 'nirvana.' " That is, neither existence nor peace exist by virtue of any intrinsic reality, and the very object of the knowledge of the intrinsic nonreality of existence is itself nirvana. So how can this be the philosophical position that claims that the emptiness that is the truthlessness of the samsaric life cycle is a nihilistic emptiness?

As for the meaning of the reference from *Praise for the Dharmadhātu*, it shows that sutras (wherein the Buddha) teaches emptiness, which is intrinsic nonreality, in order to get rid of the root of all other addictions, that is, the truth-habit regarding things, teach the nonexistence of its reified object and do not teach that there is no emptiness, which is the naturally pure realm wherein the two selves, objects of the truth-habits, are negated.

Therefore this reference becomes standard to refute ideas such as "this reference teaches there is no emptiness that is the negation of the negatee, truth, since though there is emptiness it is not truly established," and that "it is not necessary to realize the emptiness that is the suchness of the ultimate in order to exhaustively eliminate the addictions." Therefore, Nāgārjuna, from the very same *Praise*, says, "The mind can be cultivated by the three ideas, 'impermanence, emptiness, and suffering,' but the supreme cultivator of the mind is the intrinsic nonreality of things," and "One should meditate on the very lack of intrinsic reality of things as the ultimate realm," that is, that the ultimate realm to be contemplated is the very intrinsic nonreality of all things, and that such contemplation is the supreme cultivator of the mind.

Thus how can it be proper to quote this (in support of) the position that, since the emptiness that is the intrinsic realitylessness of things is a nihilistic voidness, one must employ some different, truly established emptiness as the emptiness to be contemplated? This would be like saying that, to dispel the pain of terror from mistakenly thinking there is a snake to the east, "showing there is no snake there would not serve as remedy, so one must show that there is a tree to the west!" For what one is saying here is that the realization of the truthlessness of the objects of truth-habits is no remedy to cure beings' suffering from their truth-notions about such apparent things, and that rather one must show that some other irrelevant object truly exists.

Presentation of the Two Realities—The Ground Differentiated into the Two Realities

Past scholars held many opinions about the grounds of differentiation into the two realities. Here knowable objects are the ground of differentiation, following (Śhāntideva's) statement in the *Compendium of Training*: "Knowable objects are comprised of the superficial and ultimate realities."

The number into which the two realities are differentiated

The grounds of differentiation are divided into the two realities, superficial and ultimate, according to Nāgārjuna's statement in *Wisdom*: "The reality of the social superficial and the reality of the ultimate object."[123]

The purpose of such differentiation

Here we might wonder, since the "two" in a dual differentiation must involve difference, what is the mode of difference? Here many past scholars, out of the three types of difference—actuality-difference, where both things have different real causes, as in the case of pot and cloth; differential difference, where actualities are the same and the cause of one or the other thing is unreal, as in the case of production and impermanence; and exclusive difference, where one thing negates the other—claimed that the two realities were exclusively different, a few of them maintaining they are the same in actuality but differentially different. According to the correct statement of Kamalaśhīla in the *Illumination of the Middle Way* that "the relation of identity is not precluded even when (one of the relata) is unreal," the (relation of) actual sameness and differential difference is not precluded in either the case where both causes of difference are unreal or the case where one or the other is unreal. Chandrakīrti states in the *Entrance to the Middle Way Commentary*: "This indicates that the intrinsic actuality of all things has two forms—superficial and ultimate." So each thing considered has two actualities, superficial and ultimate. It would be extremely irrational for the two realities (therefore) to be two different actualities, were they not the same actuality. And if there was no actuality to those two, they would become nonexistent. For being existent is concomitant with having either one actuality or many actualities.

Also, Nāgārjuna states in *Disclosure of the Spirit of Enlightenment* that "the superficial is explained as emptiness, and emptiness itself is the superficial, because it is definite that they are mutually indispensable, like production and impermanence." If such things as sprouts were different actualities from their own ultimate realities, they would also be different actualities from their own emptiness of truth (status) and hence would possess truth-status. Thus, as the (two, sprout and its truthlessness,) are not actually different, they are the same in actuality. A sprout, (on the other hand), though it is its own emptiness of truth, is not its own (intrinsic) ultimate reality.

Now some treatises say that the two realities are neither the same nor different. Some interpret this as intending that they lack any intrinsically real sameness or difference. Some interpret this as intending that they have neither different actualities nor identical differentials.[124]

Explaining the Meaning of Each Type—Superficial Reality and Verbal Meanings of "Superficial" and "Reality"

In *Lucid Exposition*, Chandrakīrti explains "superficial" in three ways: as "a covering over of reality," as "mutual dependence," and as "social convention." The latter of these is explained as having the nature of the expressed and its expression, the knowable and its knowledge, and so forth, but by this the superficial reality is not to be understood as including all expressible and knowables whatsoever, and not as merely the expression and cognition of subjective conventions. Now the first of the above three is the superficial represented as reality in superficial cognitions of material forms, and so on. This is also the misknowledge that reifies existence of intrinsic reality in things lacking in any intrinsically real objective status. For, truth-status being objectively impossible, truth is (merely) represented in cognition, and there is no representation of truth in a cognition free of truth-habits.

Thus Chandrakīrti states in *Entrance to the Middle Way*: "It is superficial because delusion obscures its nature; and what artificially appears therein as real was termed a 'superficial reality' by the Sage, since an artificial phenomenon is 'superficial.'" In the *Commentary* he explains that "thus what is included in the branch of existence is represented as a superficial reality by the force of addictive misknowledge. For disciples, self-enlightened sages, and bodhisattvas who have abandoned addictive misknowledge make no presumption of the reality of things that appear to them as existent, such as creations and reflections, and so on, which (they know) are not (intrinsically) real but have an artificial nature. So while they delude the naive, others understand them as superficial, merely like illusions, through the fact of their relativity."

Therefore, while things represented as existent according to the superficial reality are so presented by misknowledge, Chandrakīrti does not indicate there is no representation of superficial reality at all for disciples, sages, and bodhisattvas who have abandoned addictive misknowledge. Now the first reason for that is as explained above—that it is because, since addictive misknowledge is the truth-habit, its perceived object is impossible even conventionally, and superficial reality is concomitant with conventional existence. Therefore, if things are the superficial that is the basis of the presentation of superficial existence, they must not be what is taken as superficial by addictive misknowledge. The second reason is that, according to those who have abandoned addictive misknowledge, there is no superficial that is represented as truth by truth-presumptions, and so those creations are not established as real for them, while still they do not establish the utter lack of any superficial reality. Therefore the statement that creations are "merely superficial" for them should be understood as intending that, since among "superficial" and "reality," "reality" does not present itself to them, the word "merely" rules out "reality" without ruling out "superficial reality," and this is the intention behind the mention of both "merely superficial" and "superficial reality." Chandrakīrti's statement in *Lucid Exposition*, "That which is real according to mundane superficialities is the mundane superficial reality," and the statement in *Entrance to the Middle Way Commentary*, "That superficial whereby reality appears, things each appearing as intrinsically real while actually being devoid of intrinsic reality, is a reality that is superficial, constituted by the errors of the world, and so is (called) 'the social superficial reality,'" should both be understood as clearly referring to the reality according to the superficiality of the previously explained misknowledge, and not to the reality that has conventionally real status. For otherwise it would contradict the Dialecticist interpretation wherein (even) conventionally, intrinsically identifiable status is impossible, and also because both the negations of truth-status and the proofs of truthlessness are accomplished by means of conventions. Along these lines one should understand also the explanation of the status of the superficial by Jñānagarbha.[125]

Here one might imagine, "Well, since a true reality and a true self are real according to the superficiality maintained by the truth-habit, they become superficially real!" That would certainly be the case, I grant, if something merely true according to the superficiality of the truth-habit were to be represented as a superficial reality, but that is not what I said. I was merely explaining according to what kind of "superficiality" is it that the "reality" of "superficial reality" is a "real superficiality," as well as the mode of its corresponding "reality!"

The Nature of Superficial Reality

Each of these internal and external things has both ultimate and superficial actualities. If we illustrate this with the case of a sprout (they are, respectively,) the actuality of the sprout discovered by the rational cognition that sees the object that is the authentic knowable, thatness, and the actuality of the sprout discovered by the conventional cognition that encounters the delusive objects of false knowables. The former is the actuality of the sprout's ultimate reality and the latter is the actuality of the sprout's superficial reality. According to Chandrakīrti in the *Entrance to the Middle Way,* "All things are perceived as having two actualities, each discovered by authentic and spurious perception (respectively): the object of authentic perception is their thatness and the object of spurious perception is said to be their superficial reality." This teaches that the sprout has the two actualities of the two realities, the ultimate being encountered by the former cognition and the superficial being encountered by the latter cognition, and does not teach that one and the same actuality of the sprout has both realities depending on whichever of the two cognitions. As the *Commentary* states, "The intrinsic actuality of all things is precisely indicated as having two forms, superficial and ultimate," so the actuality of each thing is differentiated into two, an ultimate (actuality) that is discovered by the cognition that perceives the authentic object, and the superficial (actuality) that is discovered by the cognition that perceives the false.

The superficial reality is not objectively real, being real only according to the truth-habit, and so to ascertain the elimination of its objects, one must ascertain their falseness. In order to ascertain the delusive status of a superficial object such as an identified "pot," for example, one must find the view that refutes through rational cognition the conceptual object of the truth-habit concerning that object, since falsity will not be established by validating cognition without rational negation of truth. Although "pot" and "cloth" and so on are superficial realities, to establish them cognitively it is not necessary that they be established cognitively as objects belonging to the superficial reality, just as, though "pots" and "cloths" are illusory in that they appear (intrinsically real) while lacking intrinsic reality, the cognitions that establish them (as merely conventionally present) do not necessarily establish them as illusory objects.

Therefore to interpret this system as being that, according to the cognition of an alienated individual with no Middle Way view, the superficial reality of pots and cloths and so on is (what is) presented, and their ultimate reality is presented according to the (cognition of the) holy person, is not correct, for it is the opposite of (Chandrakīrti's) statement in the *Entrance to the Middle Way Commentary* that "the very thing that is the ultimate for the alienated individual is the merely superficial for the holy person who has attained the sphere of illumined experience, for (the lack of intrinsic reality of) that thing is the ultimate reality for them." Alienated individuals perceive pots and so on as (intrinsically) real, which is the same as holding them to exist ultimately, and therefore those things, pots and so on, have ultimate status according to their cognitions and are not superficial objects (for them). But such pots and so on, which according to them are ultimate in status, are superficial according to the intuitive experience of the holy persons who encounter appearances as illusory. And he mentions "merely superficial" here since such an (exalted) cognition does not represent anything as really true. That being the case, furthermore, he says "their intrinsic reality is the ultimate," and therefore one should formulate these, differentiating between "the pots and so on are superficial" and "their intrinsic reality is the holy persons' ultimate," and one should not say that "pots and so on are ultimate for the holy persons," because the rational cognition that perceives their true objectivity does not encounter any pots and so on, and because the meaning of ultimate reality is stated to be that encountered by the rational cognition that perceives the authentic object.

Categories of the Superficial

The Dogmaticist Centrists assert that the cognition that perceives intrinsically identifiable status (in things) is definite about their existence as they appear, and that there are differentiations about whether objective appearances have or do not have the intrinsically identifiable status they appear to have without there being any differentiation of subjective cognitions into authentic and spurious; according to Jñānagarbha's statement in *Distinguishing the Two Realities*, "Although both appear the same, the authentic and spurious superficial (realities) are differentiated according to whether or not they have functional efficiency." (However), this (Dialecticist Centrist) system asserts that everything that appears to have intrinsic identifiability to a person endowed with misknowledge is an appearance (only) for that cognition deluded by misknowledge, and therefore they do not differentiate superficial objects into authentic and spurious.

Chandrakīrti states in the *Entrance to the Middle Way Commentary* that "what is spurious even superficially is not the superficial reality." (But) what he means here is that a mirror image of an object is not really that object according to the superficial (cognition) of an educated social person, and so it is not a superficial reality according to that person. Nevertheless, since it is an object encountered by the perception of delusive objects that are superficial knowables, it is a superficial reality. And just as a cognition that perceives a mirror image is mistaken in its apparent object, so the appearance of intrinsically identifiable blue and so on to one with misknowledge is also erroneous as an apparent object. If a validated object is presented as true, its being erroneous contradicts its representation, but the same (erroneousness) can accompany the presentation of that validated object as superficial. Otherwise, if there were no conventionally real status (at all), then one could not present any superficial reality, and when the superficial illusory things are presented conventionally, it would be impossible to represent them as superficial realities.

According to the Dialecticist Centrist system, the six cognitions not deceived by any circumstantial causes of error and their six perceived objects, and the six cognitions opposite to them (circumstantially deceived) and their six perceived objects, are presented (respectively) as the authentic superficial and as the false superficial, including both subjects and objects together in both cases. They are presented further as true and false superficials depending on social or conventional validating cognition itself, and not in relying on the rational cognition that corresponds to the intuition of the holy persons. Therefore they do not differentiate true and false superficials (as does the) Dogmaticist Centrist system, since (for the Dialecticians) there is no question of differentiating between an ignorant person's perceptions of mirror images and so on and blue and so on by whether or not they are mistaken concerning their apparent objects.

As Chandrakīrti says in the *Entrance to the Middle Way*, "the social persons recognize what is perceived by the six sense faculties when undamaged, and they are true according to society itself; the rest are represented as false by society itself." The one exception here is the opposite to the holding of the intrinsic identifiability of persons and phenomena, which are habit-patterns arising from such as the circumstantial mental deceptions caused by wrong theories regarding both things, which (opposite tendency, that is, wisdom of selflessness) is (after all) not (usually) established by conventional validating cognition. Further, although dualistic perception arises in the objectively omniscient intuition that is free of all causes of deception by instinctual misknowledge, still it is not mistaken with regard to its perceptual objects; the reasons for this have already been explained elsewhere.[126]

Ultimate Reality: The Meaning of "Ultimate" and "Reality"

Chandrakīrti states in *Lucid Exposition*, "It is an object and it is supreme, therefore it is 'ultimate' (lit., 'supreme object'). The same thing is also 'real,' therefore it is called 'ultimate reality.' " Thus he asserts that both objectivity and supremacy constitute the "ultimate reality." The mode of reality of ultimate reality lies in its nondeceptiveness, since it does not deceive people by appearing in one way while actually being another way. Chandrakīrti, however, states in his *Sixty Reasonings Commentary* that (even) this ultimate reality is merely presented as existent in terms of social conventions. Therefore the verbal meaning of "reality" in "superficial reality" and "ultimate reality" is different, the former being "reality" in terms of the truth-habit (only).

The Nature of Ultimate Reality—Actual Meaning

The nature of ultimate reality is as explained above in terms of the *Entrance to the Middle Way* statement that it is what is discovered by the intuition of the object that is the authentic knowable. Chandrakīrti further explains in the *Entrance to the Middle Way Commentary* that "the ultimate as the very object of the special intuition of those of authentic perception is discovered as the intrinsic actuality of the self, but it (itself) is not established by its own intrinsic nature; it is a single actuality." Thus he states that, while the nature of ultimate reality is discovered by the uncontaminated intuition that encounters thatness, it has no intrinsically objective status (itself). Therefore the position that "since it is something discovered by the uncontaminated equipoise, ultimate reality has truth-status (itself)" is refuted. He calls it "the special intuition" to indicate that it is inadequate to define the ultimate as what is discovered by any type of holy intuition, but that ultimate reality is what is discovered by the special intuition that is the ontologically omniscient intuition. The meaning of "discovery" here is establishment by that (special) cognition, which is similar to the usage in the case of the superficial.

As for the process whereby that (cognition) discovers that (object), just as someone with distorted vision sees hairs falling from the sky and another without that distortion does not see such an appearance as hairs falling, so those damaged by the distortion of misknowledge perceive an intrinsic objectivity in the aggregates and so on, but those who have completely eliminated the instinct for misknowledge and those who have the intuition of the holy learner's uncontaminated equipoise by way of their perception of thatness, like the person with undistorted vision, do not perceive in the very same (aggregates and so on) even the slightest dualistic appearance, the reality that they perceive being the ultimate reality. As Chandrakīrti states in *Entrance to the Middle Way*, "Those construct a false actuality such as hairs and so on by the power of hallucination, while others, by the purity of their vision, see the very same things as suchness—this should be recognized." Further, from the *Entrance to the Middle Way Commentary*, he continues, "The lord buddhas, free from the instincts for misknowledge, see the ultimate reality in the aggregates and so on, in the same manner that the person of undistorted vision does not see hallucinated hairs." Now the ultimate that is thus perceived is the ultimate actuality involved in each thing considered as having two actualities. Further, that (very actuality) is the nirvana that is the pure intrinsic reality free of intrinsically real status of each thing under consideration, as well as the nirvana that is the truth of cessation free from whatever kind of seed of defilement. Therefore Chandrakīrti makes such statements as, in his *Sixty Reasonings Commentary*, " 'Well then—is nirvana just the superficial reality after all?' 'Yes, that's just it,' " and "therefore nirvana is construed as precisely the superficial reality." As for the meaning of such statements, the presentation of nirvana, ultimate reality, as existent is a presentation merely of existence in terms of the cognition of conventional superficial reality, but it is not that this system asserts that nirvana is superficial reality.

From the same *Entrance to the Middle Way Commentary*, Chandrakīrti explains that "three of the noble truths are superficial realities, while nirvana is ultimate reality." Here one objects that because he states that the other three truths are superficial reality and cessation is ultimate reality, and because he presents nirvana as superficially existent, his statement that there is an ultimate reality is contradicted. In answer to this objection, it is said that ultimate reality is mentioned only in terms of social conventions. Therefore all things represented as existent are presented in term of social conventions. Thus Buddha states, in the *Perfection of Wisdom in One Hundred Thousand Lines*, that "all these things are designated in dependence on social conventions and not in terms of the ultimate." Nāgārjuna states, in the *Seventy Stanzas on Emptiness*, that "duration, production, and destruction, existence and nonexistence, inferiority, equality, and superiority—the Buddha mentioned these in terms of social conventions and not in terms of the ultimate." So all statements of the Victor that present duration, production, and destruction, or existence and nonexistence, or inferiority, mediocrity, and superiority—all these are presented only in terms of social conventions and are not presented in terms of any sort of authentic objectivity, which is not just conventionally presented. Therefore master Jñānagarbha's statement in *Distinguishing the Two Realities* that "there is ultimate reality through reality in the ultimate" means that, since he explains rational cognition itself as a kind of ultimate, it is a reality according to that, as it is not deceived, and he does not intend any sort of truth-status that can withstand critical analysis, because in his treatise he refutes the truth-status in all things.

Thus if one says that "if the ultimate is not ultimately real, then the superficial is not superficially real," we accept that. But if one says that "if the former is not established in the former, then the latter is not established in the latter," it becomes tantamount to saying that "if the negation of truth

(-status) is without truth-status, then the negation ground, considered things, becomes truly established!" (and this is unacceptable), because ultimate reality itself is presented as precisely the negation of truth in considered things, (and to say that) all considered things would not be superficially established implies that they would not be falsely established (even, and not that they would retain truth-status). But even that (supposed implication) becomes extremely incoherent, because by the very fact of the lack of truth-status of all apparent considered things, the negation-ground necessarily is established as false. Therefore, while ultimacy-analyzing rational cognition need not establish something that is presented as conventionally existent, it is necessary that such a thing not be faulted by any sort of validating cognition, either conventional or rational. Chandrakīrti states in his *Sixty Reasonings Commentary* that "the four properties such as impermanence abide in the appropriative aggregates superficially, and so to hold them is not mistaken; but the four (opposite) properties such as permanence do not inhere in the aggregates even superficially, and so to hold them there is explained to be erroneous"; and in the *Entrance to the Middle Way,* "The inner essence imagined by those fundamentalists, so much troubled by the sleep of unknowing, and those things imagined as illusions and hallucinations—none of these exist even according to the social world." Thus the "self" and the "principle" imagined by these fundamentalists, and those imaginary objects such as illusions and hallucinations, are said to be not even conventionally existent, merely existing according to an erroneous cognition. It is therefore a baseless supposition to hold that these things are presented as superficially existent in the Dialecticist system, besides which, none of the other great Centrists accept them. As for Chandrakīrti's assertion in the *Entrance to the Middle Way* of the equivalence of subject and object in terms of existing or not existing, it is not merely in terms of general existence and nonexistence but also in terms of intrinsically real existence and nonexistence.

Therefore, while things presented as conventionally existent are presented as existent in terms of verbal conventions, all things presented in terms of verbal conventions are not accepted as conventionally existent. And as for the assertion that something is "merely" presented in terms of conventions, the word "merely" definitely does not exclude there being anything other than subjective conventions, nor does it exclude a (conventionally) presented things being established by a (conventional) validating cognition. Rather, this system does not present the existence (of anything) through the discovery of a referent object by investigation into the mode of being of that referent out of dissatisfaction with its being presented in terms of conventions, nor does it present (that thing) as nonexistent when no (referent) is discovered. It asserts that if anything were to be discovered by investigation through such a type of inquiry it would become endowed with truth-status, and therefore does not accept even conventionally that anything is discovered to exist through such an analytic process. Since it thus formulates the criterion for what constitutes analysis and nonanalysis into reality, it considers that if something were to exist by virtue of intrinsic identifiability, it would come to have intrinsically objective existence, not merely being established in subjectively conventional terms, and it does not accept therefore any intrinsically real, intrinsically identifiable, or intrinsically objective existence, even in conventional terms. But I have explained all this extensively elsewhere.[127]

Rebuttal of Objections

Here some argue that if the Buddha's ontologically omniscient intuition discovers ultimate reality, how does it not contradict Chandrakīrti's statement in the *Entrance to the Middle Way Commentary*: "If one objects that, 'Is not the experience of such an intrinsic reality utterly nonexistent? And so how do they perceive it?' We grant that; however, they see by the way of not seeing." He explains that the vision of reality is not seeing at all, and he quotes in support of the explanation that ultimate reality is even beyond the sphere of omniscient intuition: the explanation that mind and mental processes do not function at the buddha stage. So if the Buddha does not perceive the aggregates and so on, how does this not contradict the explanation that he knows absolutely everything, given in the context of his ten powers?

The statement about "seeing by the process of not seeing" does not mean that he does not see any kind of object at all, but rather it shows that, if these objects (advanced) by the power of the veil of misknowledge were to exist in reality, the holy, uncontaminated, equipoised intuition must perceive them, and so from the perspective of not seeing them at all, it sees their ultimate reality; because it is presented that the realization of the negation of a negatee comes from not perceiving that negatee when it should be perceived if it were to exist.

The meaning of the statement that the "supreme seeing is not seeing" is to be understood in the same way. As the *Dharma Encyclopedia* states, "Forms are not seen, sensations are not perceived, concepts are not experienced, and thoughts are not known. There is no perception of consciousness, mind, or mentality—this is the experience of the Dharma. This is the teaching of the Transcendent One. Beings say in words, 'See the sky!' But how do you see the sky? This you must examine. The seeing of the Dharma is taught by the Transcendent One to be like that. That experience cannot be explained by any other example."

Here "not seeing" refers to the five aggregates and "seeing" refers to the Dharma, which here has the meaning of "thatness," as in the statement "Who sees relativity, sees the Dharma!" Here the example is "sky," which is the mere exclusion of tangible obstruction. To see, or to experience that, is not to see any obstruction, the negatee in this case, when it could be seen if it was there. In this example, the "not seeing" refers to the obstruction and the "seeing" refers to the space. As in this example, (the seeing of reality) is not a seeing, and the last two phrases (of the quote) negate the idea that the seeing of reality is like the seeing of blue. And the statement that the five aggregates are not seen teaches that according to the vision of thatness by uncontaminated equipoise, considered things are not seen.

In Atīsha's *Entrance into the Two Realities*, it is said: "Gods! The ultimate reality transcends everything, including the sphere of the omniscient intuition supreme in all aspects, and it does not correspond to any expressions such as 'Such is the ultimate reality!'" Here, when one expresses "ultimate reality," it is explained that there is no experience in the mind, as when subject and object appear to be separate. Therefore this reference is a source for (the ultimate's being) the elimination of dualistic appearance, and not a source for (the idea that) the Buddha does not experience the ultimate.

In the *Entrance to the Middle Way Commentary*, furthermore, Chandrakīrti states: "He is called Buddha because he realizes only the intrinsic reality unaffected by any created phenomenon; because he has that experience." Thus, according to the vision of reality by the Buddha's ontologically omniscient intuition, only the ultimate reality of things is experienced without any contact with relative things.

As for the "elimination of the process of mind and mental functions," it means that the process of constructive thought is eliminated at the time of the realization of thatness, and does not show that mind and mental functions are nonexistent. As Chandrakīrti states in the *Lucid Exposition*, "'Thatness' is free of constructive thought, since it is free of those mental processes that constitute constructive thought. As the Buddha says in a sutra, 'What is ultimate reality? Where there are no processes of mind, not to mention any letters.'" Thus Chandrakīrti explains the meaning of the "lack of mental processes" as the lack of the constructive thought process. And even that is said not to be definitely eliminated at the time of the holy learner's equipoise but only at the time of buddhahood, according to the *Entrance to the Middle Way Commentary*.

Furthermore, in the *Commentary* Chandrakīrti proves that if that (ultimate) intrinsic reality were not to exist, the austerities of the bodhisattvas would be pointless, and he backs this up with scriptural references. Thus,

"What is the intrinsic reality of these things? It is that which does not depend on anything else, the intrinsic actuality realized by the wisdom free of all distortions of misknowledge. Who would ask, 'Does that (itself) exist? Or does it not exist?' If it did not exist, for what purpose would the bodhisattvas practice the path of the transcendences? For it is to realize that reality that the bodhisattvas undertake their hundreds of hardships." To support that assertion, (he quotes), "Noble son! If the ultimate were not to exist, the pure practice would be pointless, the arisal of the transcendent lords would be pointless. But because the ultimate reality does exist, bodhisattvas are said to be expert in the ultimate." Thus, if the ultimate reality were not to exist, practices for the sake of the purity of ultimate nirvana would be pointless, as the disciple would be unable to realize it, and the buddhas' visiting the world in order to cause disciples to realize it would be pointless, and the great bodhisattvas would become inexpert in ultimate reality. Therefore, since Chandrakīrti quotes such sutras to prove the existence of the ultimate reality, to hold that the interpretation of this great master advocates the ultimate reality as an unknowable object and that the holy equipoise has no intuition that realizes thatness is simply a false speculation.

Further, as for the meaning of his statement in the *Entrance to the Middle Way Commentary*, "Therefore we represent that 'thatness is realized' (only) designatively, and actually there is no knowing of a something by a someone, since both the knowable and the knower are actually unproduced." First of all, it is that the representation of the realization of thatness that differentiates between the subjectivity, intuition, and the object, thatness, is merely according to conventional cognition and not according to that intuition itself. "The knower is unproduced" means that it is without intrinsically real production, and so the whole process becomes like water being poured into water.

As for the statement that "since mind and mental functions do not penetrate into thatness, the object of intuition, it is realized only by the body," it means that the objective to be realized is thatness, the subjective means of realizing that is the subjective intuition, and the realizer, or knower, is the body of perfect beatitude.[128]

As for the way in which that body realizes thatness, it is by the process of elimination of the constructive thoughts constituting mind and mental functions, as explained above, which can be known by Chandrakīrti's statement in the *Entrance to the Middle Way Commentary* explaining that the body that realizes thatness is free of all mind and mental functions, having the nature of peace. (The idea that) the Buddha does not see the aggregates and so on is a repudiation of phenomenological omniscience and of all objective things, since "existent" and "not known by the Buddha" are mutually exclusive statements. Therefore objective things necessarily appear to phenomenological omniscience, and they do so by arising in that cognition, since the system of this master does not advocate aspectless cognition. Among the apparently objective things there are two kinds: one kind, such as the Buddha's signs and marks, which are not deceptions by the instinctual misknowledge, and a second kind, such as the impure animate and inanimate things, which are deceptions by instinctual misknowledge. The first of these kinds is not eliminated on the stage of buddhahood; the second kind is eliminated, since its cause is eliminated. As for the way in which they appear, when the Buddha's signs and marks appear to a person who has not abandoned misknowledge, they appear to have intrinsic identifiability when they actually do not, but not for the reason that the objects themselves arise by the power of instinctual misknowledge, since they appear so by the power of the subject's being deceived by instinctual misknowledge. And in that case, they do not appear so (intrinsically identifiable) to that subjectivity merely according to the fact that they appear that way to some other person, but from that person's very own point of view. On the other hand, in the phenomenologically omniscient intuition of the Buddha, things appear (also) according to (the cognition of persons) who have not abandoned misknowledge, where forms and sounds and so on appear to be intrinsically identifiable when they are not, but they appear so to the Buddha only from the point of view of their appearance to such persons deceived by misknowledge and do not appear to the Buddha from his own point of view without depending on their appearing so to other persons. Therefore the appearance of unreal forms and so on as intrinsically real also arises in the Buddha's omniscience according to their appearance for those subject to misknowledge, but without depending on such an appearance to such a person, they are not cognized as appearing in that way from a buddha's own point of view. Therefore there is no fault here that the Buddha's omniscience becomes erroneous by being aware of such appearances, for, even though such intuition does not arise from deception, their awareness is there by the key point of his intuition's necessarily having awareness of all objective knowables. Therefore, according to objective omniscience's own point of view, all phenomena appear as selfless and realityless, like false illusions, and do not appear as real, and their appearance in that intuition with the aspect of their appearance to persons subject to misknowledge is merely due to their arisal with a true appearance to other persons.

Nāgārjuna states in his *Sixty Reasonings* that "those who are expert in phenomena perceive impermanent phenomena as collections of deceptive things, selfless, empty, and isolated," and Chandrakīrti comments that "they see them in such a way since they have accomplished the ultimate." Likewise,

Jñānagarbha states in *Distinguishing the Two Realities* that "the Omniscient One directly sees all relative productions just the way they appear, devoid of any imagined objectivity." Thus the phenomenological omniscience directly sees things in reality. And again, "When he does not experience subject, object, and essence, because of his firm abiding in the nonarisal of any signs, he does not arise." Thus (the Buddha) never again arises from the samādhi wherein dualistic appearance is eradicated. Thus Jñānagarbha speaks in both ways in these two explanations.

However, although it must appear contradictory to assert both—(that he sees only nondually and that he sees things individually) and not one or the other, as long as one does not understand—they are not in fact contradictory. For although the vision of thatness and the intuition aware of all phenomena are one actuality, depending on their respective objects they can function as rational cognition and as conventional cognition without the slightest contradiction. Understanding this point depends on properly understanding how, although at the time of the elementary view, rational cognition and conventional validating cognition occur with different modes of discovering when operating on a single considered thing, they have not the slightest contradiction to each other. At the time of fruition (in buddhahood), when the two intuitions encounter their objects, if you understand well not only just that (they are not contradictory) but also how each validating cognition applies to the object, you can also understand how even though the two objects are not separately ascertained, the two subjectivities do not operate on a single basis. And this should be understood as an extremely fine point concerning the identification of the two realities.[129]

The Categories of the Ultimate

The ultimate reality is differentiated according to the *Entrance to the Middle Way Commentary* statement: "If emptiness is extensively differentiated, there are the sixteen emptinesses. Its medium differentiation is into thing-emptiness, nothing-emptiness, self-emptiness, and other-emptiness. And most briefly, (it is differentiated into) the two—personal selflessness and objective selflessness." Other treatises mention two categories, the actual ultimate and the corresponding ultimate. For example, Kamalaśhīla in the *Illumination of the Middle Way* states that "this nonproduction is termed 'ultimate' and 'corresponding ultimate,' but it is not so, since actually the ultimate transcends all fabrications." And Śhāntarakṣhita states in *Ornament of the Middle Way* that "the ultimate reality is called 'ultimate' and 'corresponding' but really it is free from the whole mass of fabrications." Jñānagarbha also speaks the same way in *Distinguishing the Two Realities*. Further, *Distinguishing the Two Realities Commentary* and *Ornament of the Middle Way* explain the negation of production and so on in the ultimate as the superficial reality.

In regard to the meaning, many old-time scholars considered this to refer to two ultimate realities, one verbal and one not verbal, the former being the emptiness that is the negation of the production and so on of material form and so on ultimately, which is a designative ultimate reality with the nature of the superficial reality, and the latter being not an object of knowledge, since it could not be the object of any sort of cognition whatsoever. But that is not the meaning of these statements. It is rather explained as follows: While it is necessary that the objective reality should be called "ultimate," there are many explanations in which the subjective rational conviction is so termed.

For example, in Jñānagarbha's *Distinguishing the Two Realities*, "reason is ultimate, since it is not deceived," and in Kamalaśhīla's *Illumination of the Middle Way*, "those statements that things are utterly unproduced ultimately" have the following meaning: the wisdoms arising from realistic learning, reflection, and meditation, since they are nonerroneous subjectivities, are called 'ultimate' because they are the ultimate of this." There are two kinds of rational cognitions: the nonconceptual intuition of the holy equipoise, without conceptual thought, and the rational cognition that encounters thatness depending on a reason, with conceptual thought and so forth. Bhāvaviveka's explanation in *Blaze of Reason* of "ultimate" as both nonconceptual intuition and as the wisdom that corresponds to that, and Kamalaśhīla's explanation, in *Illumination of the Middle Way,* of the two ultimates, have the same intention. Therefore the meaning of these treatises is not a differentiation of the objective ultimate only, that is, without differentiating the subjectivities (involved).

Now, the first (of the two kinds) is the penetration into thatness, and is the actual ultimate, as it can cut off instantaneously with regard to its object all mental fabrications both of truth(-status) and of dualistic appearance; it is what is meant by "transcending all fabrications." The second one, while it can terminate fabrications of truth with regard to its object, cannot terminate fabrications of dualistic appearance, and it is called "the corresponding ultimate" since it corresponds in form to the transcendental ultimate. Similarly, the two modes should be explained with regard to the ultimate, which is the object for the negation of ultimate production and so on of material form and so on. The objective emptiness according to the nonconceptual rational cognition is the actual ultimate free of both kinds of fabrications, while (the same thing), according to the conceptual rational cognition being free of only one kind of fabrication, is not the actual ultimate free of both kinds of fabrication, yet it is not said in general not to be the actual ultimate reality. Therefore, except that it is free of all fabrications of dualism according to a certain type of cognition, it is not possible for that truth-emptiness to be free of all fabrications of appearance, and therefore it is not the meaning of the treatises that for it to be ultimate reality it must be free of all fabrications of dualistic appearance.

Therefore the Illusionists'[130] claim that the coordination of the ground aggregates and so on, and the truth-devoid-appearance that is just the object achieved by inferential rational cognition, is the ultimate reality refers to the corresponding ultimate and not the (actual) ultimate reality. Although the understanding of freedom from true sameness and difference establishes the understanding of the truthlessness of sprouts and so on, that is not the object for such achievement for a thoughtful person who has not (yet) ceased his doubts as to whether that object exists or not in truth, and that reason does not serve as a genuine reason for the termination of his doubts. Kamalaśhīla's *Illumination of the Middle Way* states that both reason and probandum of freedom from (true) sameness and difference are merely exclusion (negations), and that it is the same whatever is taken as reason, either nonsameness, nondifference, or not both of them. This is not interpreting them as implicative negations, as one can understand from the examples used therein, and as that is certainly not the position of Śhāntarakṣhita, Kamalaśhīla, and Haribhadra. In regard to the exclusion of fabrications of the negatee in appearance, taking it as the latter of the two possibilities, exclusion or determination, and asserting that ultimate reality is merely the object encompassed by inference—none of the great Centrists take this position. You should understand in this way the detailed explanation of the systems of these masters, as I have given it in the extensive *Path of Enlightenment*. Jñānagarbha, in *Distinguishing the Two Realities Commentary*, after explaining the negation of production and so on as a corresponding ultimate, continues, "When others hold only the 'perfect,' it should be etymologized as 'also pure,' (meaning that this expression for the ultimate is itself but an analogy). If we analyze this, it is merely superficial. Why? Since the negatee (truth-status) is not existent, it is clear that there is no negation ultimately."[131]

Here the "others," that is, the Idealists, assert that they have truly established emptiness, which is the negation that negates the objective self in the negation ground. But Jñānagarbha's own system does not consider that the objective self is present as the negatee, and so he says that the negation that negates that is not really achieved. Therefore his statement that the negation of ultimate production and so on is superficial means that it is superficially existent and does not show that it is (itself) the superficial reality.

Further, from the same text, he answers the objection that "true production should actually be perceived, but it is not, and so it is like the false superficial, and so the negation of true production and so on is also the false superficial, since the phenomenon that is the negation ground should be perceived but it is not" by saying that "it is not that it is not perceived, since it is not different from the actuality of the phenomenon." Here, when blue and so on is perceived, its truth-emptiness is explained as being apparent, for although the mere negative exclusion that is truthlessness does not appear to the visual consciousness and so on, he intends it to be an implicative negation, such a thing being superficial by definition, and so it is not prevented from being the ultimate reality that is the emptiness that is the mere exclusion of truth(-status). Śhāntarakṣhita, in the *Ornament*, says that the negation of ultimate production etc. is included in the genuine superficial, being explained as being there through its correspondence with the ultimate reality. He also mentions that the ultimate is the abandonment of the entire network of fabrications concerning being and nothing.

In regard to this network of fabrications, Jñānagarbha states in *Distinguishing the Two Realities*: "Therefore, 'it is not empty, it is not nonempty, it neither exists nor does not exist, it is not nonproduced and it is not produced,' such things and so forth the Lord proclaimed." And furthermore: "Why? That is free of fabrications. Just that is free of the whole network of conceptual thoughts." Here he explains the "network of fabrications" as the network of conceptual thoughts. That is abandoned according to the direct realization of thatness. That is the actual ultimate. And what is not like that, rational cognition with its object, is the former, the corresponding (ultimate), as previously explained.

Further, in regard to the negation of true production and so on, there are both the rational cognition that negates it and the inferential object, and one should understand the method of including it in the genuine superficial on that basis. And that method of explaining the freedom from the network of assertive fabrications about the two realities is very useful in many contexts.

The Number of the Two Realities

Of necessity, when one determines that something is a false and deceptive thing, one has excluded that thing from being nondeceptive. Deceptive and nondeceptive are therefore mutually exclusive contradictories. Thus they apply to all knowables pervasively through their mutual exclusion and there is no third option. Thereby one should understand the certification of the number of the two realities. (The Buddha) stated in the *Meeting of Father and Son Sūtra*,[132] "Thus the Transcendent Lord realizes the two realities, the superficial and the ultimate. Knowable objects are all included in these superficial and ultimate realities." He states that all knowable objects comprise the two realities. He also states in the *Thatness-Teaching Samādhi Sūtra*,[133] "other than the superficial and the ultimate, there is no third reality." This is a clear statement of the certification of the number of the two realities. If you understand the differentiation of the two realities, you will not become confused about the Sage's teachings, and if you do not understand them, you will not understand the reality of the teaching. Further, you must understand it according to the determinations of the savior Nāgārjuna. Chandrakīrti says in the *Entrance to the Middle Way* that it is very important for those seeking liberation to be expert in the two realities: "There is no method for (attaining) peace for those who stray from the path of master Nāgārjunapada. They fail in both the superficial and ultimate realities, and failing there, there is no attainment of liberation. Conventional reality serves as the technique, and ultimate reality is the result of that technique. Who does not understand the differentiation between them gets involved in false paths under the influence of wrong notions."

The Categories of Transcendent Insight

When you discover the view that realizes the two selflessnesses from the above teaching of the necessary conditions for transcendent insight, you should meditate on transcendent insight.

How many transcendent insights are there?

Here I have not mainly taught the high stages of transcendent insight but have emphasized the transcendent insight to be meditated by common individuals. To completely analyze that type of transcendent insight, there are the insights of the four realities, the insights of the three doors, and the insights of the six investigations.

The insights of the four realities are stated in the *Elucidation of Intent Sūtra* as the four—"discernment" and so forth. Among them, "discernment" takes the contents of reality as its object and "investigation" takes the nature of reality as its object. The first contains examination and analysis and the second contains thorough examination and thorough analysis, since they (respectively) discern coarse and subtle objects. The identification of these four is stated in Asaṅga's *Shrāvaka Levels* and in Ratnākaraśhānti's *Instruction in Transcendent Wisdom*.

The insights of the three doors are stated in the *Elucidation of Intent Sūtra* as (the insights) arisen from signs, arisen from thorough investigation, and arisen from individual discrimination. As for the description of these three taking the import of selflessness as an example, first selflessness is identified, then taken as object, and then its significance is imprinted in the mind without engaging in repeated determinations. The second (stage of insight) consists of determinations in order to ascertain what was not previously certain. The third (stage of insight) is the analysis as above of the identified import.

The (insights of the) six investigations are the thorough investigations and individual discriminations of meaning, phenomenon, nature, orientation, time, and reason. (Insight) investigating meaning investigates (whether) "the meaning of this expression is this"; (insight) investigating phenomena considers "this is internal" or "this is external" and so on; (insight) investigating nature investigates whether "this is a particular nature or a general nature," or "this is a common nature or an uncommon nature"; (insight) investigating orientation investigates the faults and disadvantages of negative orientations and the virtues and benefits of positive orientations; (insight) investigating time investigates "such happened in the past, such happens in the present, and such will happen in the future." (Insight) investigating reason investigates through the four types of reasoning: it investigates relational reasoning by viewing how effects occur depending on causes and conditions, considering specifically the objects of superficial and ultimate realities; it investigates functional reasoning by investigating how things perform their specific functions, such as fire by burning, considering "this is the phenomenon, this is the activity, and this is the function it accomplishes"; it investigates logical reasoning by investigating how things are established without contradicting validating cognitions, considering whether "this is supported by perceptual, inferential, or scripturally testimonial validating cognitions or not"; and it investigates natural reasoning by investigating the commonsensical natures, the inconceivable natures, and the ultimate natures of things such as the heat of fire and the wetness of water, respecting those natures and not considering other (possibilities). The presentation of these (investigative insights) as sixfold is to be understood by the yogi, but they can definitely be included in three categories, as concerned with verbal meanings, with objective things, and with ultimate natures. The first investigative (insight) is in terms of the first (concern), objective investigation and particular nature investigation are concerned with the second, and general nature investigative (insight) and the other three are concerned with the third. The first-explained four insights operate through three doors and manifest six modes of investigation, and therefore the (insights of the) three doors and the (insights of the) six investigations are included in the (insights of the) four realities.

The four attitudes explained above (in the quiescence section), such as the "balancing" attitude, are explained in Asaṅga's *Shrāvaka Levels* as being common to both quiescence and insight, and thus there are also four conscious attitudes in insight.

How to Meditate on Transcendent Insight—The Meaning of Meditating on Insight Based on Quiescence

Just as (the Buddha) states in the *Elucidation of Intent Sūtra* that having first achieved quiescence one meditates on insight, the treatises of the Holy Maitreya, Asaṅga's *Bodhisattva Levels* and *Shrāvaka Levels*, Bhāvaviveka, Shāntideva, Kamalashīla's three *Stages of Meditation*, Ratnākarashānti's *Instruction in Transcendent Wisdom*, and many other treatises also state this. The intention of these statements is not that, first of all, one should generate a quiescence not oriented to the meaning of selflessness that perceives any kind of object, and then subsequently one's practice oriented toward selflessness becomes transcendent insight—because quiescence and insight are not differentiated by the objects they take up; because Ratnākarashānti explains in the *Instruction in Transcendent Wisdom* that one first generates quiescence oriented toward the reality of emptiness of subject-object duality and subsequently one generates insight through analytic meditation on the same object; and because Āryāsaṅga, when he explains insight concerned with the contents of reality, states that after generating quiescence there is a meditation of insight based on it concerned with the levels of peace,[134] which moreover is said to be a path common to non-Buddhists and Buddhists as well as to common individuals and holy persons. Therefore when one newly achieves quiescence, not having achieved it previously, it is precisely achieved by placing the mind in one point toward any object whatsoever, and is not properly practiced through repeated analysis of its chosen object. It will be achieved if practiced in the former way and it is impossible to achieve if practiced in the latter way. However, one who has already achieved quiescence in the former way can certainly continue to practice merely focused meditation as before, but if one practices an analytic meditation through the specific discrimination of wisdom, whether in the context of phenomenological or ontological concerns, one can derive ultimately a distinctive one-pointed samādhi. Thus, since that (practice) seems to achieve an especially powerful one-pointed samādhi that the former (practice) cannot, analytic meditation is recommended.

As for the way of practice, it is the procedure of first seeking quiescence and then, based on that, subsequently practicing insight, and that is the reason why quiescence and insight are differentiated by their different procedures in practice, even though they may both take the same object, such as selflessness. Especially, since the meditation of the two transcendent insights—that concerned with the levels of peace through specific discernment of the faults and virtues of the higher and lower realms, and that concerned with selflessness cultivated through analysis with the wisdom of the specific discrimination of the meaning of selflessness—is (indispensably) necessary to generate a firm and intense certainty, it has the greater power to abandon specific abandonees, (defilements and obscurations). As for the phenomenologically concerned transcendent insight, it is not only the meditation concerned with levels of peace that abandons the manifest addictions, but it is also stated by Ratnākaraśhānti in the *Instruction in Transcendent Wisdom* to be the analytic meditation that discerns the nature of the eighteen elements, by which illustration one can understand the other insights that are meditated by distinguishing objective things.

Although Ratnākaraśhānti explains in the *Instruction in Transcendent Wisdom* that one must generate quiescence and insight on the stage of yoga oriented toward the phenomenological before generating quiescence and insight oriented toward the ontological, here, following the view of Śhāntideva and Kamalaśhīla and so on, insight is generated after first generating any sort of quiescence, and I mean here the transcendent insight oriented ontologically (toward ultimate reality).

Vehicles in Terms of Which This System Applies

Well, that gradual procedure of generating such quiescence and insight, is it in terms of Individual Vehicle or Universal Vehicle, or in terms of sutra or tantra?

This system is common both to the Individual Vehicle of the disciples and self-enlightened sages and the Universal Vehicle of the transcendences, also being common to all four of the (main theoretical schools).[135] It also holds likewise for the three (lower) divisions of Tantra Vehicle; I have already explained the positions of the different tantras and their great elucidators in the *Stages of the Tantric Path*. As for the unexcelled yoga (tantras), the *Secret Union* also uses Ratnākarashānti's statement in the *Instruction in Transcendent Wisdom*: "If you examine your own mind, all things abide within it. This teaching resides in the vajra of space; there is no phenomenon and no reality." The *Secret Union* also explains the orientation toward mind only, as taught in the *Visit to Lanka Sūtra*: "Depending on mind alone, do not imagine any external objects"—this is the the orientation toward suchness and the teaching of the three stages of the yoga of nonappearance. It also appears to explain, as above, the procedure of practice of quiescence and insight through focused meditation and analytic meditation in the first two stages. Thus it accepts a similar procedure of generating (quiescence and insight) in the mental process oriented toward reality. My own interpretation is that in the context of the unexcelled yoga the procedure of generating the understanding of the view must be practiced according to the Centrist treatises. In practice, however, although sometimes there are conscious attitudes analytic of thatness during the aftermath (intuitions) of the creation stage and the perfection stage, and although the perfection-stage yogi who has achieved the ability to concentrate on the essentials in the body must definitely meditate through concentration on top of his view, when cultivating thatness in equipoise there is no practice of the analytic meditation of transcendent insight as explained in other treatises. Therefore, in that context, one should not employ one-pointed reality meditation on one's view in alternation with analytic meditation. But this is not the context to clearly teach the reasons as to why it is enough to practice in that way (placing one-pointedness on a realistic view), so I have only explained the reasons why one should do the opposite in other paths.

The Way to Meditate on Insight Based on Quiescence

If you do not discover the view of selflessness, no matter what method of meditation you practice your meditation will not stay on the import of thatness. So you must discover that view. And even if you have an understanding of the view, if you do not remember the view when you meditate on thatness and focus your meditation on that, you will have no meditation on reality. Further, if after each new session of analysis of the view you focus your mind on not holding anything at all, it is not the cultivation of reality of thatness. Further, practicing by remembering that view and just focusing on it is no more than the above practice of quiescence, and the meaning of the treatises is not just to practice insight in alternation with that. Therefore you should practice through the specific analysis by means of wisdom of the import of selflessness, as explained above.

If you practice analytic meditation by itself, the quiescence you previously generated will decline, so you should practice analytic meditation mounted on the horse of quiescence, now and then blending in periods of stabilized meditation. Moreover, if you practice analytic meditation often, your focusing decreases, so you should often return to focused meditation, engaging in abiding by itself. If the focused meditation is overdone, you become averse to analysis or you ignore the functioning of your analysis, and your mind becomes obsessed with one-pointed abiding, and so you should often return to analytic meditation. Your meditation has the greatest power if you practice quiescence and insight in balanced proportion, so that is how you should practice.

Kamalaśhīla says in the last *Stages of Meditation*, "When you meditate on insight and wisdom comes very strongly, quiescence becomes weaker and the mind becomes agitated like a candle flame in the wind, so reality will not be experienced very clearly. At that time, you should meditate on quiescence. If quiescence becomes too strong, then, like a man who has fallen asleep, you will not experience reality very clearly; therefore you should then meditate on insight." Thus it is not correct to hold that all thoughts occurring in analytic practice are substantivistic sign-habits that are truth-habits, and therefore terminate them—because, as I have repeatedly established, truth-habit thought is only one tendency of thought. If you decide that rational refutations overwhelm whatever is held by discriminating thought, this becomes the nihilistic repudiation that has overextended the rational negatee, and it is not the meaning of the sutras, as I have established. Yet you may still think, even if you do not assert it with regard to other subjects of concern, that whatever is held in cognition regarding ultimate nature is (merely the product of) substantivistic sign-habits that conceptualize truth(-status) in things. In fact, those (sign-habits) are the fault of a defective habit pattern (of mind) and do not (function) with regard to all objects cognized—because it is stated that the egocentric individual desiring liberation must investigate reality from many scriptural and rational perspectives.

Again, you may think that the meditation on thatness, as it is for the purpose of generating nondiscrimination, is not produced by analytic discrimination, since cause and effect must correspond (in their natures). The Lord himself clearly answered this (doubt), in the *Kāshyapa* chapter of the *Ratnakūṭasūtra* collection:[136] "Kashyapa, for example, when you rub two sticks together, they produce fire and are themselves completely consumed in the process. In the same way, Kashyapa, genuine analytic discrimination produces the faculty of noble wisdom and, being produced, it serves to consume that genuine discrimination itself." Here he clearly states that the noble wisdom is generated by discrimination. Similarly, Kamalaśhīla states in his middle *Stages of Meditation*, "When the yogi analyzes with wisdom and does not cognize as ultimately certain any intrinsic objectivity of anything, he (or she) enters the samādhi free of discriminative thought and realizes the utter nonexistence of the intrinsic objectivity of anything. When one does not meditate with wisdom by means of specific discrimination concerning the intrinsic objectivity of things but merely meditates exclusively on the abandonment of all conscious attitudes, one never eliminates that (particular) discrimination of that (absence of mental function) and will never realize the utter nonexistence of intrinsic objectivity, since one is devoid of the illumination of wisdom. Thus from the authentic specific discrimination arises the fire of the true wisdom of reality, like fire arisen from rubbing-sticks, which then burns the sticks of discrimination. This is what the Lord stated." Otherwise, it would never happen that the uncontaminated would arise from the contaminated, the transcendental from the mundane, a buddha from a living being, a noble person from an alienated individual, and so forth. For in all these cases the effect is dissimilar from the cause.

Nāgārjuna states in the *Disclosure of the Spirit of Enlightenment*: "Where discriminations occur, how could there be emptiness? The transcendent lords do not perceive any mind in the form of discriminated and discrimination; where there is discrimination and discriminated, there is no enlightenment." But here he teaches that enlightenment will not be attained when truth-status is perceived in discriminated and discrimination and does not negate discriminative wisdom or the mere function of discriminated and discrimination. Otherwise it would contradict his extensive determination of thatness through many discriminative analyses in that text, and also (if mere discrimination were meant) their not being seen by the Buddha means their nonexistence. Again, Nāgārjuna states in the same text: "Emptiness, called 'nonproduction,' 'emptiness,' and 'selflessness,' if it is contemplated as anything less, it does not serve as meditation on that." This does not refute meditation that takes emptiness and selflessness as intrinsically unproduced as its object, but refutes meditation on an inferior emptiness, the lesser nature that is conceived by holding those (emptinesses) as having themselves truth-status. As he states in *Praise to the Dharmadhātu*, "As you taught the nectar of emptiness to cure all mental constructions, you put down those who adhere to it (as having truth-status in itself)." Likewise, he said in the *Precious Garland*, "Thus neither self nor selflessness is apprehended in reality. Therefore the Great Sage eliminated the views of self and selflessness." Both self and selflessness have no objective status in reality, and so the view that holds both as truly existing is eliminated. But this does not refute the view of selflessness—because, as in the previous quote from *Rebuttal of Objections*, if it is not the case that there is realitylessness of intrinsically real status, then intrinsically real status would become (intrinsically) existent.

Likewise, the Buddha's statements in the *Dharma Encyclopedia*, "If the bodhisattva presumes that 'this aggregate is empty,' then he is involved with signs and has no faith in the unproduced condition," and in the *Mother of All Victors*, "If you treat material form as 'empty' and 'selfless,' then you are involved in signs and are not involved in the transcendence of wisdom," refer to the holding of truth-status in emptiness and so on.

Otherwise it would have been illogical to say "no faith in the unproduced condition," because faith would also become involvement in signs and because it would contradict the statements in the same sutra that "things should be understood as lacking intrinsic reality, and this is the engagement in the transcendent wisdom," and "when wisdom terminates the created, the uncreated, and good and evil, when not even an atom is apprehended, that is considered the transcendence of wisdom throughout the universes," and from the *King of Samādhi Sūtra*: "Who discerns selflessness in things and meditates on that discernment, that serves as cause for the attainment of the fruit of nirvana; no other cause will bring forth peace," and from the *Heart of Transcendent Wisdom Sūtra*, when Shāriputra asks, "When a bodhisattva wants to engage in the profound transcendent wisdom, how should he educate himself?" Avalokiteshvara replies that "he should truly regard these five aggregates as empty with respect to any intrinsic reality."

Therefore, according to Nāgārjuna's statement in *Praise to the Dharmadhātu*, "The principle that serves to cultivate the supreme mind is intrinsic reality-lessness," and "while the habits of 'I' and 'mine' are constructing the external world, the experiencing of the two forms of selflessness will exterminate the seeds of existence," and Chandrakīrti's statement in *Entrance to the Middle Way*, "thus by the view of the emptiness of self and property, the yogi will become liberated," so one should understand (the question). And one should cultivate the continuum of the certainty about selflessness and realitylessness.

Kamalashīla explains in the first *Stages of Meditation* that "the meaning of the statement of the *Spell for Entering Nondiscrimination*[137]—'through the lack of any thoughtful attitude, the signs of "form" and so on are abandoned'—is intended as being that 'lack of thoughtful attitude' means the nonapprehension through analytic wisdom and not just the mere absence of any thoughtful attitude, since the substantivistic adherence to form and so on from beginningless time has not been abandoned by mere lack of thoughtful attitudes, as in the case of one absorbed in the trance of unconsciousness." Therefore the scriptural statements about abandoning substantivistic sign-habits through meditating on the absence of thoughtful attitudes are explained as intending the realization through investigation by proper analytic wisdom that not even an atom is apprehended by the objective orientation of the truth-habits. He further explains in the middle *Stages of Meditation*, "If one seeks what is the mind, one realizes emptiness. If one investigates thoroughly what is that mind that realizes, one realizes its objective reality is also emptiness. Through such realization, one enters the yoga of signlessness." This teaches that one enters the reality of signlessness by first employing analytic investigation, which very clearly demonstrates that it is impossible to enter the reality of nondiscrimination by mere emptiness of thoughtful attitudes and by not analyzing the objectivity of phenomena through wisdom.

The statement from the *Jewel Cloud Sūtra* (that Kamalaśhīla quoted) explains it thusly, and he continues by saying that if the view of thatness is not found through proper analysis, it is impossible to enter nondiscrimination concerning the import of thatness. He further explains in the final *Stages of Meditation* that "the statements of inconceivability and transcendentality, and so on, are in order to refute claims of realization of the profound meaning through mere learning and reflection, showing that those (profound imports) are for the discriminating inner realization of holy persons and are inconceivable and so on for others, and also to refute the improper thinking that holds the import of the profound as (itself) having truth-status. They do not refute the proper analytic investigation by discriminating wisdom, since such refutation would contradict a great many references and reasonings. Although that (analysis) is actually conceptual thought, it is also a proper conscious attitude, and it causes nondiscriminating intuition to arise. Thus if you want that intuition, you should rely on that (analytic process)." These statements all refute the claim of the Chinese master that you cannot discover the view that determines thatness by relying on scriptural references and reasonings but you will realize thatness by absorbing yourself in the utter lack of thoughtful attitudes.[138]

It is extremely important to understand these statements well. These ways of meditation also occur in the old instructions on the stages of the path. Potowa says, in his *Collected Sayings*: "Some say that you should rationally determine intrinsic realitylessness at the time of study and reflection but meditate only on nondiscrimination at the time of meditation. But such leads to an irrelevant emptiness, which will not serve as a remedy, since it is meditated as something else. Therefore, even at the time of meditation, one should discriminatingly investigate the absence of sameness and difference, or relativity, whatever you are used to, and also fix yourself slightly in nondiscrimination. If you meditate like that, it remedies the addictions. If you want to follow the unique lord (Atīsha), and if you want to engage in transcendent wisdom's method, (you should know) that as the method of meditating on wisdom. Further, if you practice personal selflessness, you should penetrate it in that way."[139] And Atīsha said, "The one who understood emptiness, Chandrakīrti, is the disciple of Nāgārjuna, who saw the truth of reality, as predicted by the Transcendent Lord. The special instruction descended through him brings one to the realization of the truth of ultimate reality." The way of that teaching was explained by Atīsha in the *Instruction in the Middle Way* and, as Master Kamalaśhīla's intention seems similar, this (view) seems widespread. Thus, for the practice of transcendent insight, you should understand from the above the reliance on the six preparatory practices and the methods of practice in the actual sessions, after the sessions, between the sessions, and especially how to practice free of depression and excitement.

Criterion for Attainment of Insight through Meditation

If you meditate through investigation by discriminating wisdom in that way, until you have achieved the above-explained ecstatic fluency, you have a simulated transcendent insight. Once that ecstatic fluency is generated, you have the genuine transcendent insight. The actuality and method of generating fluency is as already explained. Further, this must occur without the weakening of quiescence and there is a fluency developed from that, so merely having fluency is not enough. Then what is? If you can develop ecstatic fluency through the power of the practice of analytic meditation itself, that then becomes transcendent insight. This is the same whether it involves the transcendent insight oriented toward the contents of reality or the transcendent insight oriented toward the nature of reality. As Maitreya asked in *Elucidation of the Intent*, "'Lord! Until the bodhisattva has attained physical and mental fluency, what is his thoughtful attitude that focuses thought on those well-considered things taken as inner images for his object of samādhi?' The Buddha replied, 'Maitreya! It is not transcendent insight. It should be called a coordinated attitude that simulates transcendent insight.'" And as Ratnākaraśhānti says in the *Instruction in Transcendent Wisdom*, "Who has attained that physical and mental fluency should focus on reality and should analyze with willed attention the considered meaning of reality as the object of samādhi (held) as an inner image. As long as physical and mental fluency has not been generated, it is a thoughtful attitude that simulates transcendent insight, but once they are generated it becomes transcendent insight."

If (insight) can by its own power develop fluency, it can also develop one-pointedness of mind. But this development of quiescence by the power of discriminating analytic meditation itself is a virtue of having previously achieved quiescence (in former lives). Thus when one who has (already) thoroughly achieved quiescence practices analytic meditation, one's quiescence becomes even more consummately intense, and so you should not think that the practice of analytic meditation through fine discrimination will lead to a lessened share of concentration.

Way of Integration of Quiescence and Insight

As explained in the contexts of the criteria for the achievement of both of them, you cannot integrate quiescence and insight if you have not attained both of them, so both must definitely be attained in order to integrate them.

Sometimes it happens that integration is attained from the beginning of the attainment of transcendent insight.

The pattern of that is, by the power of practicing analytic meditation relying on previous quiescence, it becomes integration (of quiescence and insight) if one has attained the thoughtful attitude that naturally applies itself without conscious motivation, as explained above in the quiescence section. As Asaṅga explains in the *Shrāvaka Levels*, "Just how are quiescence and insight mingled in equal integration and what is the path of the integration of quiescence and insight? To explain, when the nine calm states of mind are attained through equanimity, one strives to discriminate between phenomena with the higher wisdom, stabilizing oneself in that achievement of samādhi. At that time, one enters the path of discrimination between phenomena spontaneously without any effort, and one's transcendent insight becomes like the path of quiescence, without any conscious motivation perfectly pure, and it becomes completely purified, harmonious with quiescence, and combined with blissful experience." Therefore it is called "entrance into the balanced mingling of quiescence and insight" and the "path penetrating the integration of quiescence and insight." Kamalaśhīla also states in the final *Stages of Meditation*, "When depression and excitement are eliminated, and one is naturally engaged in balanced concentration, the mind emerges with extreme clarity in focus on thatness—then one relaxes one's effort and stabilizes oneself in equanimity. You should recognize that this is the attainment of the path of integration of quiescence and insight." According to these statements, this (integration) occurs after achieving the actual transcendent insight.

Ratnākaraśhānti adds from *Instruction in Transcendent Wisdom*, "After that, one perceives reality as an image occurring in reflective thought. In that very mind, when both (quiescence and insight) are experienced through the continuation of uninterrupted and unobstructed conscious attention, that is called the path of integrated quiescence and insight. Therein, quiescence and insight are combined and connected, mutually embracing each other in function." Here "unobstructed" indicates that, without needing to concentrate on nondiscrimination, that very analytic meditation itself leaves the fabrications of analysis and enters the freedom from discriminative thought by its own force. "Both are experienced" means that one experiences both a quiescence that is the perception of the image of nondiscrimination and an insight that is a perception of the images of discriminative thought. "Through the continuation" means that analytic insight and quiescence that focus on the conclusion of the analysis are not simultaneous but that, at the time of the actual quiescence derived by the force of analysis, both transcendent insight that discerns things as apprehended in their real nature and quiescence that is the samādhi that stays stably in one point on that reality function in coordination.

At such a time, quiescence and insight function in a balanced combination. For that, one must attain meditative realization, so, from within a state of undisturbed flow of thoughtlessness of firm stability one can gently analyze the import of selflessness, like a minnow darting about on the surface of unruffled still waters. Now this combination is considered a simulated integration of quiescence and insight and not the actual integration.

Such a way of the integration of quiescence and insight must be understood according to the teachings of the original treatises, and one should not rely on other explanations that presume it to be otherwise. And you should understand from my *Stages of the Path to Enlightenment* the extensive details (of the teachings) of the "stages of the path of enlightenment" (tradition) on the conclusive analyses through reasoning, the supportive scriptural references, and the processes of meditation.

Written by the Easterner Tsongkhapa Losang Drakpa Pal at Ganden Riwo monastery.

PART 4

PRAISES, PRAYERS, AND A
MYSTIC CONVERSATION

It is well known that Tsongkhapa had a special connection with Mañjuśhrī, in fact can be thought of as an emanation of that great bodhisattva. At least he always salutes Mañjuśhrī as his archetype deity and savior guru, as above in the *Destiny Fulfilled* poem, and his main instructions on the profound emptiness came directly from Mañjuśhrī. The present hymn was composed probably in 1394 during his long retreat at Oede Gungyal hermitage in Olkha, sometime after he was granted the marvelous vision of Mañjuśhrī sitting before him—his sword of wisdom connecting them, the handle in Mañjuśhrī's heart and the tip in Tsongkhapa's, the stream of rainbow nectar of the five wisdoms flowing down the blade. Or it is possible that it was written in 1398 when he again returned to this favorite hermitage, the time he wrote the *Praise to Dependent Origination*. It is a valuable work, as inspired by his constant direct visions of the bodhisattva.

The second chapter is a praise of Maitreya, known as *Brahmā's Diadem*, which was written at the behest of both Vajrapāṇī and Mañjuśhrī, with the great presence of Maitreya at Dzingji in mind. After Tsongkhapa came out of his long retreat with his eight companions in 1396, their first act was to start a movement to refurbish the great statue of Maitreya in that temple. This was one of Tsongkhapa's four major deeds, and the consecration was accompanied by numerous miraculous signs witnessed by the multitudes that attended. Tsongkhapa himself was sometimes considered an emanation of Maitreya as well as Mañjuśhrī, as by the Nyingma master Lhodrak Namkha Gyaltsen, who wrote, "Savior Maitreya, the future captain of living beings, considered the beings of this decadent age with his great compassion and visited us as Tsongkhapa, the glory of the Land of Snows—I invoke the feet of the glorious guru." But in this poem Tsongkhapa writes under the inspiration of Mañjuśhrī to Maitreya as the future light of the world, presently watching over us from his heavenly Dharma palace up in Tushita.

The third chapter is a *Prayer for Rebirth in Sukhāvati*, the western pure land of the Buddha Amitābha, so famous especially in Chinese and Japanese Buddhism. It was also written in 1395 and 1396, during the work on the Dzingji temple, also under the inspiration of Mañjuśhrī.

After the great dedication at Dzingji, Jé Tsongkhapa set out with his close followers to the south, thinking strongly of making a pilgrimage to visit the holy land of India. On the way, he was invited for a visit by the above-mentioned Lhodrak Khenchen Namkha Gyaltsen, also known as Chakdorpa, owing to his special affinity for and mystic communion with the bodhisattva Vajrapāṇī. Chakdorpa was perceived as Vajrapāṇī himself by Tsongkhapa when he was teaching Tsongkhapa a number of important teachings on the tantras as well as transmitting some important *Stages of the Path to Enlightenment* lineages that had descended through the Kadampas. And Chakdorpa saw Tsongkhapa as Mañjuśhrī himself when he received some teachings from the younger saint. The dialogue of the *Garland of Supremely Healing Nectars* included here is between the Khenchen and the bodhisattva Vajrapāṇī in the presence of Tsongkhapa, referred to by a Sanskrit name, Matibhadraśhrī, although it appears that, as with Mañjuśhrī and Umapa at first, Tsongkhapa cannot see or hear Vajrapāṇī directly. The prophecies are quite interesting, especially as they seem to bear on the present predicament of Tibet.

All these chapters I have translated myself. My thanks to Denma Lochö Rinpoche for his invaluable assistance with some difficult passages in this last chapter.

11 The Ocean of Clouds of Praises of the Guru Mañjughoṣa

'Jam dbyangs bstod sprin rgya mtsho

BY JÉ TSONGKHAPA (WRITTEN IN 1394)

Who calms the flames of ambitions for one's own pleasure with the waters
    of long-cultivated compassion,
Who cuts the net of imaginative fabrications by seeing the reality of the
    profound as it is,
Who carries with tireless heart the responsibility of helping others, to
    reveal to beings what he sees himself,
My mind is aimed at such a tutelary deity as you, O Mañjuśhrī!

Please consider for a moment these flowers of verses of praise,
stirred by the wind of faith, O Mañjughoṣha, Treasure of Wisdom,
O radiant shining mass of rays of saffron light,
like the great solid golden axial mountain,
embraced by the rays of the rising sun!
Though one were to seek strenuously everywhere,
one finds no good refuge other than in you,
when my mind thus turns itself toward you,
it is like a sun-burnt elephant plunging in the lotus pond!

Thus, expressing your excellence, when I let my mind go
toward the means of finding fulfillment of my hopes,

it is like the lowly beggar's pleasure
when he sees the beautiful gift-giver coming!

Praise of Body

Your body is tall and straight like the axial mountain,
its expanse is handsome as the banyan tree,
the complexion of your skin is pure and clear
like dust of gold, fine, smooth, and soft.
On your crown, like the tip of a victory standard,
your coiffe of long, soft, shining black hair
is bound in a beautiful turban whose crest
has five tufts, slightly leaning to the left.
Your head is massive like a shapely parasol dome,
adorned with a diadem of precious stones,
your hairline is high and well-defined,
and the spread of your brow is like the waxing moon.
Your midbrow is adorned by taintless *urṇa* tuft,
as if carved out in pure silver,
shapely, curling to the right,
clear white as a lily or as a lotus stalk.
Your eyebrows are long, even, of lustrous soft hairs,
black in color and slightly arched.
Your eyelashes are attractive as a bull's,
thick, soft, not bristly, well-proportioned.
Your eyes are long and slightly round
like the petals of the blue utpala-lotus,
beautiful, the pupils and whites unclouded,
clear as the petals of the white lotus.
Your nose is well proportioned and prominent,
your lips attractive, red as the bimba fruit,
your forty teeth white, even, and well-polished.
Your cheeks are round and full like the king of deer,
your tongue, sensitive to good taste, is soft and supple,
and can cover the entire orb of your face.
On the long lobes of your fine ears
dangle earrings adorned with many gems.
And your immaculate neck is well adorned
with a necklace of sparkling jewels.
The surfaces of your hands, feet, arches, shoulders, and neck,

are broad, round, without bulging veins,
your body completely full, with no imbalance,
its upper part as broad as Mahādeva,
your chest as wide at the slope of Meru,
your arm well rounded at the shoulder,
long and beautiful like the elephant-king's trunk.
The web of beauty on your fingers and toes
is well shaped like the king of geese.
Your nails shine with a polished red color,
their garland adorns your fingers
like new shoots on the wishing tree's branches,
soft, flexible, long, with youthful flesh.
The palms and soles of your hands and feet
are adorned with the best thousand-spoked golden wheels,
precise and complete, not jumbled together,
distinct and regular as if pressed from the same seal.
Adorned with armlet and bracelet,
your right hand holds the sword
that cuts the root of the tree of materialism,
shining forth a brilliant net of light.
Your left hand holds at your heart
the stalk of a blue utpala-lotus,
which upholds the supreme text of exact and full teaching
of the path of relativity, the sole doorway to peace.
Upon your shimmering lower robe of variegated silk,
soft and smooth, dyed with marvelous colors,
the lower hem of golden tinkling bells
makes a pleasant sound, beautifully draping.
Your organs are retracted like a superb horse,
your fine and soft body hairs
grow individually, curling to the right,
and grow upward on your body.
Their skin delicate, your calves are good and round.
Your ankles without protruding bones.
Your soles flat like a turtle's belly.
A quarter of the foot turns out, and your heel is broad.
On a seat of a perfectly round moon-disc,
on the saffron center of a six-petaled white lotus,
ankles adorned with beautiful, tinkling anklets,
your two feet are crossed in the vajra posture.

Your body is supremely beautiful, supreme body born of the superlative
  cause, ultimate store of merit,
like magic present before many beings, limitless in all pure lands,
  throughout endless space,
born on special occasions, teaching the enlightenment path even in other
  lands, your body, O Teacher,
its superb array here and elsewhere, even if all beings were to become
  omniscient, they could not express it!

As the thousand-rayed sun plunging its seven horses into the saffron ocean,
your body radiates everywhere masses of light of which one can never see
  enough,
by whatever merit I gain by this slight praise,
may the beautiful body of Mañjughoṣha never leave my sight!

When I just have beheld your body,
I weary of my long wandering in existence,
may my troublesome mind, always caught in the wrong path,
come into the power of the spirit of enlightenment!

Praise of Speech

Further, having attained an infinite store of samādhis,
with retentions, superknowledges, and doors of liberation,
may I manifest limitless physical arrays,
to see the victors in the million universes!
Then, having reached the limit of wide learning,
satisfying limitless beings with the Dharma,
may I before too long attain the supreme body
of the chief of all victors, the Lord of Speech!
Your saffron body manifesting a thousand light-rays,
as if reflecting in the surface of a polished mirror,
erect and beautiful as a curving rainbow,
I salute you Mañjughoṣha, Lord of Speech!

Your voice fills all universes everywhere in every different language,
satisfying the minds of all living beings appropriately, eclipsing even the
  luster of creators,
melody of your speech like a sphere of music, which sweet speech outlasts
  the cyclic life,

whose ear it enters, it takes away their sickness, their old age, and their
   death.

Your speech is pleasant, gentle, charming, heart-stirring,
harmonious, its sweetness is pure, stainless clear light,
worth hearing, taming the wild with sweetness,
not rough, not coarse, very calm, it pleases the ear.
Satisfying body, mind, and heart, it generates delight,
painless, all-informing, it is to be understood.
Brilliantly delightful, intensely delightful,
totally illuminating, enlightening,
rational, relevant, free of all redundancy,
its tone is sweet as a lion, an elephant, a lord of serpents,
a dragon, a gadara, a kivalina, a brahmā, a crane, a lord of swans.
Its drumbeat is not high, not low, penetrating all appropriately,
your phrases are expressive, not incomplete,
not disheartened, not feeble, pervaded with joy and insight,
cohesive, relevant, and all conclusive,
satisfying all senses, not contemptuous, not vacillating,
renowned throughout the whole thoughtless samsaric life cycle.
It clears away the three times, punishes the demon hosts,
emerging with supremacy in all its forms.
Such a voice with sixty-four qualities,
all are present even in a single statement,
and gives happiness to the hearing of the lucky
as far as space can reach.
It does not seem too loud when near, nor faint when far,
but accords with the language of each of countless disciples like a crystal
   prisming various colors,
manifests as coming from all parts of your body, such as crown, urna-hair,
   and throat,
and yet it pacifies all the notions of all those hearers, just as the Brahmā-
   voice can manifest from the sky.
Like the deep thunder within the rain-cloud
girt with its belt of beautiful red lightning.
By this merit of praising the speech of Mañjughoṣa,
may I never be parted from the hearing of your speech!

Just by hearing your stream of speech,
the lucky accept it, condemning wrong discourse,

may the well-wrought phrases reach the ultimate
in the explaining, writing, and arguing
that fascinate all the intelligent!
Easily obtaining supreme intellectual understanding
of unhindered linguistic grasp of all languages of beings,
may I achieve the triumph of cutting off all doubts
of all living beings without exception!
Never transgressing the boundaries
of the statements of your instructions,
through devoted single-pointed practice,
may I quickly achieve the mastery of speech!

Praise of Mind

Color of good gold mixed with dyes of coral,
wisdom certain of the proper color of all knowables,
Lord of Wisdom, Mañjughoṣha, refuge of beings,
may you as supreme refuge grant superlative wisdom!

Drunk on the ichor of materialism, knowledge of right and wrong
    destroyed,
completely wrecking the tree of virtue, with his trunk poisoned with
    addictions,
the mind dragged by the chains of existence, losing the female elephant of
    success,
such is the elephant of the mind hard to tame, running amok in the jungle
    of unconsciousness!

It should be bound tightly with the rope of conscience, mindfulness, and
    awareness,
driven with the goad of genuine reasoning,
and guided onto the good path of holy relativity,
praised and trodden by millions of supreme noble ones.

With the powerful force of tireless effort on that way,
by meditating again and again for limitless eons,
by the vajra of the illusion-like samādhi,
the mountain of extremisms is rendered merely a name!

Again the innumerable lord victors,
being pleased by oceans of clouds of supreme offerings,

with the sound of the brahmā-voices from their taintless throats,
grant supreme instruction taught with one intention.

This food of nectar eradicating the hundred illnesses of existence,
by constant use increases the strength of the body of intelligence
that reaches the transcendences of the energetic deeds
of the bodhisattva so very difficult to reach.

The one is no longer oppressed by extremist habits,
false appearances entirely conquered, there arises
the chief of all samādhis without hindrance—
the samādhi renowned as like a vajra.

By the power of your manifestation of that
appearance on the part of illusory objects
and the dreamlike intelligence, which knows clearly
all experience and appearance, enter the ultimate realm.

Thus, like a tree whose root is destroyed,
since you have eradicated the seeds of all habits,
how could you, refuge, ever deviate
from the truth body, as long as space shall last!

Thus while you, savior, never leave the ultimate realm at all,
the vivid vision of the many objects perfectly known individually without
    mixing,
though like reflections in a mirror, or like a rainbow in the sky,
O Intuitive One, your wisdom embraces all even in an instant!

From generosity comes wealth and not poverty,
from avarice comes poverty and not wealth!
You understand all such points of inexorable relativity,
therefore you are the chief of philosophers!

The process of evolution with its fruits of virtue and sin
of all those who move unchecked through existence,
there is nothing in it that you do not understand;
therefore there is never any parting from your speech.

The process of various attitudes such as sticking to desire,
inclining to hatred, or the reverse of these and so forth;

since you directly see all this, none of your deeds
can ever fail to accomplish the aims of beings.

Not a single one of all the categories of the eighteen elements
are hidden in the slightest from your understanding,
therefore you never exceed in the slightest
just proportion in training the faculties of disciples.

Since your understanding is never blocked in application
to the sharpness, dullness, or absence of faculties,
such as faith in those who wander in existence,
you are extremely skillful in the art of teaching Dharma.

Since you know without obscuration entirely
the paths of ascendance and transcendence
and of migrating to the wretched states,
you are the best spiritual friend of living beings.

Through all samādhis such as those of form and formless,
the lion's stretch and the terrific triumph,
you are not confused in the practice-methods of entrance and arisal,
you are consummate in all meditational concentrations.

You are skilled in the limits of the past,
since you realize in a mere instant
the memory and understanding of former lives of self and others
that have been continuous from the beginningless samsara cycle.

You are skilled in the limits of the future,
since you know very well all the places of rebirth,
having migrated through death from just this present time,
according to one's good and evil actions.

Your direct vision, completely free of blocks,
sees the nirvana that is the termination of contaminants
and the eightfold path the means of terminating them;
thus you are the best of all refuges.

Your knowledge penetrates unhindered the appropriate and the
    inappropriate, the effects of evolution,

attitudes, the universes, the degree of faculties, the paths that lead
    everywhere,
the addictions, purifications, the past abodes, deaths, migrations, births,
    and termination of contamination,
what point of knowables is not under your command, not your object?

Those who wander in existence from the beginningless,
though they frequent with powerful effort
the path of harming others to gain their own happiness,
are erring as their hardships will prove fruitless.
So you also see that those who for themselves,
even not harming others even in the slightest,
day and night strive a hundred ways for liberation,
have also turned their backs on the true path.
Thus you long practiced the good path of compassion,
the unique path of all the victors,
the mother that looks after all beings,
the door for entering the fray of the hero bodhisattvas.

You, loving one, see the great error of forsaking
others' happiness, as there's no virtue in all this world,
not accepting (their) suffering even in your dreams,
and not content even with the utmost pleasures,
and so by your primal cultivation
of the spirit of enlightenment that sees
the equality of self and others,
you hold all living beings as yourself.

Craving one's own happiness blocks the path.
Cherishing others is the treasury of all excellence.
Thus you practice again and again the method of exchange
of self and others, making all beings as your own self.

Thus You, Lord, completely nurse physical strength
frequently with the mother of compassion,
how can the very culmination of excellence
be deprived even by the bliss of peace?

Just as the king of birds soars in the heavens,
not falling to the earth, not his proper place,

by praising your mind that stays neither in existence nor in peace,
may I never be apart from the wisdom and love of Mañjughoṣha!

The view that removes all occasions for extremism.
And the compassion that sees all beings as one's only child,
having achieved them easily within my mind,
may I lead all beings onto the Supreme Vehicle!

The retention that remembers word and meaning of all teachings,
and the supreme eloquence that answers all questions,
quickly generating these, may I spread out the feast
of eloquent explanations of the masses of the Dharma!

By the glory of the mind of Mañjughoṣha
who, without calculating, fulfills the hopes
of various disciples according to their inclinations,
may I become beautiful as the autumn moon in sky!

Ceaselessly praised by limitless victors in the universes of the ten directions,
he is called Mañjughoṣha, whose sweetness fills the three realms,
and this ocean of clouds of praises, reverently expressing just a bit of his
    excellence,
who upholds it and reads it, may Mañjughoṣha quickly enter his mind!

*Composed by the learned Easterner Losang Drakpa Pal at the hermitage of
Oede Gungyal at the prince of snowy mountains in Tibet, written down by the
Buddhist scholar Bhadrapala.*

12 Brahmā's Diadem—A Praise of Maitreya

Byams pa'i bstod pa

BY JÉ TSONGKHAPA (WRITTEN IN 1395)

⚘

Reverence to the glorious Guru Mañjughoṣha!

Ever showering them with tender love,
he yet burns the friends of darkness.
Though he has cut off the toughest bonds,
he binds himself tightly with compassion.
Ever possessed of peaceful equanimity,
he cherishes others more than himself.
Bowing humbly at the feet of Mañjughoṣha,
I praise the Savior, Invincible[140] Maitreya!

Four-faced Brahmā praises him with his many mouths,
thousand-eyed Indra always looks at him with devotion,
Rati's Kāma drops his pride and bows down to him.
Reverently, I worship the Regent's[141] feet!

As sunlight opens lotuses in clear lakes,
as the clear sky star lord makes lily gardens bloom,
so the sight of his body, wreathed in auspicious signs,

captivates beings' hearts, the moment they see it.
May the lotus foot of my Savior, Lord Maitreya
grace the crown of my head in all my lives!

Devil-beater, free of all fear of life,
matchless hero, best teacher of the three realms,
always watching over beings fallen into dangers,
I worship your feet, O Leader!

With unrestricted access to the totality of facts,
your power of knowledge conquers the devil army horror,
whose thunderbolt weapons fall before you like fresh flowers,
you are dazzling with the glory of the ten powers!

You scorch the haughty brains of elephant-rivals,
sounding great roars of eloquence amid their congress,
finishing off the foxes of the false philosophers,
possessed of all four fearlessnesses,
you are the human lion!

You turn the supreme wheel of Dharma,
Unturnable even by the proud World-Creator, Passion Lord,
which neither wanderers nor priests can manifest—
you are the savior who loves the living beings!

Not even the word "error" affects your body and speech,
unfailing in memory, always focused in equality,
free of discriminations as well as thoughtless trances,
your activities are always absolutely pure!

You are completely beyond any occasion for failure
of the will, of energy, or of your memory,
of meditative concentration, wisdom, or liberation.
Therefore your realization is unexcelled!

Your wisdom unblocked and unattached in all three times,
your physical, verbal, and mental deeds are pure.
Accomplishing beings' aims to the end of the cycle,
you are involved joyfully with that responsibility.

Having perfected the mass of magnificent virtues
and conquered susceptibility to the slightest faults,
please consider for a moment the lamentable plight
of me who is the object of your compassion!

Though I have this life of leisure and opportunity
capable of liberation from the great ocean of suffering,
I am defiled by the faults of carelessness, sloth,
stupor, frivolity, and desire for gain and fame.

I waste this good body, using it for meaningless pursuits,
when it can easily achieve the supremely meaningful.
I inhabit this human flesh with the attitude of a beast,
pray look upon me with your great compassion!

Though I have won the crucial leisure so hard to find,
though I see the powerful Lord of Death whom no power can
    stop,
sending forth his messengers who cannot be escaped,
and am already seized by old age and sickness—
we beings do not remember the time of death, so uncertain,
nor that all is lost when death finally arrives,
and spend the days and months and years in vain pursuits—
it is time to have mercy on us deluded ones!

What need is there to mention the exaltation of
    transcendence?
We have no real ambition to reach even merely a high estate,
praised by the Muni as the basis of the spiritual path.
Can you really be indifferent to our plight?

Though we may have won the body fortunate with high estate,
if we do not find the unmistaken path of goodness,
with the wisdom that precisely investigates the teachings,
once again we will fall into the ocean of cyclic life.
So long enveloped by the huge dark fog of delusion,
obscuring our right discernment of the ground of ethical
    choice,
please bestow upon us the lamp of wisdom!

The rain of weapons falls upon the body,
licked by flames on the ground of molten iron,
and Yama's minions impale it on a stake,
and ladle gobs of molten brass upon the tongue.
Frozen in caves of ice in surrounding icy peaks
lashed by blizzards driven by fierce winds,
some are covered with blisters, some wounded,
others torn into many pieces.[142]

Faces covered with hair, with mouths parched,
they see a river and run to drink,
creatures prevent them, blocking them with swords and spears,
and the water seems to turn to blood and pus.
Mouths like a needle's eye, throat choked off by goiters,
even finding food and drink they cannot enjoy it.
Whatever they do eat or drink burns internally,
they live on excrement and urine, or eat their own flesh.[143]

Enveloped in the great darkness of delusion,
minds incapable of discerning right and wrong.
One killing another, controlled by gods and humans,
they suffer the misery of beating and drudgery.[144]

All peace of mind overcome by the burning fire
of their consuming jealousy of the glory of the gods,
bodies slashed and lost from the fighting,
deceived by trickery, with no fortune to see the truth.[145]

Not to mention the experience, mere hearing about these
    realms
produces terror in the heart, one shudders in general
at the fall into the great abysses
of the hells, ghosts, beasts, and titans,
having accumulated from the beginningless, and still doing so,
the unbearable evil action condemned by holy persons,
I quail in the face of this great abyss—
It is time to save me from the horror of bad migrations!

Even in the human abodes, with the high estate
of power and property, there is the worry of loss,

and the ruin of parting from excellence of fortune,
and the seeking only after the pleasures of desire.
Wanting happiness, one uses means to get it,
but afterward one will find great suffering,
so much more, from the many forms
of physical pain and mental anxiety.

Even the gods, who sport in the glory of heaven,
with beautiful bodies, adorned with jeweled ornaments,
in fine mansions surrounded by pleasure gardens,
savoring long the pleasures of desire,
finally are gripped by the signs of unwanted death.
Then they see they will unwillingly be parted
from the lovely goddesses who captivate their hearts,
from the delightful pleasure gardens,
from the nectar food, fine dress, ornaments of beauty,
and the other youthful gods, so soon!
Then they burn with fiery tongues of sorrow,
generated by the mental anguish so much more intense
than all the physical pleasures of that place.
Thus terminates the fruit gained by their striving
in actions of goodness for many lives,
and their carelessness, cause of bad states, affects them finally,
and once again they fall into the hellish realms.

Even those who have gained the form and formless heavens,
long abiding in pure bliss by power of samādhi,
without notions longing for desire, without malice,
beyond sleep and deeds of mental anguish,
free of suffering from physical and mental harm,
are not liberated from the bond of cosmic suffering,
and when the impulse of the prior samādhi ends,
again they fall down and continue their migrations.

Thus even the lords of life, gods and humans, are caught
in the ocean of existence by suffering's currents,
of birth and death and sickness and old age.
So surely it is wrong to love the mundane happiness!
So please save me from the current of existence,
I whose eye of wisdom life obscures,

mistaking suffering for happiness,
confused by perverse and foolish notions!
Stuck in the mud of desire, strayed from the path of liberation,
lost in the gloom of nescience, without the eye of wisdom,
caught in the trap of fabrications, chained in the prison of
    samsara,
tormented by evolution, I am in need of your compassion!

To stop at the cliff of the terrible samsara,
one must surely reach the stage of skill
depending on no other, by discerning rightly
the definitive and the interpretable among the boundless
    teachings,
by the power of the pure reason of correct analysis,

depending on extensive and impeccable learning—
no need to mention the subtle intention of the Victor!
But my intellectual vision becomes not very clear
even about the crude points of involvement and cessation,
and still this enemy of delusion obscures my heart
and I have no chance for liberation!

Consider this situation, clear the darkness from my heart!
Awaken my instincts left from constant practice
in the ocean of learning over many lives
of the sciences taught by the Victors and their heirs!
You, the sole eye revealing the good path to beings!

I, wretched and without protector,
abandoned by the holy ones of old,
like a guest arrived from distant regions,
it's time you cared for me with your great kindness!

You, Maitreya, who free all beings with your love,
are the refuge served with devotion again and again!
Swiftly, swiftly come and be my spiritual friend
on the Universal Vehicle in all my lives!

Before you, who constantly look out
for all beings with your great love,

if they remember your excellence with mind of faith,
daily you will come to them!

Yet even though one wishes to frequent lonely places
to enjoy the taste of solitude in isolation,
it is physically impossible to go.
Thus, you, to please the holiest of fields of merit,
with pure, high resolve filled the realms of space
with jewels, gold nuggets, and heavenly silks,
with the three robes, monk's staffs, and ascetic's bowls,
recommended by the Sage to the religious seekers,
and also emanated an excellent array of exquisite offerings
from your samādhi and your vows,
and offered them all to the Lord of Humans,
with your mind detached and free of expectations.

By the mass of pure virtue coming from that,
may I become the refuge of all beings
who have wandered so long in existence,
devoid of joy, tormented by the million pains!
May all beings who are out of contact
with the holy exaltation of the World-Leader,
take lives as monks with the pure spiritual life,
and awaken their Universal Vehicle spiritual gene!

May they obtain unwavering honesty and tolerance,
dauntless heroism and intense powerful faith,
devotion and the effort of constant practice,
and the consummate wisdom of discernment!

May the sugatas be pleased by the ceasing of doubts
through sustained practice in the ocean of wide learning,
depending on the spiritual friends, supremely skillful teachers,
kindly leading others with the art from their own insight,
having discovered the Victor's intention by the power of pure
reason,
and by putting into practice the import of their understanding!

Not transgressing the regulations of the Muni,
devoted to the Victor's heir, the spiritual friend,

extremely sharp of mind, free of faults of wrong practice,
may you have such a retinue of perfect purity!

Disturbed by the mind of dark tendencies,
obstructed in enjoying the feast of meritorious deeds,
may I never encounter even for an instant,
such an evil friend, a relative of devils!

When I train myself, with proper devotion to Śhākyamuni,
may there not even be the name of hindrance,
blocking the fulfillment of the energetic deeds,
the demonic action that follows the unlucky ones!

Thus-endowed holy and delightful persons,
may they achieve without any obstruction
all the favorable circumstances of the deeds of enlightenment,
praised by the Leader as the ornament of religious persons!

During my enlightenment deeds, may I establish
all realms of disciples in the renunciation
bound by the pure precepts, and grant them with just a thought
all the furnishings appropriate to them!

From now on throughout all my lives,
whatever I do with body, speech, and mind,
may it all become the cause of benefit
to all beings on all occasions!

Like a mother when her beloved son dies,
through the love always breaking my heart,
for all beings tormented by all sufferings,
may I give away all my wealth!

When I purify all taints of the stage of deeds in faith,
may I become like Meru amid the golden mountains,
among the common individual bodhisattvas
of the past, present, and future;
and becoming exalted through all the qualities
of the eyes, the superknowings, and great learning,
may I attain the eloquence not dependent on others!

Training in the stages of the holy bodhisattvas,
may I become like the eagle among the birds,
among all the universal beings of three times,
the great heroes abiding on the stages,
and penetrating with impeccable intuition without block,
all the points of knowables extremely vast
hard to fathom by other bodhisattvas,
may I become a treasury of energetic deeds!

When I gain the fruit of such practice,
may I perfect through practice of liberative art,
the very same sum of whatever are the body,
field and retinue, deeds, life span, and vows
of all the victors of the three times!
And this world that I contemplate from afar,
may I liberate in a single instant
by the falling of the great rain
of the nectar of the holy Dharma.

This "Brahmā's Diadem," Praise of the Savior Maitreya, the Victor, sole refuge for the whole world and the gods, was written by the learned Easterner Losang Drakpa Pal at the Retreat House Empty Mountain Sunrise at Lhodrak.

13   Prayer for Rebirth in Sukhāvati

bDe ba can gyi zhing du skye ba 'dzin pa'i smon lam (bDe smon)

BY JÉ TSONGKHAPA (WRITTEN IN 1395)

Whose outstanding deeds give endless glory to beings,
whose mere remembrance banishes the terror of the Lord of
   Death,
who considers every living being as his child with constant
   love.
I salute Amitāyus, Boundless Life, the Teacher of Gods and
   Humans!

Out of love, I will articulate as best I can
this prayer for rebirth in the Sukhāvati heaven
supreme realm highly, excellently praised
numerous times by the Lord of Sages.

The state of good and evil obscured by the fog of nescience,
life of ascendance deprived by the weapon of hatred,
bound in the prison of samsara by chains of lust and craving,
swept into the ocean of existence by the rivers of evolution,
tossed by the many billows of miseries of sickness and decay,
crushed by the burdens of unwanted sufferings,

mangled in the jaws of the unbearable monsters of the Lord of
   Death,
this is my cry of torment, I who am unprotected.
If I reverently invoke the Lord as witness to my prayer,
Amitābha, Boundless Light, Leader, sole friend of the destitute,
and the bodhisattvas, Avalokiteśhvara
and Mahāthamaprāpta, with their retinues,
who have never failed the promise of their conceiving the
   supreme spirit,
for our sake throughout limitless eons,
like the king of birds swooping through the sky,
may they come here by their love and their miraculous power!

Depending on the power of the combined focusing of the oceans of the two
stores gathered by myself and others in past, present, and future, as I approach
the time of death, may I behold directly the leader Amitābha surrounded by
his retinue, such as those two powerful sons, and may I feel intense faith
directed to the Victor with his retinue!

May I be free of sufferings of torment and being cut off, and may I remember without forgetting my faith and its objects, and so at the moment after
death, relying on the miraculous advent of the eight bodhisattvas to show
me the proper path to go to Sukhāvati, may I be reborn on a jeweled lotus in
the Sukhāvati universe just as a person with acute faculties in the Universal
Vehicle lineage!

From the moment of rebirth there, may I attain retentions, samādhis, the
unconditional spirit of enlightenment, the inexhaustible eloquence, and
the limitless store of such excellences, and pleasing the unexcelled teacher
Amitābha and the other buddhas and bodhisattvas of the ten directions, may
I truly be favored with the holy teachings of the Mahāyāna!

May I understand their import correctly, and then in each instant going without hindrance by magic power to the superlative buddha-universes, may I
completely fulfill all the energetic deeds of the bodhisattvas![146]

Then even though being born in a pure universe, still, motivated by the most
intense love, may I mainly proceed to the impure universes by means of
unhindered magical powers, and depending on teaching living beings the

Dharma according to their special lots, may I be able to establish them on the pure path praised by the Victor!

And by quickly accomplishing those miraculous deeds, may I easily attain the exaltation of buddhahood for the sake of the infinite beings!

> When the creative energy of life is released,
> may I behold clearly before my eyes,
> Amitābha surrounded by his oceanic hosts,
> and may my being be filled with faith and compassion!

> From the moment when the visions of the between[147] arise,
> may the eight bodhisattvas show the unerring path,
> and, being born in Sukhāvati, thence by emanations,
> may I lead all beings of the impure worlds!

And in all lives before attaining such supreme exaltation, may I attain only that embodiment fit to practice the perfect learning, thinking, and meditating on the verbal and realizational teachings of the Victor!

May such embodiments not lack the ornaments of the seven excellences of ascendant status! And in all those situations, may I attain the memory of lives that remembers accurately all former lives!

And in all those lives, may I experience the hollowness in all existences and be motivated by thoughts captivated by the excellence of liberation, and may I renounce the world in the religious discipline well taught by the Lord!

Having renounced, may I discover the great spirit of enlightenment by ultimately accomplishing the deeds of morality, untainted by even the smallest transgressions, and may I become like an imperturbable monk!

Further, in all those lives, understanding the processes of defilement and purification accurately, may I attain the perfect retentions that retain without forgetting all the words and meanings of the teachings, the factors of perfection!

May I attain the unimpeded pure eloquence that teaches others what I have understood myself! Further, in all those lives may I never lack attainment of the doors of samādhis such as the "Hero's March," the eyes such as the physical eye, and the superknowings such as the knowing of feats of magic!

May I attain the clear wisdom that can distinguish without confusion precisely the subtlest of the subtle facets of defilement and purification!

May I quickly attain the wisdom that can completely cease at the moment of arisal all nonunderstanding, misunderstanding, and doubting considerations!

May I attain the profound wisdom that mysteriously penetrates the words and meanings of the sutras whose measure cannot be taken by any other!

In short, may I become like the holy Mañjughoṣha who consummates all the deeds of the bodhisattvas through his wisdom of skill in liberative art, which discerns the words and meanings of the teachings, a wisdom free of all the faults of pretended wisdom!

Thus, having easily found the deep, swift, clear, and great wisdom, may I attain transcendent skill in explanation, debate, and composition concerning all the Victor's teachings, which are, respectively, the factors of sustaining the fortunate, chastising the false philosophers, and gladdening the wise!

Further, in all lives stopping all attitudes that hold my own purposes most important and all feelings of laziness and discouragement about the energetic deeds of the bodhisattvas, while reaching the ultimate of the supreme powerful heart that undertakes the purposes of others, may I become like the noble Avalokiteshvara, who consummates all bodhisattva deeds through the spirit of enlightenment, which becomes skill in liberative art!

Further, may I reach the ultimate in the bodhisattva deeds by competent skill in liberative art in conquering all demons, fundamentalists, and antagonists, while I am engaged in the purposes of myself and others, becoming like the Holy Lord of Secrets, Vajrapāṇī!

In all my lives, may I find the great enlightenment through the massive effort that never deviates an instant from the moment of the spiritual conception to the perfection of the bodhisattva deeds, whose energy abandons all laziness, and may I become like the incomparable King of the Śhakyas!

May I become in all my lives like the Buddha medicine-king, Bhaiṣhajya Guru, able to heal all pains of body, speech, and mind, just by having his name pronounced, by conquering all ills of mind and body that obstruct the achievement of enlightenment!

May I become in all my lives like the victor Amitāyus, able to overcome all untimely deaths just by having His name pronounced, having reached the ultimate in voluntary control of the life span!

When an obstacle to life is approaching, may I behold my refuge Amitāyus' manifestation of the vision of his body that conforms to the *Discipline* by means of his four activities, and may all such obstacles be eradicated the moment I see that body!

As for that manifestation of the vision of his body according to the *Discipline*, may I recognize it as the savior Amitāyus and generate a firm and nonartificial faith, and by the power of that, may I never fail to have the victor Amitāyus work openly as my spiritual friend in all my lives!

Furthermore, may the full-fledged spiritual friends of the Universal Vehicle, the root of all mundane and transcendent virtues, be pleased with me and look after me throughout all of my lives!

While he looks after me, may I attain unbreakable faith in that spiritual friend and may I only please him through all doors of activity! May I not bring about even an instant of his displeasure!

May I be not incompletely instructed by all the advice and instructions of the spiritual friend!

May I be able to understand correctly all the meanings of those teachings and to perfect them through practice!

May I not go under the influence of the nonspiritual and sinful friends even for an instant!

In all my lives, may I realize the faith of confidence in the effects of evolution, the mind of renunciation, the spirit of enlightenment, and the perfected realistic view, and may I enter uninterruptedly into the experience of effortlessness!

Whatever root of virtue I have made through my physical, verbal, and mental actions throughout all my lives, may it all serve as the cause of only the purposes of others and the pure enlightenment!

Written by the learned Easterner, Tsongkhapa Losang Drakpa Pal, at Dzingji Temple, in 1395.

14 Garland of Supremely Healing Nectars

A dialogue between Karmavajra, the Nyingma master Lhodrak Khenchen, and Bodhisattva Vajrapāṇi in the presence of Jé Tsongkhapa (at Lhodrak in 1396).

⚬

Reverence to Vajrapāṇi, Lord of the Esoteric!

"You who are the actuality of the mind of all the buddhas of past, present, and future, who are the great Vajradhāra, Lord of Secrets, who are blessed by buddhas as numerous as the Ganges River's sands, since Your memory[148] is like an elephant's, please teach the uttermost pinnacle of all vehicles!

Since You have the ornament of goodness, please teach the authentic view that abandons all abrasive and disagreeable views!

Since You are all-triumphant, please give a teaching that cuts wide open the net of doubts regarding view, contemplation, and action!

Since You are a mine of precious gems, please give a teaching that generates in our lives the inconceivable samādhi of integrated quiescence and insight!

Since You have the message of truth, please teach the instruction that pours down the great rain of Dharma that puts out the blazing fire of addictive thoughts!

Since You are ablaze with flames of wisdom, please teach the profound precept that burns the kindling of materialism and substantivism!

Since You are all beauty of form, please teach the instruction that fills the eyes with tears born of the vision of the precept that generates uncontaminated bliss!

Since You are the precious wish-granting gem, please give the extraordinary instruction that brings swift realization of the buddhas' truth body, concise in expression yet extensive in meaning, and so clear that the person of acute intelligence ceases her doubts and realizes the meaning, and the dumb cowherd can also get the words and understand the meaning—for the sake of this request of Matibhadraśhrī and for the sake of this prayer of mine, I, Karmavajra!"

When I had so petitioned, an extraordinary taste came from between my teeth and coiled around my tongue until I felt completely ecstatic! It must be thanks to You, O Guru!

Then without manifesting His body, His unconquerable voice spoke as follows: "Karmavajra! Bring these esoteric words of mine to the ear of Matibhadraśhrī![149]

"It is the intimation of Father Samantabhadra, the heart's message of Mother Samantabhadrī—this esoteric speech of mine, I Vajradhāra! To achieve the great supreme medicine, the uttermost pinnacle of all vehicles, seek out the clear light of the mind itself!"

I, Karmavajra, asked, "What is the actuality of the clear light?" He said, "Karmavajra! The clear light (is explained by) three: actuality, nature, and compassion."

Karmavajra asked, "When one meditates on the clear light, are there pitfalls? Or not?"

He said, "Your question is extremely good! If someone does not understand, there are pitfalls. I will explain four points: the pattern of error, the sign of error, its faults, and the effect of error. First, the pattern of mistaking the actuality: in general, what we call 'actuality' is the introspectively known reality that exists just like this, free from the adulteration of present artificial consciousness, originally clear emptiness wherein nothing is (intrinsically) established. When a person meditates on emptiness without focusing just on that, he falls into the error of cutting off enlightenment at emptiness by not freeing his mind from the holding of emptiness. The sign of error is that thoughts arise such as that 'above there is no Buddha, below there is no hell, the utter lack of establishment of anything is emptiness.' The fault of the error is that the mind that thinks 'everything is empty,' on the positive side, abandons all religious practice such as devotion, purification of perception, refuge-taking, spiritual conception, love, and compassion, and engages in the enterprises of this life, and on the negative side, all his practice is contaminated in the activities of sin. For one who thus engages in such perversion of the truth, there is no place to go but the Vajra Hell. The fruit of such evil activities is that, on the positive side, since such a one has distorted the truth of the virtuous orientation, he conceives the nihilistic view of the fundamentalists, and on the negative side, by distorting the orientation toward causality, he wanders in the ocean of suffering. Karmavajra! There are many who say they realize emptiness, but there are very few who actually realize the real condition of ultimate reality!

"Karmavajra! There are four (points) to the pitfalls concerning nature. First, the pattern of error concerning nature: in this clarity wherein body and intuition have the intrinsic brilliance of empty awareness, faces and arms have no categorical (intrinsic) status in the body, and colors and signs have no categorical (intrinsic) status in intuition. When a person settles on the indivisibility of clarity and emptiness as merely the clarity aspect that is the intrinsic brilliance of emptiness, and does not know the integration of the indivisibility of clarity and emptiness, it is the mistaking of awareness as illumination. The sign of this error is that all Dharma teachings go their separate ways. When you teach such a person the expression 'communion,' it does not fit into his mind. The fault of this error is that the mind that thinks 'universal illumination is substantial' does not aspire to engage in any Dharma practice and, being too extreme in verbal adherence to theories, it departs from the path of omniscience. There is no way this person will become liberated, since his illumination has become fixated. The effect of this error is that such a person becomes attached to a clear light that appears externally and therefore is reborn in the realm of form. Not knowing his inner awareness as clarity-emptiness, he migrates with his mind fixed in one orientation and has no occasion for liberation. Karmavajra! There are many who say they perceive the clear light, but there are few who cultivate illumination-emptiness as communion!

"Karmavajra! There are also four (points) in the pitfall concerning compassion. The pattern of error: this constructive thought that arises as variety, not arising as the intrinsic brilliance of clear empty awareness, no matter how it arises, never exceeds awareness-emptiness (indivisible). A person who does not understand that is said to mistake awareness as emptiness. The sign of error is that he engages exclusively in the physical, verbal, and mental activities of this life. The fault of this error is that his attitude that constructive thought does not arise in the truth-body causes everything that arises to be bound by the net of constructive thought; he becomes arrogant and his virtuous exertions are dissipated. Since his practice emphasizes bad instincts, he achieves only (the aims of) this life. Bound by the chains of dualistic suspicions and doubts, he himself binds himself. The effect of this error: not knowing the pitfalls of constructive thought, he becomes fixated in his instincts. Not knowing the evils of causality, he ends his life while still on the path of vacillation, and after death he gets lost again in the three realms. Karmavajra! There are many who say they have no constructive thoughts, but there are few who understand the criterion for the liberation (of whatever) arises."

I, Karmavajra, asked, "There is no point in not avoiding those three pitfalls; how are those three pitfalls avoided'?"

The Lord of Secrets said, "Karmavajra! This emptiness, the actuality of awareness, is not contrived by anyone, has no cause, no condition, but has been there from before the very beginning. It has no infraction or observance, it cannot be focused on or mistaken—it is buddhahood in the realm of primal perfection. Likewise, this natural clear light is effortlessly indivisible from beginningless emptiness. Its exercise is ceaseless compassion. Whatever arises lacks intrinsically real status, so you must understand all three as the great communion, buddhahood in indivisibility!"

I, Karmavajra, again asked, "What are the pitfalls in view, meditation, and action?"

The Lord of Secrets said, "Listen, Karmavajra! First, there are the five pitfalls with regard to view: the pitfall of view itself, the pitfall of place, the pitfall of companion, the pitfall of addiction, and the pitfall of partiality. First, the pitfall of view itself: the yogi in this esoteric tantric system prefers naked direct perception to the view generally taught, accepted as emptiness devoid of extremes. But there is no difference between those two if the ultimate is realized. If it is not realized, then the general view is a verbal view held in the analytic mind and does not hit on the actual import; it is an erroneous view. Not trusting in the view that is direct perception, but placing confidence in the verbal, analytic view, one thinks that there is nothing to aim at and that freedom from extremes is inactivity, and then one's actions are corrupted with regard to the principles of virtue and sin. Thinking that there is no good and bad evolution, virtue has no reward, sin brings no harm, everything is straightforward equality, one stays content with ordinariness. This is called the "view that dallies with evil," and is the root of all erroneous views. Matibhadrashrī must act in the profound integration of the view, which is intrinsic clarity of nondual direct perception with evolutionary cause and effect.

"The pitfall of place: in general, one who realizes the temporary view should go to a clear and solitary place such as a hermitage in order to enter the realm of the ultimate view. Even though one has a temporary view one needs the discipline of retreat to cultivate it. Bad places distort one's view. Tell Matibhadrashrī! The temporary view must be cultivated in retreat.

"The pitfall of friends: one who has the temporary view should associate with friends who agree with the Dharma and do not increase addictions. It is impossible not to be infected by bad actions if one associates with bad friends. They lead one into (the concerns of) this life and leave no room to cultivate the view. They are the root of the pitfall of increasing the addictions.

Karmavajra and Matibhadrashrī! If you do not want to fall into this error, cut off all attachment to unwanted friends and stay in solitude.

"Fourth, the pitfall of addictions: that person who has the temporary view, if he is not motivated to overcome the arisal of addictions, will be motivated into addictions by any external circumstance. Gathering evolutionary action even in an instant, he will engage in bad evolutionary action for a long time. Bad evolutionary action will be gathered through the influence of the five poisons with regard to all six kinds of apparent objects. The evolutionary effect of that will emerge both temporarily and ultimately, and when addictions are generated, though mindfulness of instantaneity may hold them, a loose awareness will let them go. Meditate on love and compassion for all living beings controlled by such addictions. Pray for blessings that they may be motivated into the path of overcoming those addictions. Especially, invoke the Guru from the depths of your heart. Purify the seed of addictions with mantras, and consider it essential to meditate on the archetype deity. Afterward, when you are naturally released in the view, make extensive dedicatory prayers. If you move on such a path, you will attain virtues as a result, both temporarily and ultimately. If you do not employ such a path, you will become stuck in the mud of addictions and your view will not become actuality. It is the great root of pitfalls. Karmavajra and Matibhadrashrī! If you do not want to fall into such error, employ the remedies for whatever addictions are generated. Put them into practice.

"Fifth, the pitfall of partiality: all persons who have the temporary view take refuge erroneously in sutras (by fastening on) the view given in the treatises of their own schools exclusively, and divide things into 'self' and 'other,' 'higher' and 'lower' factions, and 'good' and 'bad,' and they make Buddha's great extreme-free view into something to be grasped at and presumed on by (ordinary) persons. This is the root of errors. Karmavajra and Matibhadrashrī! If you do not want to fall into such error, you must realize the extreme-free view is a great vast emptiness!

"Now for the second point, there are five errors with regard to meditation: the error of actual meditation, the error of place, the error of friends, the error of faults, and the error of passions.

"First, the error of the actuality of meditation: although the guru nakedly identifies actuality, nature, and compassion, the disciple does not understand and cannot decide about actuality, nature, and compassion. He falls into error by not understanding the indivisibility of clarity and emptiness. Then, when he practices according to the method of his guru, he falls into the state of a human of the desire realm through his attachment to the merest particle of physical and mental bliss; he falls into the state of the deities of the pure abodes through his attachment to the mere absence of thoughts in his mind; he falls into the state of the deities of the form realm through his attachment to mere thoughtlessness in clarity; he falls into the state of desire-realm deities through his attachment to thoughtlessness in regard to bliss; and he falls into the state of the formless-realm deities through his attachment to thoughtlessness in regard to emptiness. These are the pitfalls in the three realms. If he continuously shuns sense objects, he falls into the realm of infinite space. If he ceases, without sensations, even in the feeling of falling into deep sleep he falls into the realm of absolute nothingness. If he ceases all clear illumination in his consciousness, he falls into the realm of infinite consciousness. If he generates continuously the mere shine of bliss in his clarity-awareness and utter nothingness in his perceptual awareness, he falls into the realm beyond consciousness and unconsciousness. These are called the "falling into one-sided quiescence." When one migrates via death from these, one migrates throughout the three realms and the six species. Karmavajra and Matibhadrashrī! If you do not know how to eliminate the errors of meditation, (meditation) is unnecessary, since you will just return to migration when the realms of dumb meditation are lost.

"Furthermore, if you accept body and mind as (really being) the way they are experienced by the alienated individual, you fall into the error of the ordinariness of your own being. If you adhere one-sidedly either to being or nothing, you fall into the spiritualism or the nihilism of the fundamentalists. If you accept the repudiation of all objects except for the mind, you fall into the state of the disciples and self-enlightened sages. If you accept appearance as mind, you fall into the error of the Idealists. If you accept animate and inanimate things as divine, you fall into the error of the Tantrics. What is the use of meditation when you cannot avoid the extremes of errors?"

I then asked for some method to avoid these pitfalls.

The Lord of Secrets said, "If you want to avoid these pitfalls, then, like Matibhadrashrī, first broaden yourself by learning, then in the middle concentrate (the teachings) into the essentials by means of the personal instructions identifying (realities), and finally, at the time of practice, do not fall into the above errors, and, in spite of the fact that longing and attachment arise in meditation, meditate like a rabbit lying in an eagle's nest or like an archer (waiting for his prey). And you will not fall into any pitfalls if you relax with regard to whatever appearance arises in your experience, not negating or establishing any infraction or observance or doubts or worries about whatever arises, and if you do not cling to any of it.

"Second, to show the pitfall of place and friends: the person who is meditating should meditate in a solitary and suitable place. If he stays in a crowded monastery or a place that arouses the passions, he will fall into error by the force of defilements, possessions, attachment, and aversion. If he associates with bad friends, his meditative growth and enthusiasm will be disturbed, and he is buying his own suffering. Karmavajra and Matibhadrashrī! If you practice a pure teaching, it is urgent that you use forceful means to abandon the negative influence of bad friends and bad places.

"Third, to show the pitfalls of meditation—when you cultivate your meditation, there are three (faults): depression, excitement, and distraction. There are (six) kinds of depression: because of place, because of friends, because of time, because of food, because of posture, and because of meditation. First, depression on account of place: if one stays in a forest in a low or sunken place, or in a country where solitude is disturbed or where defilements are prevalent, one's consciousness will grow stupefied, one's subtle drop becomes unclear, one's awareness dull, sleep too long, body too heavy. One should perform ablutions and confessions and go to a high and clear place and meditate in an open place or let the wind blow in the window. Contemplate snowy peaks and meditate naked, and this (type of depression) will be dispelled.

"Second, depression on account of friends arises by staying with defiled persons. Make purifications and ablutions, and this will be dispelled by protecting yourself from people who have broken their commitments and are full of defilements. Third, seasonal depressions, which come in spring and summer when you feel oppressed and depressed, are dispelled when you meditate in high places, as in the snowy mountains. Fourth, depressions caused by food and clothing come from using the defiled food and clothing of people and are dispelled by avoiding such food and clothing. Fifth, depressions caused by posture occur for beginners from meditating while walking, sitting, lying down, and so on, and are dispelled by meditating using the three postures or the vajra posture, bringing intensity to the awareness and brightness to the faculties by sitting erect and alert. Sixth, depression caused by meditation: when one meditates, by meditating with one's consciousness (focused) in the lower body, one becomes sunken down in one's physical being. That is depression, and it is dispelled by carrying one's senses, imagined as having the clarity of a lamp, through the sky, strengthening the awareness by the intense brilliance of mind itself. Karmavajra! As for the dispelling of obstacles of meditation, it is not accomplished by anyone without strong energy.

"As for the pitfall of passions, there are many thieving enemies of one who practices meditation. Generated by the root five poisons, 84,000 passions arise, which leave no room for meditation and lead one into cyclic life. One should be undistracted concerning them by imagining one is like a mother fearing the loss of her only son; one should abandon them as if they were a snake suddenly appearing in one's lap. One should hold them with mindfulness that is vigilance, practicing as in the path application (mentioned above) in the context of the view. Otherwise, in an instant, bad evolutionary action is accumulated. If you do not want to fall into such error, you should exert yourself in careful choice of action, never apart from the watchman of alertness. Again, until view and meditation are stable, practice alone like a wounded deer. Especially, it is of the utmost importance to flee from the passions, seeing them like poisonous snakes.

"There are two (points) to explain the faults of excitement: excitement on account of place and excitement on account of conditions. Excitement on account of place: when one meditates in a high and clear place, one's awareness becomes clear, one's consciousness will not stay still, and constructive thoughts become excited and spread out everywhere. If one lets them loose to spread as they will, they become influenced by passions, so awareness should be settled in between tightness and looseness. If you cannot overcome it, subdue it by the gaze of the disciples. Sometimes it can be subdued by aiming one's consciousness toward one's sitting mat. In the evening, lie down placing the mind within a black drop within an intestine-like vein in the center of the soles of the feet. When the vapor of thoughts emerges, identify it and (seal it) with PHAT. Hold the breath, and afterward let it go in relaxation. Or else it is dispelled by leaving thought to run its natural course, leaving it to proceed on its familiar path.

"Second, excitement on account of conditions: thought picks up on any sort of external circumstance and spreads the mind excitedly in the direction of the passions. Generate a will, thinking, "What's the use, it is unnecessary," and practice with love, compassion, aversion, technique, wisdom, respect, and devotion. Thereby compel oneself along the path motivation (mentioned above) in the context of the view.

"Third, there are two points in the fault of distraction: distraction through misunderstanding and distraction on account of circumstances. First, distraction from failure to understand: not knowing how to delimit the session of meditation, as much as one meditates there is no impact. Wrong views are generated toward the guru and the instructions. Not distinguishing between realization and (superficial) understanding, one's meditation becomes dumb. For that, one should invoke the guru, generate certainty about the instructions, often delimit the sessions of meditation, meditate powerfully without involvement in other affairs, and meditate by cutting off fabrications at the times of clarity. Then distraction is cut off and one's experience will increase from culmination to culmination. Second, distraction due to circumstances: here one becomes distracted by external circumstances, becoming involved in the six kinds of objects mixed with the five poisons, and one's vacillations cannot be contained by mindfulness. As a remedy for that, if one applies it suddenly, one should cut off as a whole the perception of appearances, realizing them as illusory. Karmavajra! If you want to eliminate those pitfalls, whack the pig on the snout with a club!"

Again I, Karmavajra, asked the Lord of Secrets of Secrets, "Do not the tantras harness the passions to the path?"

The Lord of Secrets said, "Of course they harness passions to the path. But none but the peacock can make a diet of poison. That person who is able to harness passions to the path, without abandoning them, is more rare than the uḍumvara flower. Even the keenest person experiences passions as friends, but in the end they will become poison, so it is important one abandons them. If, however, one first enters the realm of their abandonment as much as possible, then all passions and objects of desire arise as illusions, and lust and attachment for them do not arise. If some emerge, it is not necessary to stop them, they cause no harm. If they do not emerge, the mind to achieve them does not arise, there is no wishing. Just that is the criterion for their becoming motivations of the path. If one harnesses passions to the path before getting rid of intense attachments, it is like a fly flying around honey and becoming stuck in it. Karmavajra and Matibhadraśhrī! That is how you should take the measure of the stages and paths!

"Third, there are two pitfalls on the path of action, the pitfall of action at the wrong time and the pitfall of action in general. First, the pitfall of action at the wrong time: bee-like action precedes learning, thinking, and meditation; it is the action of a beginner and goes wrong when engaged in during the time properly spent under discipline. Deer-like action is action at the time of practice and goes wrong when engaged in at the time of discipline as one's samādhi comes under other influences. Dumb-like action is action when practice gets down to essentials and, if engaged in at the bee-like time, goes wrong when the verbal meanings are not discerned. Actions like a dove entering its nest are actions at the time one's inner experience is generated, and become obstacles to samādhi, and go wrong when there is no intensity. Madman actions are actions demonstrating one's experience, and when engaged in at the time of partial experience, being generated, go wrong because the ultimate aim is not discovered. Lion-like actions are actions when the view has become experiential and go wrong if engaged in at a time (more suited) for (further) practice, because they do not occur on the basis of reality but go wrong by being diverted through extraneous appearances. Dog-pig-like actions are actions at the time of initiation, and if engaged in at the wrong time go wrong because of the interference of one's ḍāka. If your actions do not go wrong, as one's inner perceptions arise as reality, external appearances are transformed into inconceivability and one can err in regard to the esoteric. One can achieve any kind of miraculous feat, since one can master any kind of appearance that arises. To eliminate the above types of actions, you should understand the pitfalls of action, (or else) the effect will not come forth. Karmavajra and Matibhadrashrī! You should act in accordance with the treatises on the general Dharma!

"Second, the pitfalls of action in the context of the Dharma in general: although you may be conscious about incidental acts, if they do not accord with the Dharma they do not contribute to the path of Buddha and are called 'artificial,' being erroneous actions. Karmavajra! If you do not want to err at the time of actions, you should do whatever action in such a way that it contributes to the path of enlightenment!

"Third, there are two types of pitfalls in regard to the final fruit: a temporary one and a final one. First, the temporary pitfall: if you hold the ordinary fruit of the practice of the profound instructions as supreme, your pride and arrogance are generated, and that is the error that impedes the ultimate fruit. Although you have achieved a fruit, if you do not terminate doubts, it is to mistake the fruit for a cause. Karmavajra and Matibhadrashrī! You should recognize that the cause of doubts is baseless!"

Again I, Karmavajra, asked, "If this pith teaching about awareness is intuitively realized, is the conception of the loving spirit of enlightenment necessary still? Or not?"

The Secret Lord said, "The tantras of the Mahāyāna are very much distinguished by the conception of the loving spirit of enlightenment. Still, if you do not at all remember four times the evils of the life cycle of cause and effect, such as death and impermanence, everything naturally becomes a concern of this life (only). If you do not meditate on love and compassion toward all living beings at all times, although you may nominally acclaim the Universal Vehicle, you have already fallen into the error of the disciples and self-enlightened sages. If you do not understand the moment-by-moment crisis of ethical choice concerning the subtlest aspect of cause and effect, various sins will accrue, even though your realization may be advanced. Karmavajra! If you want to live up to the Dharma honestly, you must always relate those above (spiritual conceptions) to your realization!"

Again I, Karmavajra, asked, "What is the greatest obstacle to the practice of the path?"

The Lord of Secrets said, "When you first enter the path, the obstacle is whatever circumstance leads your mind in the wrong way. Especially, for a man, women are most demonic. For a woman, men are the most demonic. For both, food and clothing are very demonic."

Again I asked, "Most tantrics nowadays say that the use of a consort has a tremendous impact. How is it in fact?"

The Lord of Secrets said, "The consort who can elicit the impact of the path is more rare than gold. Obsession with an inferior woman makes you into a sex-fiend! Purifying your perception (in regard to such a woman) makes your heart suffer. Your accumulated stores of merit and wisdom are offered to the sex-fiend. Your perverted lust is made into a divine quality. If you can, you will unite even with a dog. Faith is generated from your mouth but abandoned from your heart. Your avarice and envy become enormous. You accumulate no exalting evolutionary action and it drags you down like an iron hook. Any impact that increases the Dharma is not brought forth and you are led by the nose of lust and suffering. You practice with the hope of liberation through desire, but it only becomes a cause of increasing your passions. You hope it will be a basis of expanding your scope, but you get carried off in a bag of loss and defilement. A consort who keeps no spiritual commitment is a demoness!"

I asked, "Who then is the only one fit to consort with?"

The Lord of Secrets said, "Someone who has none of the above faults. Especially, one who is respectful of the Dharma, great-minded, persevering, great in faith and compassion, completely endowed with the six transcendences, obedient to the advice of the guru, devoted to the practitioner, who holds the tantric vows as dearly as the apple of her eye, with no urge for sex at times that are not times of power, and who observes the rules of purity. If you find such a (consort), she can serve as a friend of the path. As such (a consort) is extremely rare, and as such (a consort) has the purpose of developing a desirous person, it is the special fortune in Dharma of the keenest practitioner. Ordinary persons, since their passions go their own way, must abandon any (such ideas). If you enter the door of tantra yet do not keep your vows, better not have any hopes about buddhahood!"

Again I, Karmavajra, asked, "Since this kind of addiction concerning food, clothing, and body harms one's Dharma practice, please give men an instruction for getting the mind free of these three!"

The Lord of Secrets said, "Karmavajra! These bodies are (soon) destroyed. The length of life has been determined long ago. There is no certainty, whether you are old or young. No one gets out of death. I never saw anyone who failed to die because of their attachment to their body, no matter how beautiful. Let go of all cherishing of the body and discipline yourself in retreat. As for clothing, it is sufficient to wear even the poorest. As for food, grain and water is enough. Human beings are not capable of (much) practice of Dharma. Now if, motivated by the spirit of enlightenment of love and compassion, you accomplish some virtue, it has great power. But it is extremely rare.

"These teachings of my esoteric words are the heart's message of the ḍākinis. This esoteric speech of mine, I, Vajradhāra, have taught to Matibhadrashrī, who is blessed externally by the goddess Sarasvatī and internally by the goddess Guhyajñāneshvarī. And I seal this instruction for three years, that it not be taught to anyone else. The name of this instruction is 'The Dialogue Garland of Supremely Healing Nectars.' This medicine is as if unpalatable in the mouth of faith of the beginning disciple; even if it goes in their mouth of faith, it is as if vomited out. The application of this medicine has no superior in curing the plague of cyclic life. Having first requested this medicine, digest it without vomiting it out. If you can, you will become liberated from the fierce plague of cyclic life."

Again Karmavajra asked the Lord of Secrets, "What is the character of this Matibhadrashrī? Will he attain buddhahood? Which archetype deity looks after him? Where was he born in his former lives?"

The Lord of Secrets said, "This Losang Drakpa is a person who has extensively gathered the two stores. For seven precious lives he manifested the form of a paṇḍit and accomplished the aims of living beings. In his just previous life, he was born in Kashmir, near Shrīnagar, as the paṇḍit Matibhadrashrī, and he gathered an excellent circle of five hundred disciples. According to the perception of ordinary people, he was renowned as having attained the path of application. But even I, Vajrapāṇi, cannot measure his excellences. He is looked after by the special deities that are outer and inner goddesses, as well as by the saviors of the three types (i.e., Avalokiteshvara, Mañjushrī, and Vajrapāṇī)—these are his archetype deities. As to his buddhahood, I do not show that; it will be predicted by Avalokiteshvara and Mañjushrī. He is a person who benefits when contacted by seeing, hearing, or remembering. Other persons cannot take the measure of his character."

Again Karmavajra asked the Lord of Secrets, "How long will the teaching remain in the Land of Snows?"

(The Lord said), "From now on, the present is the time of sutras, and within that the time of sutras. Along with the discipline, it will remain for thirteen hundred years."

Again Karmavajra asked the Lord of Secrets, "What will be the state of suffering or happiness in this Tibet, the Land of Snows?"

(The Lord said), "The evil side will grow and defeat the side of good, and people from the frontiers will come into the center. On the strength of that, the frontier gods and demons will also come into the center. Then all the people in the center will go into foreign lands and the central deities and demons will also go into foreign lands. On the strength of that, the gods and demons will not be at peace with the other gods and demons. Plagues and famines will addict many people and living beings will have no happiness. You, the responsible preserving teachers, must be compassionate. Now is the time when war comes from outside and overcomes. The teaching can be restored by the scholars and monks even performing the merest portion of the necessary service. It is still possible to restore it if the techniques of reversing (the evil process) are employed. By the power of the evolutionary action of living beings, this cannot be delayed more than ten years. If the community becomes divisive, it is a sign that the worst will happen sooner. If one cultivates the samādhis of the Supreme Vehicle, such as nondiscrimination, the experience of transcendent insight will be generated, arising even more quickly if distinguished by the profound technique of compassion. If you get to the essentials in the body through the profound techniques of reciting mantras, realization will inevitably spring up in the mind, which means that the great compassion will arise through the presence of the inconceivable, supreme principle of profound art. If there is no learning, then only erroneous tantras will multiply, so learning is extremely important at the beginning stages.

"However nowadays, as for the method of spiritual conception through the blessing of contemporary meditators, of what worth is it beyond generating the merest fraction of the experience of transcendent insight? When they recite the mantras and spells of the profound tantras, they get only a few ordinary accomplishments. Rather than that, you should generate a deep adherence to the supreme accomplishment. Thus you must generate a purified perception toward everything. And, to generate an experience of perfect transcendent insight, you must rely on a guru who has himself generated a perfect transcendent insight. If you do not generate a perfect transcendent insight, you should study my esoteric teaching, for you will need to eliminate (innumerable) pitfalls. Since the view is impeded in its range of understanding for those who have no quiescence, the victors did not say that transcendent insight by itself is sufficient. It simply does not happen. The most excellent technique to elicit the experience of transcendent insight consists of the Six Yogas and the Great Perfection,[150] the extraordinary instruction of the tantra. While it is true that in general there are inconceivable various categories of causes of liberation and omniscience, they can be condensed into three types. Among my esoteric teachings, there are many. Whether or not Dharma practice serves as the path depends on the extent of the extraordinary spirit of enlightenment. The actuality of the spirit of enlightenment is great compassion. Its function is to accomplish the aims of living beings. It is extraordinary. The criterion for the perfect generation of the understanding and experience of those three (spirit, compassion, and activity) is whether all selfish motivations have ceased and exclusive thinking of altruistic concerns has been achieved."

I, Karmavajra, asked, "Is this Great Perfection the perfect view?"

The Lord of Secrets said, "The Great Perfection is an exalted view, and also the elucidation of the view by the masters Nāgārjuna and Chandrakīrti is without error. It is impossible to generate transcendent insight without relying on them. Nowadays, in U and Tsang, there are inconceivable numbers of people who are able to terminate reifications about the path of buddhahood through the power of unerring references and reasonings, and then to teach others the correct path. But there is no certainty that those who can teach this are in fact the ones called on to teach. If those who cannot teach this do the teaching, everyone, including the teacher, goes to the bad migrations! One has to feel compassion for them!"

Again Karmavajra asked the Lord of Secrets, "What will be the length of life of this Losang Drakpa? What kind of followers will he have? Going where will his accomplishments increase? In his future lives, where will he accomplish the aims of beings? Please tell me."

The Lord of Secrets said, "His accomplishment of the aims of beings will increase if he does not stay in one place. His life span can be no more than forty-five, although if he spends his time exclusively in practice, he can stay seventy-one years or maybe seventy-three. To accomplish the aims of beings, his life will become that long if he practices the meditations of White Tārā, Amitāyus, and Mañjushrī Raktayamāri, since he has a connection with Mañjushrī. If he does not do that, there is the danger that the evil side will interfere with him. The above practices are extremely precious. Of his followers there will be three who will be outstanding and many who will enter the path of accumulation. As for his path, even the holy persons cannot measure it from the predictions already made in his former lives. He will soon behold the faces of the above-mentioned archetype deities. There are three ways in which he will have these visions: the best is seeing them directly, the medium is seeing them mentally in meditation practice, and the worst is when he beholds them in dreams. Before seeing the faces of archetype deities, there will occur terrible miraculous events. Beings who are types of great demons will emerge, manifesting as archetype deities. Confronting them then, stabilize your samādhi, invite the intuition-hero and merge it into the (archetype deity). If it is a (real) archetype deity, an intense brilliance is generated. If it is a demon, it disappears. Although there will be inconceivable things such as this, that is all I can easily and understandably explain. I am not inspired to discuss how he will have visions of the archetype deities. If I do, the demons will carry it away!"

Again I asked, "This Losang Drakpa, where will he be reborn in the next life?"

(The Lord said), "He will be born in Tushita, in the presence of Maitreya, as the bodhisattva Mañjushrīgarbha. Then from Tushita, he will wish to accomplish the aims of beings in another human universe, and he will be reborn there in the form of a Dharmarāja, an enlightened king, from whom immeasurable benefit will emerge for the beings there. Third, in this universe's human realm, he will be reborn in the Licchavi community in eastern India as the paṇḍit Jñānashrī, where he will gather a following of two thousand, all of whom will attain the great accumulation path and the application path."

(Thus spoke Vajrapāṇī). Then Karmavajra said to Losang Drakpa, "The words spoken by the Lord of Secrets might not suit others' minds, so you should hide them. The greatness of your body and your virtues, though I could extol them at length, you would not have time to write down, so I have only partly transmitted them. And the questions as I asked them, and also what he said extensively on his own, as there is no more than this little bit, I have recorded."

Note: In general there are many forms of correct interpretation of the Great Adepts'[151] deeds and instructions. Likewise, among the revelations of this holy master, in the context of the view, there are three different systems of interpretation: one according to the Great Seal, one according to the Great Central Way, and one according to the Great Perfection. Each has a definite intention according to the (needs of) the disciples. Especially, this *Supremely Healing Nectar* is the best instruction given to master Tsongkhapa himself. Even the dākinis said, "*The Supremely Healing Nectar* is the supreme medicine." And Tsongkhapa himself said, "The secret speech of holy Vajrapāṇī, free of the faults of excess, omission, and error, that is the *Supremely Healing Nectar*." He often praised it in this way.[152]

PART 5

PRAISES AND AN INVOCATION

The anthology concludes with a number of poems praising and invoking Tsongkhapa, written by a number of different authors.

The first work, *Song of the Tricosmic Master*, was written by Khedrup Jé Rinpoche. In the early part of his life, Tsongkhapa was a bitter opponent of the eclectic innovations of Jé Rinpoche, but later became a chief tantric disciple and a major elucidator of Jé Rinpoche's, making his innovations even more widely accessible to and popular among Tibetans of the time. When Jé Rinpoche went to Tushita, he left his throne to Gyaltsap Jé, who in turn handed it on to the much younger Khedrup Jé.

The *Song Rapidly Invoking Blessings* is from a collection of thirty-seven songs found in the first volume of the *Collected Works* of the Seventh Dalai Lama. The First Dalai Lama was a direct disciple of Jé Tsongkhapa and attained enlightenment under his tutelage. As a result, all the Dalai Lamas wrote a number of works about Jé Rinpoche. This particular text is intended for recitation prior to meditation.

The *Praise of the Incomparable Tsongkhapa* is one of several poems about Jé Rinpoche written by the Eighth Karmapa, Mikyö Dorjé, an extremely comprehensive scholar as well as a great leader of the Karma Kagyü order.

These three poems are translated by Glenn H. Mullin and Losang N. Tsonawa, with the assistance of Geshé Ngawang Dhargé on the first and of Geshé Losang Tenpa of Ganden monastery on the second and third.

The fourth chapter, translated by myself, is a famous invocation of Tsongkhapa used for several centuries by those meditating on his teachings at the beginning of a session of practice to invoke his presence and blessings.

15   Song of the Tricosmic Master

dPal ldan sa gsum ma

BY KHEDRUP CHÖJÉ GELEK PAL SANGPO (1385–1438)

⚭

O, Jé Tsongkhapa, master of the three worlds,
who surpasses all others in compassion,
the eye through whom all beings
can receive ultimate vision,
peerless refuge of liberation seekers,
to you, a supreme and incomparable lama,
I offer my spiritual aspirations.

In the very presence of the Victorious One
you entered the ways of enlightenment.
Here in this Land of Snow Mountains
you were renowned as Losang Drakpa;
now in Tushita Pure Land you abide,
famed as Mañjuśrīgarbha, Wisdom Essence,
to you, mightiest of bodhisattvas,
I offer my spiritual aspirations.

By the force of ripening merits
you read the teachings and, without study,
understood texts even in the mystics' language.
To you of naturally perfect excellence
I offer my spiritual aspirations.

From the time your sun-like body
slipped radiantly from your mother's cloud,
you ever shunned the dancing lights
of the world and its vain fortunes;
to you I offer my spiritual aspirations.

From your very youth, you held no distaste
for the austerities of Buddhadharma,
but secured yourself in perfect discipline.
To you who for countless lifetimes knew
the power of familiarity with meditation,
I offer my spiritual aspirations.

Having unrelentingly examined in depth
the words and meanings of Buddha's teachings,
constantly and with spontaneity you practiced
the guidelines discovered therein.
To you, a treasury of vast knowledge,
I offer my spiritual aspirations.

Not satisfied with strings of empty words,
with subtle reason you fathomed that point
not perceived by millions of scholars;
to you who beheld reality itself
I offer my spiritual aspirations.

Were all logicians to analyze
your teachings a hundred times,
not even a fraction's fraction
of your words would prove wrong.
To you of flawless mind
I offer my spiritual aspirations.

Who but you have seen as they are
all the concepts contained
in the texts of the ancient masters?
To you in whom all teachings
arose as practical advice,[153]
I offer my spiritual aspirations.

When the dust clothing of the earth
is inscribed by your lotus feet,
which always rest on the crowns of sages,
that dust becomes an object
well worthy of worship; to you
I offer my spiritual aspirations.

Although a fully omniscient one
were to challenge your ethical temper,
not a hint of a flaw
could ever be discovered:
to you, a perfect renunciant,
I offer my spiritual aspirations.

Like an ocean of wish-fulfilling gems
is the immeasurable depth of your love,
beyond the measure even of clairvoyance.
To you, a gem mine of benevolence,
I offer my spiritual aspirations.

What burden of benefit to beings
is not carried by your mind so mighty,
for did you not reach the zenith
of deeds that send forth endless waves?
To you of miraculous compassion
I offer my spiritual aspirations.

If every breath that you exhale
acts only as medicine to beings,
why try to describe the effect
of your stores of merit and wisdom?
To you, friend of the three worlds,
I offer my spiritual aspirations.

Mañjushrī, the wisdom bodhisattva,
daily appeared manifestly to you
and rained ambrosial streams of teachings,
the synthesis of the minds of buddhas
of times past, the present and the future;
to you I offer my spiritual aspirations.

"In the lotus garden of the Muni's teachings
you are likened to a sun among Buddhas";
with these very words, Maitreya Buddha
praised you when in a vision he appeared;
to you I offer my spiritual aspirations.

Beholding the sublime forms of countless Buddhas,
you directly received the transforming powers
of Saraha, Luhipa, and the other Mahāsiddhas;
to you, a supreme and perfect being,
I offer my spiritual aspirations.

Having in a dream received the blessings
of Nāgārjuna and Āryadeva,
Buddhapālita and Chandrakīrti,
the real Dharma experience, profound emptiness,
arose within; to you who has abandoned
even the very instincts for confusion,
I offer my spiritual aspirations.

With subtle meditation, samādhi centered
on reality itself, clear like the sky,
you moved not for a moment postmeditation
from viewing mind as illusory;
to you I offer my spiritual aspirations.

Having mastered the oceans of tantras,
pinnacle of all Buddha's teachings,
you indeed are a perfect lama,
one with all-pervading Vajradhāra;
to you I offer my spiritual aspirations.

Master who practiced exactly as taught
the essential depths of tantra's two stages,[154]
the ultimate paths, as never before
revealed by any other in this land,
and then accomplished their whole purpose—
I offer you my spiritual aspirations.

Perfecting coarse and subtle deity yogas,
you eliminated the habitual thoughts

that conceive existence as profane.
To you whose mind never stirs away
from the blissful flow of mystic mandalas,
I offer my spiritual aspirations.

Coasting in the central channel on wind currents,
you perceived the quintessence of emptiness,
the clear light itself, great mahāmudrā,
experiencing the summit of great bliss;
to you, the one of vajra mind,
I offer my spiritual aspirations.

Due to the force of your infinite prayers,
countless disciples spontaneously were drawn
to the path that pleases all the buddhas;
to you, refuge of all the world,
I offer my spiritual aspirations.

In an era when nothing but the empty name
of "teaching" was held by teachers and students,
you brought to light the three higher trainings;[155]
to you, great bringer of the renaissance,
I offer my spiritual aspirations.

When you determined consciously to pass away,
hosts of ḍākas and ḍākinīs beyond imagination
made offerings that filled the heavens.
To you I offer my spiritual aspirations.

Mind focused on clear light of Dharmakaya,
your body turned into a luminous sphere,
in the between, the magic body yoga
fulfilled the blissful Saṃbhogakāya.
To you who gained supreme siddhi,
I offer my spiritual aspirations.

From this moment onward in all future lives,
may I sit before your lotus feet
and, hearing your eloquent teachings,
practice only as will give delight to you.
May I be blessed to abandon both

viewing this life as the only thing to crave
and yearning for happiness for myself alone.
And may I never abandon the bodhi mind,
the wish to attain buddhahood for all.[156]

With clear wisdom focusing on the subtle,
may I fathom the perfect words of Buddha
and ascend the path of knowledge.
Thus, may I arise to dispel the darkness
of the ignorance pervading the minds of beings.

May I have power to discover
the import of the many tantras
and to practice single-pointedly
the profound significance of their two stages,
unhindered by inner or outer obstacles.

In brief, may I receive your grace to understand
all the teachings of Buddha Śhākyamuni,
especially those of the peerless Vajrayāna,
just as do all the awakened beings.
Thus, may I bring light to the world.

By the virtue of this aspiration,
may I in all future lives never be
parted from you, a perfect lama,
and may I live the savor of the teachings
that arose from the depth of your experience.

Because of whatever good I have done or will do,
may you look upon me with pleasure,
and may I always unwaveringly practice
precisely in accord with your advice.

By the power of the mighty deeds
of Lama Jé Tsongkhapa, the Tantric Guru,
until enlightenment may I never fall
from the good path praised by all the buddhas.

The colophon: Written by Khedrup Chöjé Gelek Pal Zangpo, who learned a great deal by sitting for many years at the lotus feet of Jé Rinpoche.

16   A Song Rapidly Invoking Blessings

rGyal ba gnyis pa rje btsun tsong kha pa chen po la thugs rje bskul ba'i gsol 'debs byin rlabs myur 'jug

by Gyalwa Kalsang Gyatso, the Seventh
Dalai Lama (1708–1757)

⬍

Above, in actuality primal awareness
manifest as a radiant buddha mandala,
the pure land of Tushita, the joyous abode
blessed by buddhas past, present, and future.

Mountains of herbs blanketed in sweet aromas,
flowers blossoming morning, noon, and night,
a forest of trees with turquoise leaves:
reminders of the splendid body of Jé Rinpoche.

The murmur of a river swiftly flowing,
the stirring songs of birds,
the majestic sound of a Dharma teaching:
reminder of the gentle voice of Jé Rinpoche.

The blue sky freely hovering,
clear, white clouds scattered abstractly,

the young sun casting beams everywhere:
the wisdom, compassion, and power of Jé Rinpoche.

Body adorned with the marks of a buddha,
speech raining down vast and deep Dharma,
mind seeing all things in the sphere of clear light:
I recollect Jé Rinpoche, Losang Drakpa.

Fulfill your vow to benefit beings;
descend, grant protection and power.
To you I offer an ocean of all-good things.
Enjoy them within your great bliss.

On the mighty nomad mountain, quiet, easy,
a land made pure with goodness and strength,
stands your Ganden monastery,[157] prophesied by Buddha:
a monastery producing limitless awakened ones.

Your mind on bliss and void inseparable,
the flow of events appears as a rainbow.
One body sends endless clouds of emanations
to set this world ablaze with joy.

Your profound teachings bridging sutra and tantra
are jewels for those truly seeking liberation.
Even the words you used are perfect,
nakedly pointing the way for the ripe.

O Jé Lama, because of your infinite kindness
we can know all sutras and tantras as precepts,
see the entire path leading to perfection,
and correct all delusions and erring concepts.

O Master, merely hearing legends of your deeds
can place a person on the enlightening path;
with thoughts of your greatness, my heart trembling,
I fix my devoted mind on you.

Invisible father gone in great bliss,
listen to this plaintive song of this boy

still sinking down in cyclic life's quicksand,
this ill-fated son cut off from his refuge.

In terms of external appearances,
a monk is easily proud of his robes,
but if his thoughts fall only on the transient,
are his lusts not worse than a layman's?

The masses revel in dark actions
and by doing evil gain their ends.
The flashes of this degenerate age
explode in the bottom of my heart.

How glamorous and exciting to go
through the motions of practicing Dharma,
and to listen to the profound teachings;
but the mind, hard as wood, is slow to change.

The spirit, weak and uncontrolled,
staggers under the three psychic poisons,[158]
whenever an object appears to it,
a golden vessel filled with urine.

Precious humanity, the chance to be buddha;
but we create only misery with it
and throw away all hope of actually
benefiting either ourselves or others.
I, born so late, so very unfortunate,
pass my time amid evil and confusion.
Father Lama, look kindly on me;
hold me with iron hooks of compassion.

In this life, the between, and future lives,
pray be my guide, my refuge, forsake me not—
Omniscient One, stay with me always.
Care for all beings as a mother for her son.
Spiritual Father, to us who are children,
reveal clearly the mandala of your body,
magnificent with every mark of perfection.

Bestow on us the oral instructions
that render every experience meaningful.
Bless us to make our minds of one taste
with great bliss and inconceivable wisdom.

Life is impermanent like the setting sun,
wealth is like the dew on the morning grass,
praise is like the wind in a mountain pass,
a youthful body is an autumn flower.

Bless me to understand the shortcomings
of constant turns round the wheel of becoming,
and to dedicate the depths of my mind
on the path leading to ultimate knowledge.

Bestow on me transforming powers
to fill my mind with love and compassion,
to see all beings of samsara's six realms[159]
as mothers who have forever helped me.

Bestow on me transforming powers
quickly to realize the way things are,
to understand images viewed by the mind
as paintings created by the mind itself.

Help me win enlightenment this very life
through the yogic methods of tantra's two stages,
to see outer events as the sport of buddhas
and mind as exalted with bliss and void.

When to fight delusion, meditation's foe,
I retreat to a cave on a distant mountain,
a place to give birth to serenity and joy,
bless me to penetrate the innermost depth.

Grant me powers swiftly to annihilate
all inner and outer negative forces,
and power to cleanse the stains of having dwelt
far from the limits of Dharma's three bonds.[160]

O Mañjuśrī, who shows himself magically
in peaceful, ferocious, and protective forms,
may your auspicious deeds reach fruition,
and you stay a constant refuge for the world.

Bestow on me the powerful blessings
of your mysterious body, speech, and mind,
that my every physical, verbal, and mental
movement may benefit beings and the teaching.

May the thunder of sutras and tantras shake the earth,
may the sun of Tsongkhapa's "practice lineage" shine,
may all practitioners attain to power
and all sentient beings realize their wishes.

The colophon: In the year of the water dog (1742), Lama Gyalwa Kalsang Gyatso visited Ganden monastery. Inspired by the extraordinary vibration pervading the place and filled with marvel at the strength and kindness of omniscient Tsongkhapa, who had founded Ganden, Kalsang Gyatso was moved to write this song.

17 In Praise of the Incomparable Tsongkhapa

mNyam med Tsong kha pa'i bstod pa

BY GYALWA MIKYÖ DORJÉ, THE EIGHTH KARMAPA
(1507–1554)

⌘

At a time when nearly all in this Northern Land
were living in utter contradiction to Dharma,
without illusion, O Tsongkhapa, you polished the teachings—
hence I sing this praise to you of Ganden Mountain.[161]

When the teachings of the Sākya, Kagyü, Kadam,
and Nyingma orders in Tibet were in decline,
you, O Tsongkhapa, revived Buddha's teaching—
hence I sing this praise to you of Ganden Mountain.

Mañjushrī, wisdom bodhisattva, gave to you
special instructions on the thought of Nāgārjuna;
O Tsongkhapa, upholder of the Middle Way—
I sing this praise to you of Ganden Mountain.

"Mind and matter are not empty of their own natures
but are empty of truly existent mind and matter,"[162]
you, O Tsongkhapa, are Tibet's chief teacher of emptiness—
hence I sing this praise to you of Ganden Mountain.

In only a very few years you filled
this high land between China to India
with peerless holders of the saffron robes—
hence I sing this praise to you of Ganden Mountain.

Those who become your followers
and look to you and your teachings
are never again disappointed or forsaken—
hence I sing this praise to you of Ganden Mountain.

The trainees who walk in your footsteps
breath the fresh air of the Great Way;
they would die for the good of the world—
hence I sing this praise to you of Ganden Mountain.

Anyone who disparages your doctrine must face
the terrible wrath of the Dharma protectors;
O Tsongkhapa, who abides in truth's power—
I sing this praise to you of Ganden Mountain.

In person and in dreams you come to those
who but once recollect your image.
O Tsongkhapa, who watches with compassionate eyes—
I sing this praise to you of Ganden Mountain.

In order to civilize humans and spirits you spread
your teachings through Kham, Mongolia, and Turkestan;
O Tsongkhapa, you tamer of savages—
I sing this praise to you of Ganden Mountain.

For men coarse and far from the Way, you dispel
mental clouds, evil ways, and bad karma;
O Tsongkhapa, who bestows quick progress—
I sing this praise to you of Ganden Mountain.

Those who take heartfelt refuge in you,
even those with no hope for now or hereafter,
O Tsongkhapa, have their every wish fulfilled—
hence I sing this praise to you of Ganden Mountain.

Having exposed false teachings transgressing
the excellent ways well shown by Buddha,
you firmly established your bold teaching—
hence I sing this praise to you of Ganden Mountain.

Manifesting sublime austerity and discipline,
the form and fragrance of your life was incomparable;
O Tsongkhapa, self-controlled and pleasing to buddhas—
I sing this praise to you of Ganden Mountain.

By the strength of the sons of your lineage
and by my having faithfully offered this praise,
may the enlightened activity of Buddha Śhākyamuni
pervade the whole earth for ages to come.

The colophon: Once when Gyalwa Mikyö Dorjé was traveling through the Charida Pass, thoughts of the incomparable Tsongkhapa welled up within him. Overcome by profound faith, he was moved to compose the above poem.

18   Tushita's Hundred Gods

dGa' ldan lha brgya ma

An Invocation of Jé Tsongkhapa

From the heart of the savior of Tushita's hundred gods,
floating on fluffy white clouds, piled up like fresh curds,
here comes the Omniscient Lord of Dharma, Losang Drakpa!
Please come down to us, together with your sons!

In the sky before me, on a lion throne with lotus and moon
    seat,
sits the Holy Guru with his beautiful smiling face,
supreme field of merit for my mind of faith;
please stay one hundred eons to spread the teachings!

I bow to you so beneficial to see, hear, and remember,
your body of beauty, resplendent with the glory of fame,
your speech of eloquence, jewel ornament for the lucky ear,
your mind of pure genius that spans the whole range of
    knowledge!

Various delightful offerings of flowers, perfumes,
incenses, lights, and pure sweet waters, these actually presented,
and this ocean of offering-clouds created by my imagination,
I offer to you, O highest field of merit!

All the sins I have committed with body, speech, and mind,
accumulated through evolution from beginningless time,
and especially all transgressions of the three vows,
I confess each one with strong regret from depth of heart!

In this dark age, you worked for broad learning and attainment,
abandoning the eight mundane concerns to realize the great
    value
of leisure and opportunity; sincerely, O Lord Savior,
We congratulate you for all your prodigious deeds!

In the truth body's sky, you holy supreme guru,
build up the massive clouds of your wisdom and your love.
And please pour down on the earth of the deserving disciples
the great rains of the profound and magnificent Dharma!

Whatever virtue I may have gathered here,
may it long make shine the essence of the Buddha teaching,
make manifest whatever benefits the living beings,
and especially the teaching of holy Losang Drakpa!

Notes

1. The *Sukhavati Prayer* is included in part 4 below, along with a praise of Maitreya written a bit later from the same inspiration.
2. Part of the instructions given by Vajrapāṇī to Tsongkhapa through the Nyingma master Lhodrak Khenchen is included in the *Garland of Supremely Healing Nectars* in part 4 below, wherein the Khenchen is referred to by his Tantric name, Karmavajra, and Tsongkhapa by his name in Sanskrit, Matibhadrashri (one way to translate Losang Drakpa).
3. Geshé Potowa of the Kadampa lineage (1031–1105).
4. *Great Exposition of the Stages of the Teachings* refers to the *Bstan rim chen mo* by Dronlungpa Lodrö Jungné.
5. *Sustaining Buddha* is another name for the *Middle Way Commentary*.
6. This eulogy is included in part 3 below.
7. See the Insight segment of this work in part 3 below.
8. *The Four Commentaries Combined* refers to four related texts: Chandrakīrti's commentary called *Illuminating Lamp* (*Pradīpodyotana*, Toh 1785) and three commentaries on that work by Tsongkhapa—a general annotation, an abbreviated outline, and a resoution of difficult points. These four comprise the tradition for studying Guhyasamāja tantra at the two Geluk tantric colleges.
9. See part 5 below.
10. This direct form of address to Mañjushrī reflects Tsongkhapa's constant mystic conversational communication with the bodhisattva, while his use of the epithet "Wisdom Treasure" indicates his awe, making him hesitate to call his guru by his personal name. See *Song of the Mystic Experiences* in part 1.
11. The great paṇḍits of Buddhist India, Nāgārjuna (ca. 0–600 CE), Asaṅga (ca. 400 CE), Dignāga (ca. 6th century CE), Dharmakīrti (ca. 7th century CE), Āryadeva (ca. 1st century CE +), and Vasubandhu (ca. 400 CE), along with the two Vinaya masters Gunaprabha and Śīlaprabha.
12. All these works are found in the Kangyur collection. This being an anthology prepared for Dharma practitioners, the scholarly reader will please forgive our omission of precise references to the exact verses of the works cited by Tsongkhapa.

13. Various methods of interpretation used in elucidating the scientific treatises on tantra. The six parameters are interpretable meaning and definitive meaning, intentional explanation and nonintentional explanation, literal meaning, and symbolic meaning (Sanskrit, *neyārtha, nītārtha, sābhiprāyika, nirabhiprāyika, yathāruta,* and *ayathāruta*). The four interpretive procedures are literal meaning, general meaning, hidden meaning, and ultimate meaning interpretive procedures (*aksh_arārtha, samanyārtha* or *samastāṅgaṃ, garbhi,* and *kolikaṃ*).

14. Tib. *ji ltar* and *ji snyed.* The former term, lit. "like what," is synonymous with "ultimate truth," "emptiness," "thatness," "suchness," and so on. The latter, lit. "whatever findable," is synonymous with "conventional truth," and so on. The former is also the same as *gnas lugs,* "the way things are," and the latter with *snang lugs,* "the way things appear."

15. The vast teachings on the far-reaching activities of the conventional spirit of enlightenment (*bodhicitta*) and the profound teachings on the depths of emptiness, the ultimate spirit of enlightenment.

16. Vajrāsana, modern-day Bodh Gaya, Bihar, North India.

17. The perfect view; the understanding that everything is devoid of true existence or intrinsic truth-status.

18. Skt. *Prajñāpāramitāsūtra* (*Perfection of Wisdom Sūtras*) and *Guhyasamājatantra* (*Guhyasamāja Root Tantra*).

19. Many beings attain buddhahood, but only one thousand each eon manifest the twelve deeds of a universal teacher. Buddha Shākyamuni was the fourth this eon and Jé Tsongkhapa will be the eleventh.

20. The lineage gurus of emptiness meditation that Tsongkhapa received from Mañjushrī, who in turn received it from Shākyamuni. See Geshé Wangyal, *Door of Liberation,* 45–52.

21. Ibid., 52–54. The lineage gurus of enlightenment spirit meditation that Asaṅga received from Maitreya, who had received it from Shākyamuni.

22. The eighty-four Mahāsiddhas, Great Adepts. Tsongkhapa's school, later known as Geluk, synthesizes three Indian lineages: the wisdom lineage of Mañjushrī, Nāgārjuna, and so on; the art or method lineage of Maitreya, Asaṅga, and so on; and the practice lineage of the eighty-four Mahāsiddhas, such as Saraha, Tilopā, Naropā, Maitrīpā, and so on.

23. The terrific or fierce embodiment of the wisdom of emptiness. I avoid "wrathful," because however fierce the terrific deities may seem, they are not at all angry at anyone or anything (except perhaps anger itself).

24. *Bde ba can du skye ba'i smon lam* and *Mi pham mgon gyi yang dag don bstod.* See part 4 below.

25. Skt. *ārya.*

26. The Great Adept to whom Shākyamuni originally gave the Kālachakra Tantra teaching at Dhānyakaṭaka Stupa in South India. Suchandra was King of Shambhala at the time and immediately took the tantra back there up north. Thus the tantra did not appear in India until over one thousand years later.

27. The Great Prayer Festival of Lhasa, conceived and founded by Jé Tsongkhapa, continues to the present day. During the first fortnight of the lunar new year, more than twenty thousand monks would assemble to commemorate Shākyamuni's miracles at Shrāvastī. The tradition continues in the free Tibetan communities in India, though of course on a much smaller scale. Cf. *The Great Prayer*, Tangent Records, London.

28. Skt. *Mañjushrīgarbha*. Tib. *'Jam dpal snying po*.

29. *Saṃsāra*. Sometimes also "cyclic life," "cyclic existence."

30. *Nges 'byung*; *niryāṇa*.

31. *Las kyi 'bras bu*; *karmaphala*.

32. *Byang chub kyi sems*; *bodhicitta*.

33. *Rten 'brel, rten 'byung*; *pratītyasamutpāda*.

34. The perfect accomplishments are the realization of an enlightened motive of bodhicitta and a correct view of emptiness.

35. The three realms are the desire, material form, and immaterial formless realms, moving through which consciousness is preoccupied in turn with desirable sensory objects, meditative trances with a physical body, and meditative trances without any physical body, respectively. The desire realm is inhabited by hell creatures, hungry pretas, animals, humans, antigods and the first six classes of gods; the material form realm is inhabited by the next seventeen classes of "brahmabodied" gods; and the nonmaterial, formless "realm," or really "medium" (Skt. *āyātana*), is inhabited by four classes of gods who lack any material body.

36. The "Mother of the Buddhas" refers to the *Perfection of Wisdom Sūtras* (*Prajñāpāramitāsūtras*) delivered by Buddha on Vulture's Peak, and in which are begun the two Mahāyāna lineages of the teachings of the profound insight of emptiness and the vast action of bodhicitta.

37. *The Lamp on the Pathway to Enlightenment* (*Bodhipathapradīpa*) by Atisha is the forerunner of the *lamrim*, or "graded path," literature. In it the two lineages begun with the *Prajñāpāramitā Sūtras* are recombined.

38. Tsongkhapa refers here specifically to two of his forty-five spiritual teachers, namely, the Kagyü Lama Chökyop Sangpo, "most learned among the monks," and the Nyingma Lama Namkha Gyaltsen from Lhodrak, through whom he received and recombined the three strands of Atīsha's "Lam-rim" lineage.

39. There are two desirable aims, one for higher status with rebirth as a human or a god and one for the definite goodness of either liberation from suffering or full enlightenment as a buddha.

40. The nine kinds of beings are derived from the fact that beings may be reborn from any one to any other of the three realms, for example, from the desire into the desire, form, or formless realm, and so forth.

41. The power-granting king is an epithet of the wish-granting gem, a fabulous jewel that grants all worldly wishes.

42. Buddha's intended themes are renunciation, the enlightened motive of bodhicitta, and a correct view of emptiness.

43. The great mistake is to advance sectarian views; to discredit any of the Buddhist schools, vehicles, or texts; and to disclaim the validity of Buddha's teachings.

44. The initial-level motivation is to work for a better rebirth as a human, or a god, out of fear of a lower rebirth. The intermediate level is to work for liberation from cyclic existence, out of renunciation of your own suffering. The advanced level is to work for achieving the full enlightenment of a buddha in order to be able to liberate all others from their suffering. This highest level, then, is the bodhicitta motivation.

45. A yogi is someone who has joined himself or herself to actual paths, here specifically ones that lead to enlightenment.

46. The eight liberties for Dharma study are defined as freedom from the eight states of no leisure. Four of these are nonhuman states, namely, birth in the hells, as a hungry preta, as an animal, or as a long-lived god. The four human states of no leisure are birth in an uncivilized border region or among barbarians, birth where the words of Buddha are not present, birth as a deaf and dumb cretin, and birth as instinctively holding distorted views.

47. The three unfortunate states of rebirth are as a hell creature, a hungry preta, and an animal.

48. The Three Jewels of refuge are the buddhas, their Dharma teachings, and the Sangha assembly of those who realize them.

49. The eight ripened favorable qualities of a human rebirth most conducive for Dharma study and practice are having (1) a long life, (2) a handsome and healthy body, (3) a good, reputable family, (4) prosperity, (5) honesty and credibility of speech, (6) a strong influence on others, (7) birth as a male, and (8) a powerful body and mind.

50. The four opponent powers for cleansing yourself of sinful karmic debts are (1) feeling sincere regret about your previously committed nonvirtue, (2) invoking what you must rely on, namely, the Three Jewels of refuge and a bodichitta motivation, (3) your commitment to turn away from ever doing such nonvirtue again, and (4) the power of whatever virtuous actions you do to oppose your nonvirtue.

51. The two collections are of merit and of insight, the former resulting in your attainment of the form bodies of a buddha and the latter in the wisdom bodies or Dharmakāya.

52. The causal Mahāyāna Vehicle is that of Sūtrayāna. The resultant Mahāyāna Vehicle is that of Tantrayāna.

53. Maitreya, *Ornament of the Mahāyāna Sūtras*; *Mahāyānasūtrālamkāra*.

54. Nāgārjuna, *Suhṛllekha*, 117.

55. Āryadeva, *Catuḥśataka*, V 4.

56. Kamalaśīla, *Madhyamakāloka*.

57. Nāgārjuna, *Mūlaamadhyamakakārikā*, *Vaidalyaprakaraṇa*, *Vigrahavyāvartanī*, *Śūnyatāsaptati*, *Yuktiṣaṣṭikā*, and *Ratnāvalī*.

58. *Smṛtyupasthānasūtra*.

59. Nāgārjuna, *Ratnāvalī*, 4:71.9. Ibid., 2:19–20.
60. Ibid., 2:9–20.
61. Nāgārjuna, *Mūlamadhyamakakārikā*, 24:1.
62. Ibid., 24:20.
63. Ibid., 24:14.
64. Ibid., 24:9.
65. Śhākyamuni Buddha, *Ratnaguṇasaṃcayagāthā*.
66. Nāgārjuna, *Ratnāvalī*, 4:71.
67. Tsongkhapa, *Gsung thor bu*, vol. *kha*, 160A3–169B3.
68. Sadāprarudita searched far and wide to find a master who could teach him emptiness and the perfection of wisdom. When he finally located such a guru, namely, Dharmodgata, Sadāprarudita was so poor that he offered to cut off and sell some flesh from his body in order to obtain an offering for requesting these teachings. This account is related in *The Sūtra on the Perfection of Wisdom in Eight Thousand Lines (Aṣṭasāhasrikāprajñāpāramitāsūtra)*, parts 30–32.
69. Once a set of teachings about a certain phenomenon has been understood intellectually, it should be subjected for validation to the four kinds of logic or reasoning in examination meditation. These four are: (1) contextual reasoning, looking at the causes and circumstances or at the supporting factors for a certain phenomenon in order to see if they can in fact produce or serve as a basis or context to account for it; (2) functional reasoning, checking if a phenomenon or practice actually does produce its claimed effects; (3) logical reasoning, ensuring that the teaching is not contradicted by either valid bare perception, inference, or scriptural authority; and (4) commonsense reasoning, ascertaining whether or not something fits into what is commonly accepted as the nature of things.
70. The three types of laziness are procrastination, being attached to trivial matters, and delusions of incapability. With joyous effort and enthusiasm for virtue, these can be overcome and a state of enlightenment gradually attained.
71. Skt. *Prāsaṅgika Mādhyamaka* and *Svātāntrika Mādhyamaka*.
72. Tib. *rten 'byung*, Skt. *pratītyasamutpāda*, also translatable as "dependent origination," "relativistic occurrence," and so on.
73. Tib. *ma rig pa*, Skt. *avidyā*. Not merely a failure to know something, which we mean by ignorance, but a knowing something wrongly, a thinking we know rightly when we misknow.
74. *Blo dang ldan pa*, that is, bodhisattvas.
75. *Rang bzhin, Svabhāva*.
76. *Mu stegs pa, Tīrthika*. A somewhat derogatory term for non-Buddhists, as referring to those who seek salvation by frequenting holy places, bathing in sacred waters, and invoking various outside agencies to solve their problems.
77. *Sgro 'dogs pa* and *skur 'debs pa, samāropa* and *apavāda*, that is, the mental reification of merely relative things as intrinsically real things and the repudiation of even the relative reality of absolutely realityless things; that is, a way of describing the two extremisms of absolutism and nihilism.

78. The kumuda lily blooms at night, opening its bright white petals for the moon's rays, as most flowers bloom in sunlight, at least according to Indian literary convention. This is the key to this exquisite metaphor, where the white lilies of Nāgārjuna's teachings need the moon-rays of Chandra(kīrti)'s elucidation to bloom in all their beauty in the mind, as Tsongkhapa attains the complete relief of perfect enlightenment.

79. Tib. *chung ngu*, lit. "lesser," but the *bsdus don* (above as *Lines of Experience)* is really the "lesser" and this the "medium."

80. Maitreya is here speaking in dialogue with the Buddha, as recorded in *Elucidation of the Intent.*

81. *Madhyamabhāvanākrama,* by Kamalaśhīla, eighth century. During his debates with the Chinese Hvashang Mahāyāna at Samyay monastery, Kamalaśhīla composed three texts on the *Stages of Meditation.*

82. Skt. *prāṇa.*

83. Tib. *chos nyid* and *chos can.*

84. This being the context of the Unexcelled Yoga Tantras, the distinctive subjectivity is the great bliss inuition itself.

85. This passage is abstruse, but we assume that fluency can only arise through the fitness of the neural wind energies brought about by quiescence. Hence, fluency implies the combination of quiescence with discriminating wisdom.

86. *Madhyamakahṛdaya,* the first great work on comparative ideologies *(grub mtha)* in history, in which Bhavya covers all major schools of philosophy in the 500s in India.

87. Jñānakīrti, author of *Entrance to the Truth* (*Tattvāvatāra*).

88. *Shing rta chen po, mahāratha.* Common epic epithet for a warrior in the *Mahābhārata* and so on, used in the later Indo-Tibetan literature for the great champions of philosophy, Nāgārjuna and Asaṅga, and sometimes for other highly respected teachers.

89. Āryadeva was Nāgārjuna's closest disciple and Dharma heir, which means his dates are as confused as his teacher's. His *Four Hundred Stanzas (on Yoga Practice)* is of the same importance as Nāgārjuna's *Wisdom: Root Verses of the Middle Way,* and his *Lamp of Integrated Practices* is fundamental for *Guhyasamāja* studies after Nāgārjuna's *Five Stages* (Tibetan historians consider that the Nāgārjuna and Āryadeva who wrote the philosophical works also wrote the tantric works, as they consider tantra to be just as old as exoteric Universal Vehicle teachings). Buddhapālita is usually placed in the fifth century, a contemporary of Bhāvaviveka, both from South India, in the days when Kañci was a major Buddhist center. Buddhapālita elucidated the *Wisdom* from a dialectical point of view, and Bhavya criticized that method, providing a more systematic, dogmatic approach. Chandrakīrti (ca. 600) then rebutted Bhavya's critique, and the formal Dialecticist school was founded, according to Tibetan historians of philosophy. Śhāntarakṣita (ninth century) then came along and continued Bhāvaviveka's dogmatic approach, while relating more

closely with the Idealists' positions on the status of external objects, at least conventionally.

90. The expression "foundation treatise," or "paradigm treatise" (*gzhung phyi mo*), is interesting, since the *Transcendent Wisdom Scripture* herself is known as the *Mother of All Victors* (*Jinamātā*). Thus, since the works of Nāgārjuna and Āryadeva, the noble father and son, give birth to transcendent wisdom, who gives birth to buddhahood, they are like the mothers of the mother, that is, grandmothers.

91. Sautrāntika.

92. Yogācāra.

93. Māyānyāyasiddhi (*Sgyu ma rigs grub pa*).

94. Apratiṣṭhitavādi.

95. Rngog blo ldan shes rab, great translator of *Entrance to the Middle Way* and many other works (1059–1109).

96. Tib. *dbu ma pa*, Skt. *Mādhyamaka*. I translate this as "Centrist"—less awkward than "Middle-ist" and still accurate to the meaning of the school.

97. Atiśha (eleventh century) was the great Bengali master who spent twelve years in Tibet, starting a tradition of teaching and practice that was Tsongkhapa's own central inspiration.

98. People tend to refer to Nāgārjuna's basic work as the *Basic Middle Way Verses*, which is the translation of the work's subtitle, *Mūlamadhyamakakārikā*. Its actual name is simply *Prajñā* (*Wisdom*).

99. Vaibhāṣika is the individual vehicle philosophical school that relies on the clear science (*abhidharma*) text, the *Great Exposition* (*Mahāvibhāṣha*).

100. *Mūlamadhyamakavṛttiprasannapadā*.

101. Respectively, *svarūpasiddha* (*rang gi ngo bos grub pa*), *svalakṣaṇasiddha* (*rang mtshan gyis grub pa*), and *svabhāvasiddha* (*rang bzhin gyis garb pa*).

102. *Upāliparipṛcchāsūtra* from the *Ratnakuṭa* collection.

103. *Yuktiṣaṣṭikā*. Sixty verses giving various logical arguments for dependent origination.

104. *Dgag bya (nishedhya)*, the "to-be-negated."

105. *Vijñānavāda*.

106. *'Jig lta lhan skyes*.

107. That is, in Tsongkhapa's *Essence of True Eloquence*.

108. *Bdag gir 'dzin pa*.

109. *Nyon mongs can gyi ma rig pa*.

110. *Bden 'dzin*.

111. *Kleśajñeyāvaraṇa*.

112. *Svasaṃvitti*, a self-aware cognition, aware of itself at the same time as it cognizes other objects, posited by Idealists.

113. In the part of the *Path of Enlightenment* above on the Individual Vehicle practitioner, considered the mediocre person, better than the self-seeking worldling and worse than the altruistic bodhisattva.

114. This remarkable finding is further elaborated in the *Essence of True Eloquence,* providing extraordinary insight into the relationship between the enlightened and unenlightened mind, as Tsongkhapa says there that the unenlightened person has only the first and third of the three types of cognitions, whereas the enlightened person has all three types. This is very thought provoking.

115. In the *Great Stages of the Path* and elsewhere. Basically, it involves learning to observe the false sense of "I," the "I" that dominates one's experience and that becomes most evident in moments of righteous indignation—for example, when one is falsely accused—this is when the sense of "I," "I," "I," the feeling "I did not!" rises up powerfully from the heart. This is the time to catch the sense of "I" and see how it dominates our lives. It is the first key, since we have to identify the negatee before we can negate it.

116. *Jinamātāsūtra,* that is, the *100,000 Prajñāpāramitāsūtra* (the *Perfection of Wisdom in One Hundred Thousand Lines*).

117. The big difference between Western transcendent noumena and Buddhist transcendent ultimates, such as emptiness and nirvana, is that the former are considered in principle to be inaccessible to human cognition, whereas the latter are the proper objects of human transcendent wisdom (*prajñāpāramitā*).

118. *Tha snyad shes pa* (*vyāvahārikajñāna*) and *rigs shes* (*yuktijñāna*).

119. *Mtshan 'dzin* (*nimittagrāha*), the holding of things as having intrinsic identity or significance, seizing them as self-signifying signs. This way of describing the concept-dominated, naive realist experience of the world has no parallel in Western epistemology until the work of Wittgenstein, who first clearly described how we project our concepts on the world and then "read them off" it, as if they were really objectively embedded there. He calls this deep mental habit "substantivism."

120. *Skye mched, āyatana.*

121. Thesis = emptiness of intrinsic reality (this refutes absolutism), and reason = because of relativity (this refutes nihilism).

122. Tsongkhapa is especially critical of the Jonangpa school here.

123. *Lokasaṃvṛti* and *paramārtha.*

124. *Ldog pa, vyāvṛtti,* a term describing conceptualization as differential, that is, differentiating its designandum from everything other than it. It is used by Dignaga to safeguard against the tendency to substantivism, that is, reifying linguistic categories into reality.

125. Jñānagarbha, author of *Distinguishing the Two Realities* (*Satyadvayavibhaṅga*).

126. In the *Essence of True Eloquence* and in the *Elucidation of the Middle Way Intention,* Tsongkhapa's commentary on the *Entrance to the Middle Way.*

127. Especially in the *Essence of True Eloquence,* where Jé Rinpoche gives his most concise definition of intrinsic identity as involved in the presentation of the radical conventionality of the superficial reality wherein all intrinsic identities are absent.

128. *Saṃbhogakāya.*

129. This passage seems elusive in its point that the Buddha's absolute and relative intuitions can operate simultaneously on one object while never confusing that object's emptiness and its appearance in conventional cognition, perhaps because it does elude a dualistic grasp. The analogy of the mirror is the only thing that helps here: when we observe a reflection in a mirror, we pay attention to its details without forgetting that it is only a reflection in a mirror. The awareness of its illusory nature and the awareness of the details of what is reflected do not disturb each other and occur simultaneously—the former best considered a steady intuition, the latter a conceptually guided perception. Of course, this is only an analogy, the actuality of a buddha's cognitive-dissonance-embracing omniscience being ultimately inexpressible.

130. These *Sgyu ma rigs grub-pas* assert that the ultimate is the coordination of considered phenomena and truthless appearance.

131. Parentheses required here because of the difficulty of conveying the etymology of the Skt. *samyak* and Tib. *yang dag.*

132. *Pitāputrasamāgamasūtra* of the *Ratnakuṭa* collection.

133. *Tattvanirdeśasamādhisūtra.* Not in Tibetan canon but quoted in Chandrakīrti's *Entrance to the Middle Way.*

134. *Zhe rags kyi rnam pa can.*

135. Rationalists, Scripturalists, Idealists, and Centrists (*Vaibhāṣhika, Sautrāntika, Vijñānavāda,* and *Mādhyamaka*).

136. The *Kāśyapaparivarta* of the *Ratnakuṭasutra* collection.

137. *Avikalpapraveśadhāraṇī.*

138. Kamalaśhīla's opponent at the Samye debate was a renegade Ch'an teacher who taught a simplistic meditation of mere thoughtlessness as the ultimate practice. His view is just as incorrect in terms of the critical sayings of the great Ch'an masters, such as Ma Tzu, Pai Chang, Huang Po, Lin Chi, and so on as it was for Kamalaśhīla. Thus the Hvashang's position should not be considered as typical of all Ch'an and Zen.

139. *Collected Sayings* (*Be'u bum sngon po*) was compiled by Potowa's student Geshé Dölpa. Published as *The Blue Compendium* in *Stages of the Buddha's Teachings: Three Key Texts: Dölpa, Gampopa, and Sakya Paṇḍita.* Translated by Ulrike Roesler, Ken Holmes, and David P. Jackson (Boston: Wisdom Publications, 2015, in association with the Library of Tibetan Classics), quote on 87–88.

140. Ajitanātha. Skt. *nātha*, Tib. *mgon po*, refers to someone who "protects" the soul (mutating, supersubtle incarnational continuum) of a person, and so saves them from incarnating in the woeful states of hell, preta, or animal, and hence has a more important status than a "protector" from mundane problems.

141. That is, the regent of Śhākyamuni in Tushita until he descends to earth and leaves the next buddha as his regent.

142. Images of the hells.

143. Preta realms, little better than hells, where beings languish tormented by unsat-isfied desires.

144. Beasts, dumb animals.

145. Asuras, or antigods, or titans.

146. Note how the Buddhist attainment of heaven is not an end in itself but involves even the aspiration to use the heavenly favorable circumstances to learn, contemplate, and meditate, thereby achieving exalted accomplishments and then reemanating back into the realms of suffering sentient beings throughout the universes in order to benefit them.

147. *Bar do.*

148. Lit. "ear," referring to the fact that Vajrapāṇi has heard every esoteric teaching from all buddhas, never forgetting a single one.

149. It seems that Tsongkhapa cannot himself directly see Vajrapāṇi at this point in his life.

150. Nāropa's six yogas teachings and Padmasambhava's Great Perfection teachings.

151. The Mahāsiddhas.

152. There is a note appended in the Tashi Lhunpo edition that purports to soothe anyone who might have been offended by Vajrapāṇi's equation of the Great Perfection with the Great Middle Way of Nāgārjuna and Candrakīrti.

153. This line touches on the spearhead of the Geluk approach to Buddhism: learning as much as possible but doing so in terms of one's own personal practice. The Geluk tradition has been condemned by a number of Western scholars as being overly intellectual. Rather, it would be more accurate to say that, although the Geluk intellectual discipline is extremely vigorous—top scholars may study sixteen hours a day for forty years—this discipline is never allowed to deviate from actual practice. Tsongkhapa dedicates many pages in the opening part of his *Lam rim chen mo* to this theme. In fact "taking all teachings as personal advice" is one of the four great qualifications of Tsongkhapa's tradition. See H. H. the Dalai Lama, *The Path to Enlightenment*, ed. and trans. Glenn H. Mullin (Ithaca, NY: Snow Lion Publications, 1995).

154. The two stages of tantra: the creation (or generation) stage (*bskyed rim*), wherein one develops the pride of being a buddha-deity, a visionary samādhi on the supporting and supported mandalas and the eight siddhis, or magical powers, and the perfection (or completion) stage (*rdzogs rim*), wherein one practices with the perfect bodymind and environment created previously and attains the perfect accomplishment or magical power of the great seal (*mahāmudrā*), which is the buddha-experience of the whole of emptiness-relativity's reality as an ecstatic embrace, also called "bliss-void indivisible."

155. The higher trainings or educations in ethics, meditation, and wisdom. Perhaps Tsongkhapa's greatest contribution to Tibetan Buddhism was his emphasis on using the three higher educations—the essence of the Individual Vehicle—as bases and supplements to tantric practice. Of course, these three were known in Tibet before Tsongkhapa's time, but only in words. Therefore the great translator Taktsang Lotsawa wrote: "Some, clinging to the Individual Vehicle doctrines, abandoned the tantras. Others, loving the tantric system, disparaged

the Individual Vehicle. But you, Tsongkhapa, are the sage who saw how to put every teaching given by Buddha perfectly into practice." Taktsang Lotsawa continues: "You practised all sūtras and tantras, but specialised in Vajrayāna; you practised all tantric systems, but specialized in unexcelled tantra; you practised all stages of unexcelled tantra, but placed special emphasis on the peerless illusory body yoga. O Tsongkhapa, unmatched treasury of teachings, I bow to you." Losang Trinlé Namgyal quotes Taktsang Lotsawa in his biography of Tsongkhapa. See Losang Trinlé Namgyal, *Beautiful Ornament of the Buddha's Teachings* (*Thub bstan mdzes pa'i rgyan*) (Sarnath, India: Mongolian Lama Guru Deva, 1967), 618.

156. The bodhi-mind, spirit of enlightenment, or Universal Vehicle attitude, is of two types: conventional and ultimate. Conventional bodhi-mind is also subdivided into two: the wishing bodhi-mind, which yearns for enlightenment as the most practical way to benefit all sentient beings, and the venturing bodhi-mind, which ventures into the practices of the six perfections and four ways of amassing trainees. Ultimate bodhi-mind is the bodhi-mind that understands emptiness.

157. The monastery built by Tsongkhapa. The Ganden Throne Holder is the official head of the Geluk order.

158. Attachment, hostility, and ignorance.

159. The realms of hell beings, ghosts, animals, humans, antigods, and gods.

160. Tibetan: *sDom pa gsum*. The three vows are those of the Individual Vehicle (*Hīnayāna*), Universal Vehicle (*Mahāyāna*), and Vajra Vehicle, or the individual liberation (*prātimokṣa*) vows, the bodhisattva vows, and the tantric vows.

161. The first, third, and fourth verses of this song were quoted in "A Cooling Raindrop," a biography of Tsongkhapa published in the British journal *Vajra*, no. 3 (September 1976).

162. During the time of Tsongkhapa, many Tibetans were mistaking emptiness for a vacuum-like state similar to the experience of the formless realms. Tsongkhapa proved that such a "voidness" was not the intention of Buddha, Nāgārjuna, Āryadeva, or Chandrakīrti, and that the liberation achieved by realizing it and settling down in it is a short-lived freedom. This sentence, quoted from Jé Rinpoche, points to the true emptiness.

Bibliography

Works Referenced in the Texts

KANGYUR (CANONICAL SCRIPTURES)

Close Contemplations Sūtra. Smṛtyupasthanasūtra. Dam pa'i chos dran pa nye bar gzhag pa'i mdo. Toh 287.

Elucidation of Intent Sūtra. Saṃdhinirmocanasūtra. Mdo sde dgongs pa nges 'grel. Toh 106.

Guhyasamāja Root Tantra. Guhyasamājatantra. Gsang ba 'dus pa'i rgyud. Toh 442.

Heart of Transcendent Wisdom Sūtra. Prajñāpāramitāhṛdaya. Shes rab snying po. Toh 21/531.

Hevajra Tantra. Hevajratantra. Kye'i rdo rje rgyud. Toh 417.

Hymn of the Names of Mañjushrī. Mañjuśrīnāmasaṃgīti. 'Jam dpal gyi mtshan yang dag par brjod pa'i dge ba'i rtsa ba bsngo ba. Toh 360.

Jewel Cloud Sūtra. Ratnameghasūtra. Dkon mchog sprin gyi mdo. Toh 231.

Kālachakra Tantra. Dus kyi 'khor lo'i rgyud. Toh 362.

Kāshyapa Chapter. Kāśyapaparivarta. 'Od srungs kyis zhus pa. Toh 87.

King of Samādhis Sūtra. Samādhirājasūtra. Ting nge 'dzin rgyal po'i mdo. Toh 127.

Meeting of Father and Son Sūtra. Pitāputrasamāgamasūtra. Yab dang sras mjal ba'i mdo. Toh 60.

Mother of All Victors. Jinamātāsūtra (the *Perfection of Wisdom in One Hundred Thousand Lines; 100,000 Prajñāpāramitāsūtra*). *Śatasāhasrikāprajñāpāramitā. Shes rab kyi pha rol tu phyin pa stong phrag brgya pa.* Toh 8.

Perfection of Wisdom Sūtras. Prajñāpāramitāsūtras. Shes rab kyi pha rol phyin pa'i mdo. (This is a general reference to a category of twenty-three sutras. Most common reference is to the *Perfection of Wisdom in Eight Thousand Lines*.)

Perfection of Wisdom in Eight Thousand Lines. Aṣṭasāhasrikāprajñāpāramitā. Shes rab kyi pha rol tu phyin pa brgyad stong pa. Toh 12.

Questions of Nāga King Anavatapta Sūtra. Anavataptanāgarājapariprcchāsūtra Klu'i rgyal po ma dros pas zhus pa'i mdo. Toh 156.

Questions of Sagaramati Sūtra. Sagaramatiparipṛcchāsūtra. Blos gros rgya mtsho zhus pa'i mdo. Toh 152.

Questions of Upāli Sūtra. Upāliparipṛcchāsūtra. Nye bar 'khor gyis zhus pa'i mdo. Toh 68.

Secret of the Tathāgatas Sūtra. Tathāgataguhyakasūtra. De bzhin gshegs pa'i gsang ba'i mdo. Toh 47.

Spell for Entering Nondiscrimination. Avikalpapraveśadhāraṇī. Rnam par mi rtog par 'jug pa'i gzungs. Toh 142.

Sūtra on the Three Heaps of Doctrine. Triskandhakasūtra. Phung po gsum pa'i mdo. Toh 284.

Thatness-Teaching Samādhi Sūtra. Tattvanirdeśasamādhisūtra. De kho na nyid ting nge 'dzin nges par bstan pa'i mdo. (Not in Tibetan canon but quoted in Chandrakīrti's *Entrance to the Middle Way.*)

Verse Summary of the Perfection of Wisdom. Ratnaguṇasaṃcayagāthā. Sdud pa tshigs su bcad pa. Toh 13.

Visit to Lanka Sūtra. Laṅkāvatārasūtra. Lang kar gshegs pa'i mdo. Toh 107.

TENGYUR (CANONICAL TREATISES)

Āryadeva. *Four Hundred Stanzas. Catuḥśatakaśastra. Bstan bcos bzhi brgya pa.* Toh 3846.

Āryaśhūra. *Former Birth Tales. Jātakamāla. Skyes pa'i rabs kyi rgyud.* Toh 4150.

———. *Lamp of Integrated Practices. Caryāmelāpakapradīpa. Spyod pa bsdus pa'i sgron me.* Toh 1803.

Asaṅga. *Actuality of the Stages. Bhūmivastu. Dngos gzhi sa mang po.* Toh 4035.

———. *Bodhisattva Levels. Bodhisattvabhūmi. Byang chub sems dpa'i sa.* Toh 4037.

———. *Compendium of Scientific Knowledge. Abhidharmasamuccaya. Chos mngon pa kun las btus pa.* Toh 4049.

———. *Shrāvaka Levels. Śhrāvakabhūmi. Nyan thos kyi sa.* Toh 4036.

Aśhvagoṣha (a.k.a. Mātṛceṭa). *Fifty Stanzas on the Guru. Gurupāṅkāśikā. Bla ma lnga bcu pa.* Toh 3721.

———. *Praises Extolling the Praiseworthy. Varṇārhavarṇastotra. Bstod par mi nus par bstod pa.* Toh 1138.

Atīsha. *Entrance into the Two Realities. Satyadvayāvatāra. Bden pa gnyis la 'jug pa.* Toh 3902/4467.

———. *Instruction in the Middle Way. Madhyamakopadeśa. Dbu ma'i man ngag.* Toh 3929.

———. *Lamp on the Path to Enlightenment. Bodhipathapradīpa. Byang chub lam gyi sgron ma.* Toh 3947/4465.

Bhāvaviveka. *Blaze of Reason. Tarkajvālā. Rtog ge 'bar ba.* Toh 3856.

———. *Essence of the Middle Way. Madhyamakahṛdaya. Dbu ma'i snying po'i tshig le'ur byas pa.* Toh 3855.

Chandrakīrti. *Commentary to the Four Hundred Stanzas. Catuḥśataktīkā. Bzhi brgya pa'i rgya cher 'grel pa.* Toh 3865.

———. *Entrance to the Middle Way. Madhyamakāvatāra. Dbu ma la 'jug pa zhes bya ba'i tshig le'ur byas pa. Dbu ma la 'jug pa.* Toh 3861.

———. *Entrance to the Middle Way Commentary. Madhyamakāvatārabhāṣya. Dbu ma la 'jug pa'i bshad pa.* Toh 3862.

———. *Lucid Exposition. Prasannapadā. Tshig gsal ba.* Toh 3860.

———. *Middle Way Commentary. Madhyamakakārikāvṛtti. Du ma rtsa ba'i 'grel bu ddha pā li ta.* Toh 3842.

———. *Sixty Reasonings Commentary. Yuktiṣaṣṭikāvṛtti. Rigs pa drug bcu pa'i 'grel pa.* Toh 3864.

Dharmakīrti. *Commentary on the Compendium of Valid Cognition. Pramāṇavārttika. Tshad ma rnam 'grel.* Toh 4210.

Guṇaprabha. *Monastic Discipline Sūtra. Vinayasūtra. 'Dul ba'i mdo.* Toh 4117.

Jñānagarbha. *Distinguishing the Two Realities. Satyadvayavibhaṅga. Bden pa gnyis rnam par 'byed pa.* Toh 3881.

———. *Distinguishing the Two Realities Commentary. Satyadvayavibhaṅgavṛtti. Bden gnyis rnam par 'byed pa'i 'grel ba.* Toh 3882.

Jñānakīrti. *Entrance to the Truth. Tattvāvatāra. De kho na nyid la 'jugs pa.* Toh 3709.

Kamalaśhīla. *Illumination of the Middle Way. Madhyamakāloka. Dbu ma snang ba.* Toh 3887.

———. *Stages of Meditation. Bhāvanākrama. Bsgom pa'i rim pa.* Toh 3915-17.

Maitreya. *Distinguishing the Middle from the Extremes. Madhyāntavibhāga. Dbus dang mtha' rnam par 'byed pa.* Toh 4021.

———. *Distinguishing Phenomena from Their True Nature. Dharmadharmatāvibhaṅga. Chos dang chos nyid rnam par 'byed pa.* Toh 4022.

———. *Mahāyāna Treatise on the Ultimate Continuum (Buddha Nature). Mahāyānottaratantraśāstra. Theg pa chen po'i rgyud bla ma'i bstan bcos.* Toh 4024.

———. *Ornament of the Mahāyāna Sūtras. Mahāyānasūtrālaṃkāra. Theg pa then po'i mdo sde rgyan.* Toh 4020.

———. *Ornament of Realizations. Abhisamayālaṃkāra. Mngon par rtogs pa'i rgyan.* Toh 3786.

Nāgabodhi. *Guhyasamāja Mandala Rite. Guhyasamājamaṇḍalaviṃśatividhi. Gsang ba 'dus pa'i dkyil 'kor gyi cho ga nyi shu pa.* Toh 1810.

Nāgārjuna. *Disclosure of the Spirit of Enlightenment. Bodhicittavivaraṇa. Byang chub sems kyi 'grel pa.* Toh 1800.

———. *The Five Stages. Pañcakrama. Rim pa lnga pa.* Toh 1802.

———. *The Friendly Letter. Suhṛllekha. Bshes pa'i spring yig.* Toh 4182.

———. *Praise for the Dharmadhātu. Dharmadhātustava. Chos kyi dbyings su bstod pa.* Toh 1118.

———. *Precious Garland. Ratnāvalī. Dbu ma rin chen phreng ba.* Toh 4158.

———. *Rebuttal of Objections. Vigrahavyāvartanī. Rtsod pa bzlog pa.* Toh 3828.

———. *Seventy Stanzas on Emptiness. Śūnyatāsaptati. Stong pa nyid bdun cu pa.* Toh 3826.

———. *Sixty Reasonings. Yuktiṣaṣṭikā. Rigs pa drug cu pa.* Toh 3825.

———. *A Thorough Investigation. Vaidalyasūtra. Zhib mo rnam par 'thag pa'i mdo.* Toh 3826.

———. *Transcendental Praise. Lokātītastava. 'Jig rten las 'das par bstod pa.* Toh 1120.

———. *Wisdom: Root Verses on the Middle Way. Mūlamadhyamakakārikā. Dbu ma rtsa ba tshig le'ur byas pa shes rab.* Toh 3824.Ratnākaraśhānti. *Instruction in Transcendent Wisdom. Prajñāpāramitopadeśa. Shes rab kyi pha rol tu phyin pa'i man ngag.* Toh 4079.

Śhāntarakṣhita. *Ornament of the Middle Way. Madhyamakālaṃkāra. Dbu ma rgyan.* Toh 3884.

Śhāntideva. *Compendium of Training. Śhikṣāsamuccaya. Bslab pa kun las btus pa.* Toh 3940.

———. *Entrance to the Bodhisattva's Way of Life. Bodhicaryāvatāra. Byang chub sems dpa'i spyod pa la 'jug pa.* Toh 3871.

Vasubhandu. *Methodology of Elucidation. Vyākhyāyukti. Rnam par bshad pa'i rigs pa.* Toh 4061.

———. *Treasury of Scientific Knowledge. Abhidharmakośha. Chos mngon pa'i mdzod.* Toh 4089.

TIBETAN WORKS

Dharma Encyclopedia. Dharmasaṃgraha. In the Chinese canon, but not the Tibetan. *Dharma Samgraha: An Ancient Collection of Buddhist Technical Terms.* Translated by Kenjiu Kasawara. Varanasi, India: Pilgrims Publishing, 1999.

Geshé Ngawang Wangyal. *Door of Liberation.* New York: Girodias, 1973. Republished as *Door of Liberation: Essential Teachings of the Tibetan Buddhist Tradition.* Boston: Wisdom Publications, 1995.

Losang Trinlé Namgyal. *Beautiful Ornament of the Buddha's Teachings. Thub bstan mdzes pa'i rgyan.* Sarnath, India: Mongolian Lama Guru Deva, 1967.

Potowa. *Collected Sayings. Be'u bum sngon po.* Published as *The Blue Compendium,* in *Stages of the Buddha's Teachings: Three Key Texts: Dölpa, Gampopa, and Sakya Paṇḍita.* Translated by Ulrike Roesler, Ken Holmes, and David P. Jackson. The Library of Tibetan Classics, vol. 10. Somerville, MA: Wisdom Publications, 2015 (in association with the Institute of Tibetan Classics).

Tsongkhapa. *Elucidation of the Middle Way Intention. Dbu ma la 'jug pa'i rnam bshad dgongs pa rab gsal.*

———. *Essence of Good Eloquence* (*Legs bshad snying po*), or *In Praise to Dependent Origination* (*Rten 'brel bstod pa*).

———. *Essence of True Eloquence: An Analysis of Interpretable and Definitive Teachings. Drang nges legs bshad snying po.*

———. *Golden Rosary of Eloquent Teaching. Legs bshad gser 'phreng.*

———. *Great Exposition of the Secret Mantra Stages. Sngags rim chen mo.*

———. *Great Exposition on the Stages of the Path to Enlightenment. Lam rim chen mo.*

————. *Lines of Experience (of the Stages of the Path to Enlightenment)*. *Lam rim nyams mgur*. Also known as the *Summary Points of the Graded Path* (*Lam rim bsdus don*).

————. *Middle-Length Stages of the Path to Enlightenment*. *Lam rim chung ba*.

————. *Ocean of Reasoning*. *Ṭik chen rigs pa'i rgya mtsho*.

————. *Praise to Dependent Origination*. *Rten 'brel stod pa*.

SECONDARY SOURCES

H. H. the Dalai Lama. *The Path to Enlightenment*. Edited and translated by Glenn H. Mullin. Ithaca, NY: Snow Lion Publications, 1995.

Index

A

Abhidharma. *See* Scientific Knowledge (Abhidharma)
absolutism, 56, 88, 135–36, 137, 239n77
absurd consequences, 81, 108, 126
accomplishments, perfect, 59, 237n34
Āchārya Vīra. *See* Aśhvaghoṣha (a.k.a. Mātṛceṭa)
action tantra, 37
Actuality of the Stages (Asaṅga), 109
addictions
  arisal of, 119–21
  eliminating, 121, 122, 199
  to food, clothing, body, 208, 209
  intellectual and subconscious, relationship between, 118–19
  pitfall of increasing, 202–3
  to pleasure, 55
  subconscious, 117
  See also under misknowledge
adopting and rejecting, discriminating between, 61, 68, 72
advice, practical, 67, 218, 244n153
aggregates, five
  buddha's perceptions of, 150, 151, 152
  in objective selflessness, 133–34
  and personal self, reasonings on, 123–24, 125–27
  selflessness of, variant views on, 115, 116
  truth-habit of, 118, 119

aims, two desirable, 60, 70, 71, 100, 184, 237n39
altruistic mind, 12, 24. *See also* spirit of enlightenment (*bodhicitta*)
ambrosia (in vision of Mañjuśhrī), 21, 46, 171, 219
Amdo Province, 9, 12
Amitābha/Amitāyus, 3, 11, 45, 172, 193–94, 195, 197, 212
analogies and metaphors
  conch shells, 9, 16
  hairs falling from sky, distorted perception of, 147–48
  king of birds, 181–82, 194
  for Mañjuśhrī, 174–82
  medicine, 68–69, 210, 219
  mine of precious gems, 199, 219
  mirror images, 129, 130, 133, 136, 145–46, 179, 243n129
  nectar eradicating illness, 179
  night-lily garden, 101, 240n78
  paintings, 226
  for path of action, 207
  for pitfalls in meditation, 204, 205
  power-granting king, 60, 237n41
  rabbit's horns, 79, 128, 131, 136
  rainbows, 179
  rope as snake, 114
  rubbing-sticks and fire, 163, 164
  sky, 150–51

About the Author

Robert Thurman is the Jé Tsong Khapa Professor of Indo-Tibetan Buddhist Studies in the Department of Religion at Columbia University, the president of Tibet House US, a nonprofit organization dedicated to the preservation and promotion of Tibetan civilization, and president of the American Institute of Buddhist Studies, a nonprofit affiliated with the Center for Buddhist Studies at Columbia University and dedicated to the publication of translations of important artistic and scientific treatises from the Tibetan Tengyur. He is considered the leading American expert on Tibetan Buddhism and is the author of many books on Tibet, Buddhism, art, politics, and culture, including *The Central Philosophy of Tibet, Circling the Sacred Mountain, Essential Tibetan Buddhism, The Tibetan Book of the Dead, Wisdom and Compassion: The Sacred Art of Tibet, Worlds of Transformation, Inner Revolution, Infinite Life, The Jewel Tree of Tibet, Why the Dalai Lama Matters*, and, with Sharon Salzberg, *Love Your Enemies*.

What to Read Next
from Wisdom Publications

Tsongkhapa's Praise for Dependent Relativity
Tsongkhapa, Lobsang Gyatso, and Geshe Graham Woodhouse

"In this elegant text, the ven Geshe Graham Woodhouse translates Tsong-khapa's jewel-like masterpiece. The radiance of Tsongkhapa's poetry is refracted and enhanced by the brilliant and lucid commentary of the late Gen Losang Gyatso."—Dr. Jay Garfield, Dorris Silbert Professor in Humanities and Professor of Philosophy at Smith College

The Two Truths Debate
Tsongkhapa and Gorampa on the Middle Way
Sonam Thakchoe
Foreword by Jay Garfield

"A vivid tour through the scenery of the conventional and the ultimate in two worldviews by a well-versed guide—stimulating, provocative, and comprehensive."—Jeffrey Hopkins

The Splendor of an Autumn Moon
The Devotional Verse of Tsongkhapa
Tsongkhapa and Gavin Kilty

"Some of the most inspiring verses ever written."—Geshe Thupten Jinpa, PhD, founder, Institute for Tibetan Classics

***Steps on the Path to Enlightenment* series**
Geshe Lhundub Sopa

An elegant five-volume comprehensive commentary on the Lamrim Chenmo by the renowned Buddhist scholar, Geshe Lhundub Sopa.

About Wisdom Publications

Wisdom Publications is the leading publisher of classic and contemporary Buddhist books and practical works on mindfulness. To learn more about us or to explore our other books, please visit our website at wisdompubs.org or contact us at the address below.

Wisdom Publications
199 Elm Street
Somerville, MA 02144 USA

We are a 501(c)(3) organization, and donations in support of our mission are tax deductible.

Wisdom Publications is affiliated with the Foundation for the Preservation of the Mahayana Tradition (FPMT).